TREES OF RAMAYANA

Editor
Felix Bast

Today & Tomorrow's Printers and Publishers
4436/7, Ansari Road, Daryaganj, New Delhi - 110 002
Ph : 23242621; 23241021; Fax 23242621;
E-mail: ttppindia@gmail.com; info@ttpp.in
Web : ttpp.in

ISBN: 9789391734671

Published by

Today and Tomorrow's Printers and Publishers

4436/7, Ansari Road, Daryaganj, New Delhi - 110 002

Ph : 23242621; 23241021; Fax 23242621

Dedication

We dedicate this work to our beloved teacher and great nature lover, Professor Raghavendra Prasad Tiwari, Vice Chancellor of Central University of Punjab. Prof. Tiwari have shown us all how to lead an unpretentious lifestyle centred on sustainability and environmentalism, the way sages in Ramayana have been living in the golden days of Bharat. Thank you, Sir.

Preface

Ramayana, the Indian epic written in Sanskrit by Maharishi Valmiki in 7th Century BCE, is an influential ancient text deeply ingrained in Indian culture and civilization. The ancient text of Ramayana offers immense potential for conservation ecologists. First, it serves as a snapshot of the floristic diversity of the Indian subcontinent encompassing undivided countries, including present-day India, Pakistan, Bengladesh, Nepal, Bhutan and Sri Lanka, when the text was written almost 2800 years ago. Many species since then might have gone extinct; this issue highlights the importance of careful textual analysis combining the fields of literature and botany. Second, assessing the flora of Ramayana offers avenues for ethnobotanical research. Interrelationships of humans and plants, as holistically depicted in Ramayana, had been the original culture of India; flora is intricately intertwined with every aspect of Indian life even today. For instance, consider Indian traditional medicine, Ayurveda. Ayurvedic medicinal products are almost entirely derived from plant materials with minimal processing.

In Kerala, where I was born, we have the so-called *sarpa kaavu*- the sacred grove, at a corner of our ancestral property. An untouched forest surrounding the central stone carving of serpentine God *naga*. The myth integrated with religion is that *naga kopa*, the divine retribution, will haunt if one tries to cut any plant from that area. I feel immensely thankful for this myth that we have a patch of ancient forest preserved on our property even today. Sacred groves are ubiquitous throughout Kerala and in several other locations in India, especially in North-East India. Our ancestors had been conserving these sacred groves for hundreds of years. Let us move that spirit forward. Instead of trying to conquer her with all the vanity of modernity, let us humbly surrender to her immense yet dreary glory. An ancient Sanskrit verse from Purana goes

(meaning: It is better to think of remedy before the problem arises. It is of no use to cry when the house is set on fire.) Yes, our actions are responsible for the consequences.

This book is a collection of academic term papers that my students of MSc Botany 2019 batch at the Central University of Punjab wrote as part of their Ecology, Environment and Biodiversity course. The term papers have been edited and revised at length to ensure the flow, uniformity in structure and logical cohesiveness. The result is what you are holding in your hands right now; the very first book on the Trees of Ramayana, an in-depth inspection of selected 20 trees mentioned in the classical Indian text. Several features of this book render this work unique.

1. The context in Ramayana in Sanskrit verses presented in the beginning of each chapter

2. An original image of the tree is provided

3. Taxonomic hierarchy is provided, along with local names in Indian regional languages as well as morphological characteristics of the trees

4. A detailed description of habitat, varieties and related species is presented.

5. Cultural and mythological significance is provided.

6. Economic/medicinal and ecological values provided

The book is written in a non-technical language accessible to all, making this an ideal read for all dendrophiles (people who love trees).

I hope you will find this book helpful. I would love to know your feedbacks about this work including corrections required/suggested topics for future edition-if any. I have initiated a Facebook community of lifelong learners accessible here: https://bit.ly/yaifb Please post your feedback about the book in this group, as well as on the listings of Amazon, Flipkart, and Goodrads.

Happy reading and learning!

(Felix Bast) Twitter: @ExaltFibs

Contents

Trees of Ramayana (2022): 1-11
Editor: Felix Bast
Today & Tomorrow's Printers and Publishers (India)

Chapter-1

Jackfruit tree (*Artocarpus heterophyllus*)

Malay Kumar Mohanta

आम्रजम्ब्वसनैर्लोध्रैः प्रियालैः पनसैर्धवैः।

अङ्कोलैर्भव्यतिनिशैर्बिल्वतिन्दुक वेणुभिः॥2.94.8॥

काश्मर्यरिष्टवरुणैर्मधूकैस्तिलकैस्तथा।

बदर्यामलकैर्नीपैर्वेत्रधन्वनबीजकैः॥2.94.9॥

पुष्पवद्भिः फलोपेतैश्छायावद्भिर्मनोरमैः।

एवमादिभिराकीर्णः श्रियं पुष्यत्ययं गिरिः॥2.94.10॥

The above sloka is mentioned in the Ayodhya Kanda, sarga-94, sloka-9 of Valmiki's Ramayana. Here Lord Rama describes Sita about his delight in the beautiful nature around Chitrakuta Mountain. This mountain is covered with various kinds of trees filled with flowers, heavily loaded with fruits and providing shades, for example- mango, rose apples, asanas, lodhras, priyalas, jackfruit trees, dhavas, ankolas, lovely tinisas, bilva trees, tinduka, and bamboo, kashmaya, arishta and Varuna, madhukas, tilaka trees, badari and myrobalan trees, nipa trees, cane, danvas, and pomegranate trees. The mountain looks splendid.

Figure: *Artocarpus heterophyllus* (Jackfruit tree), Date of capture: 20/04/2020, GPS coordinates: N 21°50'41.22204" E 86°56'17.35512" Address: Chitrada, India, Odisha-757018. © Malay Kumar Mohanta

Taxonomic identification:

Kingdom- Plantae

Class: Dicotyledonae

Order: Rosales

Family: Moraceae

Genus: Artocarpus

Species: *Artocarpus heterophyllus*

Local names of the tree:

Sanskrit- Panasa, Atibruhatphala, Kantaphala, Hindi- Kathal, Panas, Malayalam- Chakka, Tamil- Palae, Telugu- Panasa, Gujarati- Phanas, Kannada- Havasu, Bengali- Kathal, German- Jackfruchtbaum, Fililino- Nancas,langka, Indonesian- Nangka,nongko, Spanish- Pan de Fruta, jacueiro,buen pan, rima, jaca, English- Jack tree, Jackfruit, Jacquir

Morphological Characteristics:

Artocarpus heterophyllus is an evergreen tree. The shape of the canopy is conical or pyramidal in younger trees and becomes more spread and denser in older trees. The lifespan of the jackfruit tree is 60-70 years. The jackfruit tree belongs to the family *Moraceae* which contains nearly about 50 species.it is a tetraploid plant i.e., 2n=56. The tree provides a dense shade. Near the ground heavy side branching is seen. The jackfruit tree is a medium-sized tree and can easily reach up to 10-20 m in height and have a relatively short trunk which can be 30-80 cm in diameter. The bark of this tree is rough, uneven, somewhat scaly, and reddish-brown. All parts of the tree secrete white gummy latex when subjected to injury.

Leaves are alternate and spirally arranged on the horizontal branches. The measurements arc (4-25; 2-12) cm, generally divided into a petiole and a leaf blade. The length of the petiole is 1 to 3 inches long. The leaf blade is leathery and is (7-15) inches in length and (3-7) inches wide. The shape varies from oblong to ovate. The leaf edges in young leaves are irregularly split or lobed. When the trees become old the leaves are rounded and appear dark green with a smooth leaf margin. The leaf blade has a distinct main nerve and several 6-8 lateral nerves. The stipules are ovate shaped and of length 1.5 to 8 cm.

It is a monoecious tree where both male and female inflorescences (Spikes) are found on the same tree. Male and female inflorescences are borne individually on short, stout stems that come out from older branches and the trunk. The inflorescences are cylindrical to ellipsoidal or pear-shaped and pedunculated. It is 10-12 in length and 5-7 cm in width. Initially, the inflorescences are completely enveloped in egg-shaped cover sheets which gradually slough off. The flowers are small and situated on the fleshy rachis. The male flowers are greenish, hairy, and sometimes sterile. These are found on younger branches above the female inflorescences. The perianth found in these male inflorescences ends with two membranes of 1to 1.5milimeter thick. The stamens are prominent and straight having characteristic yellowish color and rounded shape. After the pollen distribution, the stamens become greyish and within a few days it falls off from the trees. All the male inflorescences also fall off simultaneously. The female flowers are green in color and have hairy and tubular perianth. The base of these female inflorescences is generally fleshy. The female flowers contain an ovary having broad, capitate, or rarely bilobed scar. The flowering period varies from December to February or March.

The fruit is ellipsoidal to roundish in shape. It is multiple types of fruit that are formed from the fusion of the ovaries of multiple flowers. The fruit generally grows on a long and thick stem on the trunk. They vary in size and their color changes from yellowish-green to yellow initially and later yellowish-brown when ripened. The outer covering is very thick and hard, having numerous spines like hexagonal tubercles. The size of the fruit varies from 30 to 100cm in length and 15 to 50 cm in diameter. The weight of the fruit ranges from 10-45 kg. In the ancient Sanskrit language Jackfruit is referred to as 'Atibruhatphala' (Ati-very, bruhat-big, phala-fruit) and 'Kantaphala' (Kanta-thorny, phala-fruit) because of the above features. The fruit consists of whitish fibrous rachis 5-10cm thick and its shape is ellipsoidal to ovate. Light brownish achenes of 3cm length and 1.5 to 2 cm in diameter are found. Seeds are light brown. Numerous seeds ranging from 100-500 have been found in a single fruit. The seed coat is thin, waxy, and consists of easily removable testa and brownish tegmen. The cotyledons are generally unequal in size and the endosperm is found in low amounts. Generally, the fruits become mature during the rainy season from July to August. The achenes are bean-shaped and coated with distinct yellowish aril (seed coat, flesh) having an intense sweet taste at maturity of the fruit. The pulp is covered by undeveloped perianths which are narrow strands of numerous fibers. When cut into pieces, the inner part releases a gummy liquid which is very sticky to the skin. Oil and other solvents like kerosene are used to clean the hands after cutting the pulp. The fully ripened Jackfruit has a strong pleasant aroma/fragrance. When the pulp is opened in a ripened fruit the smell resembles the odor of a combination of pineapple and banana.

Varieties:

In south India, Jackfruits are of two different types- 1- Koozha chakka (small, fibrous, soft, mushy but very sweet carpels) 2- Koozha pazham (commercially very important). These are also named differently in different areas like Barka, or Berka (soft, can be broken open with hands, very sweet) and Kapa or Kapiya (crisp and cut open with a knife). In Thailand, the equivalent types are known as Kha-nun nang (firm; best) and kha-nun lamoud (soft). Different varieties have been found depending on the climatic condition and other factors. Horticultural Research Institute of Saharanpur, India in 1961 reported several excellent varieties of jackfruits such as 'Safeda', 'Khaja', 'Bhusila', 'Bhadaiyam', 'Handia' and others. The Fruit Experimental Station at Burlier had collected 54 jackfruit clones from different parts of the world and ultimately selected 'T Najar Jack' for its best quality as well as yield.

Season:

In Asia, depending on the climate regions jackfruits ripen principally from March to June, April to Sept., or June to August. However, in some areas, it has been seen the ripening of fruits during the off-season like Sept to Dec.

Climate and soil:

The jackfruit tree is adapted only to humid tropical and subtropical climates. It is very sensitive to frost and cannot withstand drought. If rainfall is not sufficient, then it requires proper irrigation. In India, it flourishes in the foothills of Himalayan Mountains and from sea level to an altitude of 1500m (5000 ft) in the south. However, the jackfruit grown above 1200m (4000ft) is of very poor quality and is only used for cooking. Jackfruit tree mainly is in the rich, deep soil of medium to open texture and sometimes in laterite soil and gravel soil.

Storage:

After ripening, jackfruit deteriorates very quickly. So, for storage, jackfruit should be kept at 52° to 55°F for 3 to 6 weeks and relative humidity must be maintained to 85-95%.

Invasive species:

In Brazil's Tijuca Forest National Park in Rio de Janeiro, jackfruit has become an invasive species. During the mid-nineteenth century when the planting was beginning in the Tijuca which is an artificial secondary forest, Jackfruit was spread extensively because its fruit naturally falls to the ground and open, and is eaten by small mammals like the common marmoset and coati. The seeds are then dispersed randomly by these animals and give rise to jackfruit trees which compete with the native tree species.

Other related species:

Chempedak (*A. integer*)

Lakoocha (*A. lakoocha*)

Kwai muk (*A. lingnanensis*)

Breadfruit (*A. Altilis*)

Dugdug (*A. mariannensis*)

Breadnut (*A. camansi*)

Cultural significance:

For centuries the jackfruit has portrayed a significant role in Indian agriculture. The evidence from archaeological findings suggests that the jackfruit was cultivated in India around 3000 to 6000 years ago. During Hindu ceremonies in Kerala, a wooden plank known as Avani palinka is used as the Priest's seat which is made from the woods of a jackfruit tree. Jackfruit wood is prized in Vietnam for making Buddhist statues in temples. Buddhist Forest Monastics in Southeast Asia use hardwood as a dye and give the robes of the monks during those traditions. In India and Nepal during the eleventh day of Shravan, fruits and flowers are offered to Lord Vishnu. In Malabar, dried branches are used to produce fire by friction during religious ceremonies. Jackfruit is the national fruit of Bangladesh. In India, it is the state fruit of Kerala and Tamil Nadu.

The mythological story associated with tree:

In Hindu mythology jackfruit has also been mentioned. Once Lord Shiva went to the jungle for a hunt and heard a very sweet voice. When he realized the voice was coming from a tribal girl, he was stunned. She was immensely beautiful and her name was 'Koolivaka'. Lord Shiva got attracted to her beauty and became lustful. He came near to her and informed about his desire and told her to wait for him until he returned from his hunt.

Koolivaka was a devotee of Goddess Parvathi. So, she prayed to save her from this situation as she was afraid, she would displease Devi if she had a relationship with Lord Shiva. The goddess revealed that in her previous birth she was Manaswini who was a servant of the Goddess. She was cursed to be born in an outcast family as one day she was found while breastfeeding baby Lord Vinayaka. After requesting so much Devi realized and to lessen the effect of the curse, she said she would get the chance to be a mother of a son of Lord Shiva and breast-feed him. Devi Parvathy also said that she would take the form of 'Koolivaka' and deceive Lord Shiva. A son would be born from their holy union and would kill Jalandhara, a powerful Asura.

Thereafter, Devi turned into 'Koolivaka' and began swinging on a vine attached to a jackfruit tree while waiting for Lord Shiva to return. Through their holy union, a child was born who was known as 'Chathan'. They gave the child to 'Koolivaka' to raise him and for his protection, a buffalo was arranged by Lord Shiva. When Chathan grew up, he went for Kailas. Before reaching Kailas he thought that he would not be allowed by Nandikeshwar, so he took the form of Lord Vishnu and entered into Kailash. Lord Shiva and Parvathi became very happy to see their son and hugged him. Later blessed him and told him that he would be known as Vishnu Maya as he took the form of Lord Vishnu by Maya/illusions. After a few days, Chathan fulfilled his destiny by killing Jalandhara on the battleground.

The economic value of jackfruit:

As food:

The nutritional value of jackfruit is very high i.e., per 100g yields a total of 397KJ or 95 Kcal (Mukprasirt and Sajjaanantakul, 2004). Water constitutes the major portion i.e., 74%, then carbohydrate (23%), protein (2%), and fat (1%). Vitamins are also abundant in jackfruit like Vitamin C, Vitamin B6, riboflavin, niacin, pantothenic acid, thiamine, Vitamin E, and minerals like potassium, calcium, iron, magnesium, phosphorous, sodium, manganese, and zinc. The starch content of jackfruit seeds is rather high (Singh et al., 1991). It can be used in making a variety of dishes like cakes, custards or mixed with ice as *es teler* (Indonesian fruit cocktail) or as desserts like halo-halo in the Philippines. In southern India, jackfruits are used in making traditional breakfasts like idli along with rice as an ingredient. Its leaves are used as a wrapper for steaming. Jackfruit dosas are also made by grinding the pulp along with the batter. Ripe jackfruit arils are used as jackfruit chips when fried or dried properly (Jagadeesh et. al, 2006). Pureed jackfruit is also made into baby food, jams, jellies, and juices (Roy and Joshi, 1995). Fruit salad and ice-creams have also been made from mature jackfruits other than used as vegetables for making curry (Narasimham, 1990). Ripe Jackfruit is also used for the production of wine as it contains a good number of fermentable sugars (Amit and Ambarish, 2010). The local tribes of Nagaland, Tripura, and other eastern hilly areas of India consume jackfruit wine. It contains nearly 7% to 8% (v/v) alcohol. Seeds of the ripened fruit are edible and have a milky, sweet taste often compared to Brazil nuts. They are used as snacks in the roasted, baked, or even boiled form (Morton, 1987). When the seeds are roasted the flavor is comparable to chestnuts. Seeds are also used in dessert making. In Java, generally, the seeds are cooked and seasoned with salt. In India, young jackfruits are cooked along with lentils and vegetables in the form of curry. For vegans, jackfruits are an alternate substitute for meat. The seeds are also used in curry.

As fodder:

Cattle, goats, and other animals feed on the leaves. They also eat the fallen fruits. The waste obtained after removing the flesh is considered good fodder for pigs and cattle.

Timber:

The woods are used for building furniture and the construction of houses. Special features of this wood are that it is termite-proof. It resembles Mahogany and is considered to be superior to teak. Wood is used as timber. The jackfruit tree's wood is highly significant in Sri Lanka, and it is also exported to many areas of the world, including Europe. The wood is used mostly for the manufacture of household furniture like tables, chairs, and doors, windows and rooftops, etc.

Craft wood/tools:

The jackfruit wood is also used for the production of musical instruments. In India, it is used to make classical string instruments like Veena and drums, mridangam, thimila, and kanjira. In Indonesia, hardwood is used in the production drum whereas in the Philippines the softwood is used in the body of Kutiyapi, a type of string instrument.

Rope/cordage/string:

The inner bark is very useful in making cordage or cloth.

Fuelwood:

Branches and trunks are used as fuelwood.

Wrapping:

In India, leaves are used as wrapping material for the food while cooking and are also woven together to form plates.

Resin/gum/latex:

For repairing china and earthenware, heated latex can be used as glue. It contains nearly 82.6 to 86.4% resins that may have used in varnishes. The sticky latex is also used as birdlime for trapping birds as well as insects. These latexes also have bacteriolytic properties just like papaya trees.

Tannin/ dye:

In the bark, 3.3% tannins are obtained. It yields a dye when boiled with alum, sawdust, or wood chips. The dye is usually used for giving characteristics color to the robes that are used by Buddhist Priests.

Soil stabilization:

Jackfruit trees are cultivated in farms to control soil erosion. Crop shade/overstory: A jackfruit tree provides dense shade, so it is used during the cultivation of coffee, betelnut, pepper, and cardamom as a shade tree.

Medicinal value:

All parts of the Jackfruit tree are considered to have medicinal properties. The seeds and pulp tonic of Jackfruit have nutritious value and the Chinese thought that it is very much useful in overcoming the effects of alcohol on the body (Morton, 1987). Jackfruit has diverse medicinal uses because of its antioxidant, anti-inflammatory, anti-microbial, anti-cancer, and anti-fungal properties. Jackfruit contains a huge amount of vitamin-C and antioxidant which helps to improve the immunity of the body and to fight against infections (Umesh et. al, 2010). It helps in replenishing energy as 100g serving provides 95Kcal of energy. It also has a lot of carbohydrates in it. The sugars found in jackfruit are easily digestible and are healthy for the body. Per 100 g of ripe Jackfruit, the pulp contains approximately 18.9 grams of carbohydrates, 1.9 grams of protein, 0.1 grams of fat, and 77% moisture content, 1.1 g dietary fiber, 0.8 g total mineral content, 20 mg calcium, 30 mg phosphorus, 500 mg iron, 30 mg thiamine, and 84 calories (Samaddar 1985). Jackfruit is abundant in antioxidants, phytonutrients, and flavonoids. The presence of these antioxidants helps in eliminating the toxins as well as the free radicals produced by the body which were harmful. Jackfruit helps in losing body weight as it is low in calories and fat-free. The presence of an enormous amount of calcium strengthens the bones. Jackfruit also improves blood quality due to the presence of iron and other minerals. Iron helps in curing anemia (Singh et. al, 2010). Copper (10.45 mg) plays a crucial role in thyroid metabolism in the body, especially in hormone production and absorption and jackfruit have good amounts of coppers (Gunasena and others 1996). Vitamin A or beta carotene is found in the jackfruit. So, Jackfruit is also beneficial for enhancing vision. Mainly it reduces the risk of cataracts as well as degeneration of the retina. It also protects the eyes from bacterial and viral infections. Jackfruit has a rich source of phytonutrients that helps in preventing cancer as well as provides other health benefits (Ko FN et. al, 1998). Natural phenolic compounds including simple molecules like phenolic acids, phenylpropanoids, and flavonoids to complex polymerized compounds like lignins, melanins, and tannins are also obtained from Jackfruits, which have tremendous medicinal use (Soobratte et. al, 2005). The powder obtained from the Jackfruit seed is a good source of manganese as well as magnesium elements (Barua and Boruah 2004). Two lectins i.e., jacalin and artocarpin also obtained from the seeds. It has been proved that Jacalin has potential applications for being useful in the evaluation of the immune status of patients who are infected with human immunodeficiency virus 1 (Haq 2006). The presence of an enormous amount of dietary fiber content i.e., 3.6 g/100 g in the jackfruit prevents constipation and helps in producing smooth bowel movements. It also eliminates carcinogenic chemicals from the colon and protects the mucous membranes of the colon (Siddappa, 1957). Jackfruit seed is found to reduce the LDL (Low-density lipoprotein) level and increase the HDL (High-density lipoprotein) level. LDL mainly causes blockage of arteries by waxy deposition and restricts the normal blood flow and causes the rise in blood pressure as well as increases the risk of heart attack or stroke (Esmaillzadeh and Azadbakht, 2008). The presence of potassium also reduces blood pressure. Jackfruit also controls the blood sugar level. Fever and diarrhea are also treated using the root extract. The leaves are very much useful in traditional treatment for recovering skin diseases and healing wounds. The ash of the jackfruit leaves is also very useful in curing ulcers (V. M. Vaidya Gogte, 2000).

References:

Ahmed, K., Malek, M., Jahan, K., & Salamatullah, K. (1986). Nutritive value of Food Stuff 3rd edn Institute of Nutrition and Food Science. *University of Dhaka, Bangladesh*, 16-17.

Baliga, M. S., Shivashankara, A. R., Haniadka, R., Dsouza, J., & Bhat, H. P. (2011). Phytochemistry, nutritional and pharmacological properties of Artocarpus heterophyllus Lam (jackfruit): A review. *Food research international*, *44*(7), 1800-1811.

Gohain Barua, A., & Boruah, B. R. (2004). Minerals and functional groups present in the jackfruit seed: a spectroscopic investigation. *International journal of food sciences and nutrition*, *55*(6), 479-483.

Elevitch, C. R., & Manner, H. I. (2006). Artocarpus heterophyllus (jackfruit). *Species profiles for Pacific Island agroforestry*, *10*, 1-25.

Esmaillzadeh, A., & Azadbakht, L. (2008). Food intake patterns may explain the high prevalence of cardiovascular risk factors among Iranian women. *The Journal of nutrition*, *138*(8), 1469-1475.

Haq, N. (2006). *Jackfruit: Artocarpus heterophyllus* (Vol. 10). Crops for the Future.

Jagadeesh, S. L., Reddy, B. S., Swamy, G. S. K., Gorbal, K., Hegde, L., & Raghavan, G. S. V. (2007). Chemical composition of jackfruit (Artocarpus heterophyllus Lam.) selections of Western Ghats of India. *Food Chemistry*, *102*(1), 361-365.

Ko, F. N., Cheng, Z. J., Lin, C. N., & Teng, C. M. (1998). Scavenger and antioxidant properties of prenylflavonoids isolated from Artocarpus heterophyllus. *Free Radical biology and medicine*, *25*(2), 160-168.

Lin, C. N., Lu, C. M., & Huang, P. L. (1995). Flavonoids from Artocarpus heterophyllus. *Phytochemistry*, *39*(6), 1447-1451.

Morton, J. F. (1987). *Fruits of warm climates*. JF Morton.

Leon, J., & Shaw, P. E. (1990). Spondias: the red mombin and related fruits. *Fruits of tropical and subtropical origin*, 116-126.

Prakash, O., Kumar, R., Mishra, A., & Gupta, R. (2009). *Artocarpus heterophyllus* (Jackfruit): an overview. *Pharmacognosy Reviews*, *3*(6), 353.

Samaddar HM. 1985, Jackfruit. In: Bose TK, Mishra SK, editors. Fruits of India: tropical and subtropical. Calcutta, India: Naya Prokash. p 638–49.

Siddappa GS. 1957. Development of products from jackfruit canned jackfruit, frozen canned jackfruit, and jackfruit jam. J Sci Ind Res 9(11):166–99.

Singh A, Kumar S, Singh IS. 1991. Functional properties of jackfruit seed flour. Lebensm – Wissu Technol 24:373–4

Soobrattee MA, Neergheen VS, Luximon Ramma A, Aruma OI, Bahorun T. 2005. Phenolics as potential antioxidant therapeutic agents: mechanism and action. Mutation Res 579:200–13.

Swami, S. B., Thakor, N. J., Haldankar, P. M., & Kalse, S. B. (2012). Jackfruit and its many functional components as related to human health: a review. *Comprehensive Reviews in Food Science and Food Safety*, *11*(6), 565-576.

Umesh JB, Panaskar Shrimant N, Bapat VA. 2010. Evaluation of antioxidant capacity and phenol content in jackfruit (Artocarpus heterophyllus Lam.) fruit pulp. Plant Foods Hum Nutr 65:99–104.

V. M. Vaidya Gogte, Ayurvedic Pharmacology and therapeutic use of medicinal plants, (Swami Prakashananda Ayurvedic Research center, Mumbai, 2000) 656-657.

Trees of Ramayana (2022): 13-22
Editor: Felix Bast
Today & Tomorrow's Printers and Publishers (India)

Chapter- 2

NEEM TREE (*Azadirachta indica)*

Rupali Patel

आम्रं छित्वा कुठारेण निम्बं परिचरेत्तु यः।

यश्चैनं पयसा सिञ्चेन्नैवास्य मधुरो भवेत्।।2.35.16।।

The above Shloka mentioned in Ayodhya Kanda, Chapter [Sarga] 35, Verse- 16 of Valmiki Ramayana says that "Who should look after a neem tree after cutting down a mango tree (i.e. no one)? Anyone, even with milk, may water the neem tree; indeed then neem does not become sweet" (Joshi 2010). In the epic Ramayana, as Kaikeyi had asked for her boons, that is exile to Rama and throne to Bharata. The king, Dasaratha fell unconsciously; Sumantra, his charioteer, was knocked out as well. All of the palace's women and occupants were in tears. Sumantra regained consciousness after a long period of unconsciousness; she angrily started to torment Kaikeyi with his word-arrows. Here she compares Dasaratha's decision to enthrone Rama, like the mango, and to offer Bharata the throne in exchange for Rama's exile like Nimbam (neem tree). No matter how much milk you pour into the neem tree, it does not acquire sweetness.

Figure: Neem Tree Date of capture: - 20/04/2020, GPS coordinates-Longitude- 83¯ 59’49”, Latitude- 21¯ 34’21”, Locality- Talab, Dist- Sambalpur, Odisha, India. © Rupali Patel

Taxonomy

Kingdom - Plantae

Division - Angiosperms

Order - Sapindales

Family - Meliaceae

Genus - Azadirachta

Species - A. indica

Taxonomic relation with other plants

Neem belongs to the Meliaceae family or the mahogany family which consists of flowering plants of mostly trees and shrubs, with some exceptions, like herbaceous plants in order Sapindales. Trees under this family, are characterized by alternate, usually pinnate leaves without stipules, and by syncarpy, means bisexual (but mostly cryptically unisexual). Flowers are borne in panicles, cymes, spikes, or clusters. Most species are evergreen, although some are deciduous, either in the dry season or in winter. This family includes about 53 genera and about 600 discovered species, with distribution in tropics. For example, one genus (*Toona*) extends north into temperate China and south into South-East Australia. Another one is *Synoum* which extends into South-East Australia. Likewise, *Melia* extends near to far north. The neem tree and its cousin the Chinaberry (*Melia azedarach*), is extremely similar in appearance.

Regional names of neem tree

Neem is known by many different names. Names are Nimm (in Punjabi), Arya Veppu (in Malayalam), Azad Dirakht (in Persian), Nimba (in Sanskrit, Marathi, and Odia), DogonYaro (in some Nigerian languages), Margosa, Neeb (in Arabic), Nimtree, Vepu, Vempu, Vepa (in Telugu), Bevu (in Kannada), Kohomba (in Sinhala), Vembu (in Tamil), Tamar(in Burmese), sau dau, xoan An Do(in Vietnamese), Paraiso (in Spanish) and Indian Liliac (in English).

Morphological characteristics:-

With a binomial name, *Azadirachta indica*, the tree can grow up to 15-20 meters, sometimes up to 35-40 meters. Girth is about 2.5-3 meters. Dense and round canopy can cover as much as 20 m. across, with spreading branches, having dark green leaves. Their bark is of dark grey with light-colored crevices. Pinnate leaves are arranged in branches, oppositely. An individual leaf is roughly 20-40 cm long, having features like bright green and oblique at the base or slightly curved, coarsely toothed with a pointed tip. The petioles are short. Small, white, bisexual flowers found with honey-like scent. Due to this honey-like scent, they can attract bees. They are arranged in an axillary fashion. The inflorescence, which is branched to the third degree, can bear 150-250 flowers. An individual flower is roughly 5-6 mm long and 8-11 mm wide. In neem, flowering begins from March to June. Fruit is a smooth ellipsoidal olive-like drupe having a length of 2 cm. When it ripes, exocarp (fruit skin) becomes thin, with mesocarp (sweet pulp), yellow or greenish-yellow surrounding a seed. The white, inner hard shell, which is endocarp, contains one, rarely two or three, elongated seeds (kernels) having a brown coat. The lifespan of the tree is 150-200 years.

Habitat:-

Neem tree habitats are dry and hot. The tree can resist temperature up to 122¯ Fahrenheit; but cannot cope up with cold, as the temperature below 40¯ Fahrenheit may cause leaves to fall and can kill the tree. It grows well in a temperature range of 50 to 98 degrees Fahrenheit. Known for drought tolerance, this tree can survive as little as 6 inches of annual rainfall, but grows best when it receives 18-47 inches per year. It can tolerate dry periods lasting seven to eight months. It grows between sea level and 2,300 feet in the wild. Also, this tree can cope up with infertile, rocky, and dry soils, though it grows best on deep, sandy soils, where it can extend its taproots. The problem with Neem is that waterlogging mostly kills its roots. Due to this reason, clay or silty clay soils that hold water, whether all year or seasonally, are unsuitable for survival. It cannot cope with salty soil. Soil with a pH level of 5-8 can be tolerated, but the tree best thrives in soil with a 6.2-7 pH level. Natural habitat is seasonally dry, deciduous woodlands, but neem colonized other environments as well. Suited to full-sun or partial-shade sites with well-drained soil, neem tree grows quickly to 50 to 75 feet tall and wide.

Geographical origin and Evolution

The bush forest of Assam and Myanmar (formerly known as Burma) is the original habitat of neem trees (where it is common throughout the central dry zone and the Siwalik Hills), although they can grow mostly in dry, subtropical, and tropical climates. However the exact origin is uncertain; in some botanists' opinion, this tree is native to the whole Indian subcontinent. Neem trees are also found in the Siwalik Hills, Carnate, and Deccan regions of India. Neem trees are cultivated throughout the country, like in India, Sudan, and Australia.

In the annals of the ancient system of medicine, which dates back to 10,000 B.C. to 4,000 B.C, the first medicinal plant mentioned as well as found a place, according to ancient Tamil literature is neem or margosa. The first documentation of the tree in the text is mentioned as advantageous medicinal properties. According to proofs, also found in Indus Valley Civilization. Neem evolved in south-east Asia.

Distribution

Found in dry forest areas throughout all of South and Southeast Asia, including India, Pakistan, Sri Lanka, Thailand, Malaysia, and Indonesia. Neem was introduced to Africa, in the early 20th century. Now the tree is well established in at least 30 countries. In India, mainly found in Assam, Karnataka, Madhya Pradesh, Meghalaya, Odisha, Punjab, Tamil Nadu, Rajasthan, and Uttar Pradesh.

World-wide top Exporters

Leading producers of neem products are countries like India, the United States, and Australia. Talking about the neem oil, it is estimated that India's neem trees bear about 3.5 million tonnes of kernels each year and it produces about 700000 tons of oil that can be recoverable. In the late 1980s, yearly production was barely 150000 tonnes. But, in the current situation, India has tremendously increased its production of neem oil. According to Global Neem Oil Market 2020, the top companies in the global neem oil market competition are East India Distilleries (EID) Parry Limited (a public company headquartered in Chennai, South India), Neeming Australia Private Limited (in Bengaluru, Karnataka, India), P.J. Margo Private Limited, Agro Extract Limited, Ozone Biotech Private Limited, GreeNeem Agri Private Limited, and Fortune Biotech Limited.

Cultural significance

"It is believed that planting a neem tree in the house ensures a passage to heaven. The leaves of neem are strung on the main entrance to the house to keep away evil spirits, pests, and diseases" (Krishna & Amirthalingam, 2014). The neem leaves are laid on the room floors of measles, mumps, or chickenpox patients. Also, leaves are hung on the doorway to announce the presence of Sitala in the house. According to beliefs, Sitala is one of the seven goddess sisters and her presence means that someone in the house is affected by smallpox. In Hindu culture, neem is worshipped as Goddess Durga, also known as Parvati (wife of God Shiva). In some parts of India, the tree itself is thought to be a goddess, as Neemari Devi. This tree is associated with Goddess Sitala in the northern states and Goddess Mariamman in the southern states, as both of them, associated with giving and healing of skin ailments like smallpox. The beautiful and famous deities of the world-famous Ratha Yatra of Odisha are formed from neem woods. In every 19th year, a ritual called "Naba-kalebara", which involves replacing existing wooden idols of God Jagannath, Balabhadra, Subhadra, and Sudarshan Chakra, with newly carved ones. This ritual starts in the month of "Chaitra" (March-April) and ends a few weeks before the Ratha Yatra. No other neem tree but a "Daru Brahma" neem tree is chosen to sculpt the images of the idols. In those places, where there is no temple, a neem tree is worshipped since Devi is supposed to dwell within the tree. Also, local deities in villages with no temple are placed under the shadow of a neem tree. Neem leaves are used in the feast connected with the Lima rites after death, by certain tribes of Odisha. The neem tree is regarded as a symbol of the female and is ceremoniously married to an Aswattha (*Ficus religiosa*) tree, which is symbolic of the male. In villages of India, usually, these two trees are grown side by side with a platform built around them. On the platform, coiled snake stones are placed, which are a symbol of fertility. This symbolic notion of sexes, changes in Rajasthan and Punjab. Here, the Neem tree is considered as a male. Since women in "purdah" (means curtain) do not show their face to strange men, so in these areas, they cover their face with a veil on passing a neem tree. During "Gudi Padwa", which is the New Year in Maharashtra, the ancient practice of drinking neem juice on that day, before celebrating festivities, is found.

Legends and Stories

Many folktales are associated with neem trees. A legend concerning the powerful medicinal properties of the Neem is:

"A woman whose spouse was preparing to depart on a long journey, wished to ensure his early return, so she consulted a medical practitioner who told her that she must encourage her spouse to sleep beneath a tamarind tree on the way out and under a neem tree on the way back. Her husband also agreed to do so. The tamarind is said to emit harmful acid vapors. So, the unfortunate man found himself too sick to continue his travels. He returned earlier however, the healing power of the neem trees beneath which he slept each night had had such an impact that by the time he arrived home, he was feeling much better, in this way his sickness was cured" (Cowen 1952).

Ecological Importance

It naturalizes along sandy riverbanks in Australia. In the Sahara, it is grown in overgrazed, open land to help prevent desertification. Due to the high value of its seeds, wood, bark, and leaves, Neem trees are grown in plantations of tropical countries throughout the world. In towns and cities, it is grown as a shade tree, along the streets, and in parks. This ornamental shade tree is used for large gardens, amusement parks and also can grow in containers indoors.

Flora and Fauna associated with Neem tree

Some birds directly feed on neem fruit. Yellow-vented Bulbul (*Pycnonotus goiavier analis*), is a common feeder and feeds on young fruit. It is prone to plucking ripe fruit, taking to the roofs of houses, to remove the outer covering of fruit before swallowing the pulp and seed. Another bird, Black-naped Oriole (*Oriolus Chinensis*) also feeds on young fruits. These birds often bring their juveniles to the tree and feed them many mouthfuls. Common Myna (*Acridotheres tristis*) is an occasional feeder (Singh 2012). Some other visiting birds are Asian Glossy Starling (*Aplonis panayansis strigata*), Pink-necked Green-pigeon (*Treron vernans*), Lineated Barbet (*Meglaima lineata hodgsoni*), and Asian Koel (*Eudynamys scolopacea*).

Economic importance of this family

Species under this family are generally useful for soap-making, insecticides, vegetable oil, and most importantly, highly prized wood. Some economically important genera and species are *Carapa, Cedrela,* and *Entandrophragma. Carapa* is found in South America and Africa; includes the "crab-wood trees" like *Carapa procera* with a common name andiroba. Timber is important for furniture making. The oil extracted, called andiroba oil which is used to repel mosquitoes by forming an oil-seed cake can be made into balls and burnt, or it can be combined with annatto (Bixa Orellana) and used topically to offer protection from mosquito bites.*Cedrela odorata*, another species found in Central and South America; its timber is also known as Spanish-cedar. Because it is inherently termite and rot resistant, the fragrant wood is in high demand in the American tropics. *Entandrophragma* plants are found in tropical Africa. This taxon includes *E. cylindricum* (commonly known as Sapele) and *E. utile* (commonly known as sipo). The timber of few species is best traded as tropical hardwood. *Guarea*, also known as "pink mahogany" is found in tropical Africa, Central, and South America and includes *Guarea thompsonii* and *Guarea cedrata.* Its timber is very important. African species Pink Mahogany and South American species called cramantee or American musk-wood possibly because hallucinations, if accidentally ingested. Its bark can be used as an expectorant, named "cocillana". *Khaya,* another member, including Ivory Coast Mahogany and Senegal Mahogany, is found in Tropical Africa. Here also, its timber is most important. The timber of *Khaya* is called "African mahogany" and interestingly properties close to genuine mahogany. *Melia azedarach,* also called chinaberry or white cedar, is found in Indo-Malaya and Australasia. The main utility is its timber, which is of medium density and color ranges from light brown to dark red. This species' tough five-grooved seeds were widely used for making rosaries and other products requiring beads. Hummingbirds come and feed on the tree and also help in pollinating flowers. In Kenya, it is used as "fodder trees". *Sandoricum koetjape* (Santol), is common in Southeast Asia and South Asia and is grown for its edible fruit. Pulp of fruit, is eaten in both ways, either raw or simply spices added. This species is used in Filipino and Thai cuisine as an ingredient to make dishes. *Swietenia* is the classic "mahogany" genus and is found in Tropical America. Its timber is most useful. The fruits are called "sky fruit", as they seem to hang upwards from the tree. These sky fruits are used as a natural remedy that improves blood circulation and skin. *Toona,* including the genus of "toon tree" species, like *Toona ciliate,* are found in Tropical Asia, Malaysia, and Australia.

Some species of this genus used as ornamental plants like *Toona Sinensis*. It also provides valuable hardwood, of species *Toona ciliate. Toona Sinensis* is used in Chinese traditional medicine and eaten as a vegetable in China.

Uses of Neem and its products

In most parts of India, neem is used as a vegetable. The tender shoots and flowers of the tree are eaten as a vegetable in India. In Tamil Nadu, a soup-like dish, locally known as "Veppampoo charu", is made of the flower of neem. In West Bengal, young neem leaves are fried in oil with tiny pieces of Brinjal. The dish is called "neem began bhaja" and is served as an appetizer as the first course of a Bengali meal. It's usually served with rice. In Odisha, neem flower is used as an ingredient to prepare a dish, called "Nimba bhaja". For its medicinal properties, in India, it is used for over two millennia, and also mentioned in Ramayana, for its bitter taste. Neem products are believed by Siddha and ayurvedic practitioners to be antifungal, antidiabetic, antibacterial, antiviral, contraceptive, and sedative. Neem oil is used to promote healthy hair as well as enhance liver function, blood detoxification, and blood sugar control. Dermatitis, commonly known as eczema, is a group of illnesses characterized by skin irritation. Neem leaves have been used to treat this condition. These diseases are characterized by itchiness, red skin, and rash. Neem helps in treating Psoriasis (Kumar & Navaratnam, 2013). Neem, a key ingredient in non-pesticidal management (NPM) and thus provides an alternative to synthetic pesticides. Its seeds are powdered and soaked overnight in water and sprayed onto the crop. This powder is applied repeatedly, at least every ten days. As a result, it protects the crop from damage. In response to the above treatment, insects starve and die within a few days. Neem also lowers the number of nuisance insects that emerge from their eggs. Southern armyworm has been successfully controlled with neem-based fertilizers. Neem cake is used as a fertilizer. Neem oil is shown to protect from termite attack by working as an eco-friendly and economical agent.

Neem oil is also used for making polymeric resins. This statement is proved by the synthesis of various alkyd resins from neem oil, using a monoglyceride and their utilization for the preparation of PU coatings. The alkyds are prepared from the reaction of conventional divalent acid materials like phthalic and maleic anhydrides with monoglyceride of neem oil. In construction work, the juice of this plant is a potential ingredient for preparing wall plaster mixture. According to the "Samarangana Sutradhara", a Sanskrit book dealing with "Silpa-sastra" of Hindu science of art and construction, today, the timber of neem is used to make furniture from its termite-resistant wood.

Among other uses, the wood of the neem tree is used to make handicrafts like hair combs. This generates a source of income for villagers. It is a common belief that regular use of a hair comb, made from neem wood can control hair loss, dandruff, and other scalp problems. In toiletries, neem oil is used for preparing products such as bathing soaps, shampoos, balms, and creams. Nowadays, it is used in toothpaste also. In animal treatment, used to treat sweet itch and mud fever diseases in horses. Traditionally, slender neem twigs (called "datun"), are first chewed as a toothbrush and then split as a tongue cleaner. This practice is still prevalent in rural India. It is effective in reducing dental plaque (in which a mass of bacteria, which grows on surfaces within the mouth and later leads to dental decay) and gingivitis (a disease that causes inflammation of the gums). Apart from this in modern dentistry, it is used as an endodontic irritant against *E. faecalis* and Anticaries against *S. mutans* in dental erosion therapy. Neem can be used in cancer therapy, by arresting tumor cell growth and its proliferation. This can be achieved by affecting the expression of the p53 gene. Products that are also used in immunomodulation is as having anti-inflammatory and anti-microbial properties

In cosmetics, powdered neem leaves are a major component of natural facial cream. Purified neem oil is used as nail polish. Neem leaves, boiled in water, can be used as a very cost-effective bird repellent, especially for sparrows. To use it as resin, exudate can be trapped from the trunk, by wounding the bark. This high protein material, called "neem glue", is used as a food additive, in some parts of Odisha. As neem bark contains 14% tannin, for this reason, yields a strong fiber that can be commonly woven into ropes. This practice is prevalent in villages of India. People also promote apiculture by planting neem trees. Due to its antibacterial, antifungal properties, it is used in neem oil soap manufacturing plants, in India. Also, crude oil is used to produce coarse laundry soaps. In musical instruments, neem wood is considered best for the body of the "Dayan", which is the right-hand drum, of the tabla.

Oldest and Famous neem trees

A neem tree at Secunderabad Mahakali Temple has been standing strong for the past 300 years and for believers, it has become an integral component of temple worship.Devi Koli Temple, in Tamilnadu, has a neem tree that is more than 100 years old. These are few examples, as neem tree's average lifespan is 200 years. So there are many undocumented trees in India. Neem, due to its healing properties from diseases, is called "Sarva Roga Nivarini", in Vedas. Each part of this tree is precious. That's why its name is found in precious ancient texts like Ramayana. This tree is an integral part of Indian culture in various ways. Every village in India has neem trees that are worshiped by folks. In the modern world, the export of neem trees and their products is an important source of income for the Indian population. This shows progress along with the preservation of nature and our ancient culture.

REFERENCE

Kumar, V. S., & Navaratnam, V. (2013). Neem (*Azadirachta indica*): Prehistory to contemporary medicinal uses to humankind. Asian pacific journal of tropical biomedicine, 3(7), 505-514.

Joshi, S. (2010, December 19). Don't ax your good projects. *Practical Sanskrit* blog.

http://PracticalSanskrit.com

Singh, A. (2012, October 30). Neem (*Azadirachta indica*) - An Important Source for Garden Birds. 30/10/2012. Bird Ecology Study Group (BESG). *Feeding-plants.*

Krishna, N. & Amirthalingam, M. (2014). Sacred plants of India. Penguin Books of India Pvt. Ltd.

Cowen, D.V. (1952). Flowering Trees and Shrubs in India. Thacker & Co. Ltd. 3rd edition.

Trees of Ramayana (2022): 23-33
Editor: Felix Bast
Today & Tomorrow's Printers and Publishers (India)

Chapter-3

Bamboo tree (*Bambusa*)

Ananya Pradhan

आम्रं छित्वा कुठारेण निम्बं परिचरेत्तु यः।

यश्चैनं पयसा सिञ्चेन्नैवास्य मधुरो भवेत्।।2.35.16।।

The above Shloka mentioned in Sarga 55 of Ayodhya Kanda states that during Rama's exile, the first camp was in Chitrakuta forest, which is located on the borders of Chitrakuta district of Uttar Pradesh and Satna district of Madhya Pradesh. The shloka means- "Then they both made a big wooden float by joining logs of wood, spreading bamboo on it and covering it with the (fragrant roots of) Ushira bushes."

पर्णशालां सुविपुलां तत्र सङ्खातमृत्तिकाम्।

सुस्तम्भां मस्करैर्दीर्घैः कृतवंशां सुशोभनाम्।।3.15. 21।।

शमीशाखाभिरास्तीर्य दृढपाशावपाशिताम्।

कुशकाशशरैः पर्णैस्सुपरिच्छादितां तथा।।3.15.22।।

समीकृततलां रम्यां चकार लघुविक्रमः।

निवासं राघवस्यार्थे प्रेक्षणीयमनुत्तमम्।।3.15.23।।

This Shloka mentioned in Sarga 15 of Aranya Kanda states that Lakshmana built a very spacious straw cottage there leveling and raising the clay for the raised floor of the cottage, strongly pillared with long bamboos, branches of Shami trees firmly twines with jute strands and with cross laid bamboos for thatching, and over that blades of kusha grass and leaves of kasha are spread and well over covered for the roof. In Aranya Kanda, the Panchavati forest is mentioned where Sri Ram stayed during forest exile and from where Devi Sita was kidnapped. It is situated on the Godavari's banks.

(Figure: Bamboo tree (*Bambusa vulgaris*), Date of Capture- 20/04/2020, GPS coordinates- 20R"42'47"N & 86R"26'2"E, Locality- Kalyanpur village, Dist: Jajpur, Odisha, India). © Ananya Pradhan

Taxonomy

Kingdom: Plantae

Subkingdom: Tracheobionta

Superdivision: Spermatophyta

Division: Magnoliophyta

Class: Liliopsida

Subclass: Commelinidae

Order: Cyperales

Family: Poaceae

Genus: *Bambus*

Species- *Vulgaris/ balcooa/ bambos/ tulda/ blumeana/ polymorpha/ ventricosa/ multiplex/ textilis/ pallida/ chungii etc.*

Botanical name: Bambusa

Common name: Bamboo, Varan

Sanskrit name: Vamsa

Local name: Baunsa (Odia), Bamsa gacha (Bengali), Munkil MaramMaram (Tamil), Veduru cettu (Telugu), Mula Maram (Malayalam), Bansa da rukha (Punjabi), Bans (Rajasthani), Bhaluka (Assamese)

Morphological Characteristics

Bamboos are members of the grass family. Like other grass, bamboos have jointed stems, small flowers enclosed in structures known as spikelet, a specially modified embryo within the seed, and a grain-like fruit. Many bamboos have tall, somewhat arched stems, but others have shrubby, or slender and twining. The largest bamboo reaches 30 meters in height and 30 cm in diameter while the smallest ones have delicate stems no more than 10 cm tall. Bamboo often grows at low elevations, but many species grow in mountain forests, and some range up to 4300 meters elevation in equatorial highlands. It will grow 1-2 blocks taller when Bone Meal is used on it. Maximum 12-16 blocks tall bamboo can grow (Y.C. Tripathi, 2008). To maintain the desired height pruning is necessary. Topping is a form of pruning. Removing the top bamboo will result in new leaves sprouting from the cut rather than cane regrowth. As a result, chopping a bamboo grove to the ground will not eliminate it, stalks eventually regrow, but form the base rather than from cut canes (Bahadur, K.N., 1979).

Canopy

The canopy, in addition to attracting a diverse range of animals, plays an essential role in controlling regional and global climate since it is the primary location of heat, water vapor, and atmospheric gases exchange. Forest community structure and dynamics are influenced by interactions between forest canopy features and plants in the forest understory. The dwarf bamboo *Bashania fangiana* Yi dominates the underbrush of a mixed canopy of evergreen *Abies fanoniana* and deciduous Betula utilis in the mountains of southwestern China. Bamboo canopy is used in different crafts in a different community (Biozhen, C., & Hexian, J., 2010; Ben-Zhi, Z. et al., 2005).

Longevity

Bamboo produces new canes in the spring. For around 60 days, the shoots emerge out of the ground and grow in height and diameter. During these 60 days, it will develop limbs and leaves. Bamboo does not show secondary growth like trees or most floras. It will emerge in new foliage every year and a cane generally lives for 10 years. It uses more energy to produce more plants and expand the root structure because it is a colony plant. It takes around three years for bamboo to establish itself. As the colony grows closer to maturity, the new shoots that emerge in the spring will continue to grow bigger and more numerous from year to year. It takes a variable number of years (4-5) for distinct species to reach their highest size. This is completely dependent on species selection, sunlight, soil, climate, and water conditions. Temperature bamboo typically seeds on 75-year cycles and the viability of the seeds are very short. A bamboo bush can live for a century or longer. An average can live up to 15 years depending on the species, but to generalize, 7 to 10 years is more common. The shorter plant and smaller plants will begin to die off a little faster as the grove matures because of sunlight's absence. Even after being subjected to lower temperatures, several bamboos will survive. While it may be distressing to see the beautiful foliage or culms die due to extreme cold, it is comforting in most situations to see the bamboo bounce back, the following spring with new culms. This happens only when the bamboo is subjected to temperatures below those recommended for the species or to extreme wind chills (Kurz, S., 1876). So it is always important to choose an appropriate species according to the climate zone and application.

Flower character:

The flowering of bamboo is an intriguing phenomenon. Depending on the species most bamboos flower once every 60 to 130 years. Depending on species, bamboo can exhibit gregarious flowering, sporadic flowering, or annual flowering. Gregarious flowering is the most common and impressive pattern of bamboo flowering. Genetically this flowering cycle is pre-programmed into each species. When a bamboo blossoms profusely, it expends a great deal of energy in the production of flowers and seeds. Sporadic flowering is when bamboo flowers sporadically (Y. C. Tripathi, 2008). Generally, environmental factors rather than genetics brought sporadic flowering. Sporadic blooming does not occur on a large scale, and unlike gregarious flowering, the bamboo seldom dies after flowering. It usually affects a single plant or a small group of plants in a specific region.

Fruit

Bamboo blossom is a natural occurrence in which bamboos bloom and become laden with bamboo seeds in a specific spot. In China, Myanmar, and India this is commonly found. Bamboos usually have a life cycle of around 40 to 80 years, varying among species. Normally bamboo grows from bamboo shoots at the roots. They start to blossom, at infrequent intervals for most species. Flowers produce fruit, after blossom (called bamboo rice in parts of India and China). Following this, the bamboo forests die out. The death of bamboo occurs in a large area since a bamboo forest usually grows from a single bamboo. The shoots are the edible part for humans, which is the fast-growing portion of the grass. Flowering bamboo provides an abundant supply of bamboo fruits. Many researchers are investigating the nutritional properties of the fruits belonging to the bamboo *Melocanna baccifera,* locally known as Muli. Muli bamboo is distributed across northeast India, Nepal, Bangladesh, and its flowers once every 40 to 50 years (Balaji Govindan et al., 2016). In the bamboo fruiting season, its fruits are savoured by rodents, which feed on the grains from nearby agricultural fields. In addition to the massive crop loss that the rats cause, they vigorously multiply, leading to the outbreak of diseases. Another study by the researchers found that they have a high nutritional and medicinal value with rich antioxidant properties (Jeeva S., et al., 2009).

Habitat and distribution

The majority of bamboo species are found in tropical and mild temperate regions. Many species may be found in a variety of settings, from hot tropical areas to cold alpine regions and cloud forests in the highlands. In the Asia Pacific region, they occur across East Asia, from north to 50N latitude in Sakhalin, to the south to northern Australia, and west to India and the Himalayas (Soderstrom and Calderon, 1979). Bamboo shows endemic populations in China, Japan, Korea, India, and Australia. Bamboo's natural range in the Americas extends from southern Argentina and central Chile's beech forests, through South American tropical rainforests, and up to the Andes in Ecuador near 4300 meters (L.G. Clark, 2015). Bamboo is also endemic to Central America and Mexico, as well as the United States' south-eastern states. Bambusa and Dendrocalamus thrive in tropical circumstances in India, but Arundinaria and its relatives thrive in temperate conditions and are widely found at higher altitudes in the western and eastern Himalayas. Dendrocalamus is predominant in dry deciduous forests, while the distribution of bamboo is governed largely by rainfall, temperature, height, and soil characteristics are all factors to consider. The majority of bamboos require a temperature range of 8 to 36 degrees celsius, a minimum annual rainfall of 1000mm, and high atmospheric humidity for good growth

Evolution

Tropical woody bamboos (Bambuseae), temperate woody bamboos (Arundinariae), and herbaceous bamboos (Olyreae) are three distinct and comprise lineages of Bambusoideae (Poaceae). Bambuseae and Olyreae have a sister relationship which is generally supported by chloroplast markers. This suggests two things, either at least two origins of the woody bamboo in this subfamily or its loss of Olyreae. There was a phylogenomic study on chloroplast genome (plastome) presented using the coding and non-coding regions of 13 complete plastomes from the Bambuseae, 8 from Olyreae, and 10 from Arundinarieae (Bedell PE, 1997; Bahadur, K.N., 1979). Trees generated using full plastome sequences support the monophyletic relationship between Bambuseae and Olyreae. In addition to these relationships, several unique plastome features are uncovered including the first mitogenome to plastogenome horizontal gene transfer observed in monocot. From Neotropical woody bamboos and the first full plastome phylogenomic study performed within the herbaceous bamboos, this study presents the first published plastomes. Although the phylogenomic tree presented in the study is largely robust, additional studies using nuclear genes support monopoly in woody bamboos as well as hybridization among previous woody bamboo lineages. Flowering pattern, molecular marker, protein decoding, geographical distribution, plant adaptation, and plastome phylogenomic analysis make sure the Bambusa evolution as a grass family. The species of bamboo evolved from prehistoric grasses between thirty and forty million years ago, long after the extinction of the dinosaurs. There are a variety of genesis stories of bamboo among them there is an interesting story of bamboo. Mambu is a Malay word, from which the word bamboo originated. Malaya is the national language of Malaysia and Indonesia. In the late 16th century "Bamboes" the Dutch name, often got its Bambuse Neo Latin name. When bamboo explodes in the open fire, it resembles a sound by claiming that the original Malayan word was Bambu. The air in the empty internode compartments will expand when they are sealed when bamboo is heated and cause an explosive bam-boom sound. Some studies have reported some fossils of bamboo culms, namely *Bambusiculmus tirapensis sp.* Nov. and *Bambusiculmus makumensis sp.* Nov. from the late Oligocene and two new impressions of bamboo leaves, namely *Bambusium deomaressions sp.* Nov. and *Bambusium makumensis sp.* Nov. from northeast India the late Miocene to Pliocene sediments (Eduardo

Ruiz-Sanchez, 2015). The culm fossils reported here represent the earliest records of bamboo from Asia thereby indicating that bamboos probably dispersed to Asia from India after the establishment of land connections between the Indian and Eurasian plates. During the Miocene in Asia, the Neogene bamboos indicate the diversification of their ecological niche. Since the late Oligocene, the present fossils also reveal their adaptation to a monsoonal climate.

Taxonomy with related plant

Bambusa vulgaris (bamboo) is used in papermaking and the manufacture of ornamental objects and handicrafts. It's also utilized to make a variety of things, including hunting and fishing equipment, household or personal items, gasoline, and lightning. Bamboo extracts can also be used to treat inflammatory disorders (L. G. Clark et al., 2015).

Dendrocalamus giganteus (bamboo) is used in construction and paper making as well. The bamboo's young shoots are used to make vegetable items. The culms are used to make furniture, buckets, vases, matting, boards, rural housing, and water pipes (Bahadur, K.N. 1979).

Cultural significance

In different cultures bamboo is a symbol of oriental beauty like Chinese culture. It symbolizes the character of morals, integrity, modesty, and loyalty. Green plantain trees make bamboo houses for a lovely picture. Bamboo has been used in architectural art. Artists praised bamboo in their paintings, calligraphy, and poetry for thousands of years, generations. Deep mountains surrounded by bamboo forests are often used by many ancient scholars who chose to live. Now they are using it for making papers (Kurz, S., 1876). According to Japanese culture, in the case of an earthquake, people were instructed to run into the bamboo groves since the bamboo's strong root system would keep the ground together. Bamboo and sasa are used in festivals to ward off evil. In India, kenbah and kenmynsaw villages that fall under the East Khasi Hills districts of Meghalaya use bamboo in their domestic and economic sphere and also in their folklore and life cycle rituals. The close connection between bamboo and khasi is evident from its presence in their belief, customs, and traditions (Varmah, J.C.; Bahadur, K.N., 1980).

Legend story

In Japan, there is an ancient tale about bamboo. "Taketori Monogatari (a Bamboo Cutter's Tale)," also renowned as "Kaguya-Hime

(The Princess Kaguya)," is the earliest Kana writing narrative writing and one of Japan's greatest treasured stories. Kaguya- Hime, the whole story is all about whom, who is found inside a bamboo stalk. She becomes a beautiful woman when an old man and woman raise her. She never marries, although many young men propose to her. She returns to the moon, eventually on an evening when the moon is full, as it was her place of birth. Many celebrations utilize bamboo and sasa to fend off evil. People put their wishes on strips of paper of various colors and hang them on sasa during Tanabata (July 7). Ancient Chinese people designated the plum, orchid, and bamboo, and chrysanthemum as the "four gentlemen", and pine, bamboo, and plum as the "three friends in winter" (Tania Yeromiyan, 2021). People think its deep root denotes steadiness and persistence; its tall, straight stem represents honor; its hollow interior and clean exterior exemplify modesty.

Medicinal value

From the dawn of time, bamboo has been inextricably linked to humanity. They're well-known for their industrial applications, a lesser-known fact of bamboo is the usage of its young shoots can be consumed fresh, fermented, or canned as a food. The young shoots are not only tasty, but they're also high in nutrients like proteins, carbs, minerals, and fiber, and they're low in fat and sugar. They also include phytosterols and a high fiber content, making them nutraceuticals or natural medicines that are gaining the attention of both health advocates and scientists. Without the application of fertilizers, the shoots are free from residual toxicity. Modern research has revealed that bamboo has several health benefits: promoting weight reduction, boosting appetite and digestion, and treating cardiovascular and cancer illnesses. The shoots have anticancer, antibacterial, and antiviral properties, according to reports. Due to the phenolic compounds, shoots have antioxidant capacity (Biozhen, C., & Hexian, J., 2010). Bamboo shoots can be one of them, by which the health consciousness among consumers increases the trends. Bamboo fiber is now widely used in breakfast cereals, pasta, snacks, fruit juices, frozen desserts, meat products, and many other products (Kurz, S., 1876).

Economic importance

For farmers planting bamboo is beneficial because it has a low initial cost, so it reduces the investment burden. Being different from timber trees, it is easy to pay back because it has great economic value. Fresh bamboo and dried bamboo leaves are used differently like wrapping material and organic fertilizer respectively. In western countries, bamboo shoot is used as food due to its high nutritional value. Fresh bamboo leaves are used for wrapping material, dried bamboo leaves are used as a type of organic fertilizer. Bamboo culm is utilized as a construction material and in the creation of handicrafts. The bamboo root is used. Bamboo is used for making clothes, accessories, furniture, rugs, diapers, toys, durable utensils, musical instruments, etc. Many buyers are prepared to pay a 15% extra for bamboo items since they are fresh and environmentally beneficial. The government in China, India, and Indonesia are encouraging the farmers to develop bamboo to replace timber trees. Bamboo charcoal has a lot of special functions like that of wood charcoal. Bamboo charcoal has good adsorption capacity and is used to purify air and water because of its bigger specific surface area (Qisheng et al., 2009). The bamboo ecosystem plays an important role in forest CO2 sequestration. 4.05 percent of total carbon inventory is done by bamboo (Deying et al., 2003). The bamboo forest is very much useful in urban areas. It is a beautiful thing which is especially cleaning urban air, soil, and water and shielding communities from industry and heavily tracked areas.

Ecological importance

Bamboo forest functions as carbon sinks, produce oxygen, regulate water levels in watersheds, control soil erosion, conserve biodiversity, provide oxygen matter, beautify the landscape and essentially contribute to the purification and regulation of the environment (Ben-Zhi, Z., et al., 2005). That's why we can say that bamboo forests have many environmental benefits.

Tourism

Tourism contributed to 26 percent of the GDP of Chishui in the year 2015. The tourist industry employs about 50 thousand people in the area. Bamboo is also known for tourism because there are six well-known scenic spots and it supports the ecotourism industry in Chishui. Bamboo-themed parks and national bamboo Sea Park are among them. The bamboo sea park covers 11,200 hectares, a magnificent sight. In 1993 that part offered a picturesque view of the bamboo-covered landscape. The park, which employs over 100 employees, receives almost 200,000 visitors each year. The park contains different shops which sell locally created bamboo products like handicrafts, shoots, souvenirs, utensils, and juices. This national bamboo park sets an example, how bamboo creates economic opportunities and supports climate change mitigation. The remarkable bamboo from small and medium bamboo-based units to ecotourism became an important element of the people's lives in Chishui. In India, Tripura is highly cultivated area of bamboo. That area covers with a clean, large natural environment because of the dense forest. It reflects the perfectly placed bamboo-based eco-tourism opportunity like the tree house recreation, tribal tourism, and village immersion tours (Subhashish Chakraborty, 2020).

Conservation

An account of their irregular flowering and seedling nature, bamboos set great importance on conservation. The strategy for conservation of rare and threatened bamboo species can be broadly classified in two ways: 1) in situ conservation: involves prevention measures against the exploitation of edible shoots, culm extraction of rare species, fencing of the area in seeding year, restriction on clear-felling and declaration of bamboo sanctuary for lesser-known species. This method helps in preserving interspecific and intraspecific genetic variability. Therefore, areas rich in species diversity need to be marked for taking conservation measures of economically important, rare, and vulnerable species 2) ex situ conservation: this involves seed banks, clone banks, bamboo gardens, and cryopreservation. Several botanical gardens and arboreta in the topics are maintaining a rich collection of bamboos for botanical conservation and study. Fine collections of bamboo exist at Royal Botanical Garden, Peradeniya, Hopei, Botanical Garden of Tokyo, etc. ICFRE Dehradun, research wings of the different states and some universities which are maintaining inter and intraspecies collection of bamboos as per the regional priority so that they can conserve the resources and promote their use in that region (Baozhen, C., & Hexian, J., 2010). The intraspecies cohorts of bamboos raised from the seeds of clumps that have flowered at different periods by maintaining a proper record will serve as a useful gene pool for planting those areas which flower gregariously in the days to come.

References

Bahadur, K.N. (1979). Taxonomy of bamboos. *Indian Journal of Forestry*, 2(3), 222-241.

Baozhen, C., & Hexian, J. (2010). Biological characteristics of Bamboo and Its Application in Scenic Gardening [J]. *World Bamboo and Rattan, 4.*

Bedell PE (1997) Taxonomy of bamboos. *APC Publications, New Delhi,* p 150

Ben-Zhi, Z., Mao-Yi, F., Jin-Zhong, X., Xiao-sheng, Y., & Zheng-Cai, L. (2005). Ecological functions of the bamboo forest: research and application. *Journal of Forestry Research, 16(2), 143-147.*

B. Govindan, A. J. Johnson, S. N. A. Nair, B. Gopakumar, K. S. L. Mallampalli, R. Venkatraman, K. C. Koshy, and S. Baby. (2016). Nutritional properties of the largest bamboo fruit *Melocanna baccifera* and its ecological significance. *Scientific report,* 6: 26135.

Deying, L. Z. F. M. X. (2003). Bamboo Ecosystem and Carbon Dioxide Sequestration [J]. *Journal of Bamboo Research, 4.*

Eduardo Ruiz-Sanchez, Lakshmi Attigala, Mel Duvall, William P Wysocki (2015). Evolution of Bamboo. *Article in BMC Evolutionary Biology,* DOI: 10.1186/s12862-015-0321-5.

Jeeva S., Kiruba S., Lalthruatluanga H., Prasad M. N. V. & Rao R. R. (2009). Flowering of *Melocanna baccifera* (Bambusaceae) in northeastern India. *Curr. Sci.* 96, 1165–1166.

Kurz, S. (1876). Bamboo and its use. *Indian Forester*, 1, 219-235.

L. G. Clark, X. Londono, and E. R. Sanchez. (2015). Bamboo Taxonomy and Habitat. *Biological Science, Bamboo* (pp. 1-30).

Qisheng, Z. H. A. N. G., & JIABIN, Z.H.O.U. (2009). Outstanding Functions of Bamboo Charcoal [J]. *World Bamboo and Rattan, 5.*

Varmah, J.C.; Bahadur, K.N. (1980). Country report and status of research on bamboos in India. *Indian Forest Rec., ns, Bot*, 6(1), 1-28.

Yogesh Chandra Tripathi. (2008). Bamboo identification. *Advanced Research Center for Bamboo and Rattan, Aizwal (Mizoram)*, 02.

Trees of Ramayana (2022): 35-50
Editor: Felix Bast
Today & Tomorrow's Printers and Publishers (India)

Chapter-4

Coconut Tree (*Cocus nucifera)*

Sarbani Roy

कदल्याढकिसम्बाधं नारिकेलोपशोभितम्।

सालैस्तालैस्तमालैश्च पुष्पितैस्तरुभिर्वृतम्।।3.35.13।।

In the shloka number-13 of chapter-35 (Life in Dandakvan: from Chitrakoot to Panchvati) in Book-3 of Valmiki's Ramayana published by Gita Press, the tree was mentioned during Ravana's journey from Lanka to Panchavati along the seacoast. The Shloka means -"The entire place was surrounded with banana plants, and coconut trees as well as sal, and Tamala trees blossomed and were looking extremely beautiful, and the entire scenic beauty was captivating." When Ravana mounted pushpak viman and traveled along the aerial route from Lanka, he went surveying coastline crested with mountains, and was crowded with thousands of trees bearing varieties of flowers, and fruits. The great sages lived in their hermitages and areas were surrounded by ponds with sparkling water depicting its purity, and adding up to the mesmerizing beauty of nature. The coastline was charming with swans, herons, frogs, and canes. It was embellished with coconut, Sal, palm trees looking fascinating with plantain grooves (Amirthalingam et al., 2013).

Figure: Coconut Tree (*Cocus nucifera*). Leaf fronds crowned at top of the trunk in a rosette pattern, GPS coordinates: 21°50'39.96528" N-86°56'21.86268" E, Locality: Chitrada, Odisha, India, Date of capture: 20-04-2020. © Sarbani Roy

Taxonomic Position

Domain: Eukaryota

Kingdom: Plantae

Division: Spermatophyta

Subdivision: Angiospermae

Class: Monocotyledonae

Order: Arecales

Family: Arecaceae

Genus: *Cocos*

Species: *C. nucifera*

Other Names

Botanical Name: *Cocos nucifera* L.

Common Name: Coconut palm, Copra

Local Name: Sanskrit- Narikela, Hindi- Nariyal, Bengali- Narkel, Malayalam- Thengu, Tamil- Ney, Telugu- Narikelamu, Odia- Nadia, Punjabi-Narial

Trade Name: Coconut

Eppo Code: CCNNU

Morphological Characteristics

Coconut is a monocotyledon belonging to the palm family of order Palmae, and the single existing species of the genus. It is a perennial tree. It is a single species of the genus that is woody and propagated through seed. Trees are usually erect, and unbranched. The trunk appears light greyish brown. In some regions old leaves fall, forming scars that occur in ring patterns. The inflorescence is a spadix that is branched and enclosed in a sheath.

The height of the tree varies from 25-30 m, but dwarf varieties also exist. Trunks are slender, and slightly swollen at the base, and reach a diameter of 30-40 cm. The canopy is usually dense, having an 8-9 m diameter. A single unbranched stem bears a crown of fronds, which grows aerially from a solitary growth point and is crowned with a terminal crown of leaves. In a mature healthy coconut tree, fronds appear spherical and are evenly distributed in all directions starting from the growing tip. Coconut trees that are heavily loaded with nuts pushing the horizontal frond downwards, and canopy appear X-shaped where no fronds are held in a horizontal position.

Stem arises from a swollen base called bole. Usually, it is smooth in texture, erect, and sometimes slightly leaned, light greyish (Chan, and Elevitch, 2006). It grows in the center from a terminal bud present at the top. Initially, it germinates, during the first growth years, and forms very short internodes. Later this sprouts and produces many adventitious roots. Finally, the stem develops fully, and attains its width at the end of the fourth year., and then it emerges from the ground, and elongates. Lateral growth does not occur as it is devoid of cambium, and wounds remain visible as they are uncovered. The diameter remains the same under normal conditions. The cortex consists of parenchymatous tissue enclosing vascular bundles at the center and is more widely spaced than at the periphery.

Leaves appear on the top of the tree in a rosette pattern. Up to the age of one year, leaves are entire which progressively become pinnate about 4-6 m long, and pinnae are 60-90 cm long. Leaves are widely recognized as paripinnate arranged in a single plane with 200-250 linear-lanceolate leaflets on either side of the rachis (Chan, and Elevitch, 2006). The expanded base of the petiole forms a base for the fronds to attach to the stem. Petiole marks a quarter of the length of the frond of 4.5-5.5 m.

Leaflets are 1.5-5 cm wide, and 50-150 cm long. The length of leaves depends on age, variety, and growing condition. The youngest leaves are wrapped together and folded, and the oldest leaves are present in the lowest whorls, and few leaves before dropping that are on verge of withering along the stem. Leaf stalks are thorn less, and 1-2 cm long. Leaf-blades are covered with cuticles. The lower epidermis is thinner and contains stomata. Primarily, trees produce 12-18 leaves per year. But as tree senesce about 2.5 years 30-35 leaves occur in the crown.

Inflorescence develops at the axils of the leaf and is spadix. Before opening at about 33 months initiation of spadix begins. 1 m long spadix occurs in spear shape. It is enclosed within a sheath and develops inside it which later splits open. The spikes are closely situated to the main axis with length 1-1.5 m, and flowers on 40-60 spikelets. Each spike at its base contains few, and the rest is scattered with male flowers. 200-300 male flowers are born on each spike with just 1 or 2 female flowers (Jay, 1974). Thus, spadix contains only 50-60 female flowers and thousands of male flowers.

Coconut is monoecious with axillary flowers. Male flowers and female flowers form within spathe which upon flowering splits opens along the length. Flowers are borne in clusters emerging from canoe-shaped sheaths present among the leaves. They are minute slight yellow. Both male and female contain six perianths, in the former are smaller, and numerous surrounded by six stamens, and the latter are fewer, larger globose in structure arranged in two whorls. It has a tricarpous ovary with each having a single ovule. The stigma is trifid. At the time of pollination following fertilization, one carpel develops into seed, and two degenerates. Perianth persists at the base after the maturation of fruit (Chan, and Elevitch, 2006; Perera et al., 2010). The protogynous condition occurs thus encouraging cross-pollination. Female flowers become receptive soon after the completion of anthesis. But, pollination occurs on the same coconut tree between flowers of successive spadices. Under favorable conditions, the first flowering occurs 4-5 years after plantation. Upon maturity, at the axil of the leaf, a spadix is produced. Throughout the year except for the drought condition 12-15 spadices are produced in regular intervals. However, the duration of the male phase of the coconut tree is about 18-22 days vary according to the growing environmental condition.

Fruits are large and fibrous drupes. Its shape is ovoid and is 40 cm long and 30cm wide. From the outside in, it consists of exocarp that is thin, hard usually green, yellow or bronze-gold that turns brown upon maturity

(Orwa et al., 2009); a thicker layer of fibrous mesocarp, husk from which coir is obtained at maturity; a shell that is hard endocarp covering seed; white kernel called endosperm in the solid form filled in seeds adhered to the seed coat, copra derived this; and large water-filled cavity in form of liquid endosperm called coconut milk. The size and shape of fruit vary among different varieties. It takes 12 months for the fruit to mature, and takes 5-6 years to produce the first mature fruit after planting. After this, fruits are produced throughout the year, and more are produced in areas with seasonal rainfall.

Shell and kernel make the seed. It is surrounded by an intact husk. Seed Nuts are usually harvested for planting only. These are smaller than the fruit in appearance but weigh less. Husk usually dries with partial loss of water from the cavity. The nut contains three micropyles, and remains viable up to 120 days in floating condition, and germinates upon landfall, and can move 10 m inland without the assistance of man. But when seeds are disseminated by people, the spread is limited to coasts. However, distribution is panning tropical to people primarily of inland spread.

Although being monocot it has profuse adventitious roots rather than taproot arising from the base of the stem. The first root develops at germination, and later starts radiating forms more rootlets about 2000-4000 per coconut tree with a diameter of about 1 cm. Pneumatophores are present on the first roots (Pannetier, and Buffard-Morel, 2012). The root grows normally covered with soil and develops secondary roots. The cycle continues as the old root dies, and the new growth. Physical characteristics of soil and water table decide the depth of the root. Root hair is absent. The cortex is covered with hypodermis that is thick, hard, and impervious to water. A root cap protects the tip of the root. Minerals are absorbed behind the root tip in the white zone.

Habitat

C. nucifera thrives on sandy soil and is highly salinity tolerant. It thrives at altitudes of 520-900 meters in tropical and subtropical regions of the world. Mostly growth is well-preferred in areas with regular rainfall and abundant sunlight. They colonize the coastline in the tropics. The annual temperature of about 21-30 ! (Orwa et al., 2009), and regular rainfall about 1000-1500 mm with abundant sunlight, and 80-90% humidity are better for the growth (Chan, and Elevitch, 2006). For successful growth, the warm condition is required and is intolerant to cold. The soil should be deep alluvial or loamy which is found along the seashore. Soil should be well aerated and drained while sandy soil is mostly preferred. But coconut trees can tolerate variance in soil texture, and adapt to heavier texture. It occurs in both terrestrial and littoral habitats. Inland it has been introduced by humans, and is planted, and cultivated in many places across the world.

Geographical Distribution

It is native to the littoral zone in Southeast Asia including Malaysia, Indonesia, the Philippines, and Melanesia (USDA-ARS, 2014). Across the world, it is a common component of coastal ecosystems and an island. It is rather an invasion or possibly native to the Central America Pacific Coast. Earlier it was carried along currents in the tropic during the prehistoric time from eastward to tropical Pacific island, and from westward to coastal Sri Lanka, India, East Africa, and tropical islands in the Indian Ocean such as Mauritius, Andaman, Seychelles. In these regions of the sandy coralline coast, coconut trees were established on their own.

At present, it has wide pan tropical distribution occurring in about more than 80 countries across Asia, Africa, Oceania, and America. In all tropical, and subtropical regions 23' north, and south of the equator, it is a ubiquitous sight. Outside it flowers develop normally but fail to form fruit. At present, through the involvement of people, it is grown over a wide soil variety and spreads up to an altitude of 600 m equators. Now in the world, it occurs in the following countries: Southeast Asia (Burma, Indonesia, Malaysia, Singapore, Philippines, South China, Thailand, and Vietnam); Africa (Ghana, Ivory Coast, Kenya, Ghana, Madagascar, Cameroon, Nigeria, Tanzania); Caribbean (Brazil, Venezuela, Mexico, Ecuador, Jamaica); Melanesia (Fiji, Vanuatu, Solomon Island, Papua new guinea);, and regions of Micronesia, and Polynesia (Flora of China Editorial Committee, 2014; Govaerts et al., 2014; Henderson et al., 1995).

It is primarily found in India's southern regions, as well as along the coasts of the Bay of Bengal, Indian Ocean, and Arabian Sea. In Kerala, the climatic condition suits the growth of trees, and thus dense canopy is obtained in the state. Also the Indian subcontinent including Bangladesh, Sri Lanka, Andaman, and Nicobar Island, Seychelles has well vegetation cover distribution. Traditionally it is cultivated in different states of India such as Kerala, Karnataka, Tamil Nadu, Goa, Maharashtra, Odisha, Gujarat, West Bengal, and Puducherry. According to the 2014-15 statistics, the Coconut Development Board of Government of India 90% of total production in the country is from four states. Other states account for the rest of production. Production per hectare exceeds Tamil Nadu even though Kerala has the largest production (India Biodiversity, 2104).

Evolution

The origin of the coconut tree is the subject of controversy and is virtually unknown. Back in the 4th century BC it was featured in Sanskrit writings and is known as Sriphala: god's fruit. Between 1st century AD to 4th century AD in early Tamil literature coconut trees were frequently mentioned. In the Hindu epic stories such as Ramayana, Mahabharata, and Puranas it was also featured. Such literary evidence suggests that it occurred in ancient times. Many stories such as 'One thousand and one-night coconut ' were mentioned as he bought, and sold during his voyage. In 545, Topographic Christiana was also mentioned as a drupe. In 1280, Marco Polo named it as nux indica in the west whereas Sumatra termed it as Indian nut. In 1510, Ludovico di Verthema described it using Thenga (in Malayalam). Finally, in March 1521 Antonia Pigafetta described it completely in his journal.

Evolutionary history and fossil distribution seem ambiguous and are still unclear. Concerning its origin, there are 2 type of thought; some authorities claim it is native to Indo-Pacific, while others claim its origin is in north-western South America. Fossil records obtained 15 million years ago from New Zealand indicate that small, coconut-like plants grew there in the back. Rajasthan & Maharashtra, India has discovered even older fossils, suggests that it was native to west-central India. Moreover, fossils are putative and are difficult to locate. Back in the Pliocene, the first fossil was identified from New Zealand in 1926 following which evolved endemically (Berry, 1926). In India, from Deccan traps fossils were traced. The earliest known fossil is *C. binoriensis*. Apart from these two countries, fossil records have been obtained from Columbia and Australia.

In the 6th century, it became known to the western world. In lands of Western-Pacific, it originated and distributed both towards east, and west. From the Indian Ocean, it was imported to Egypt. When Marco Polo traveled through India he recognized it as Pharaoh's nut. It was also introduced into Spain and Portugal during the mid 16th century. It was also dispersed to other parts through ocean currents. It is believed that 4500 years ago aboriginal selection, Niu vai was introduced by Polynesians into the Pacific. At the same time about 3000 years ago, the Island of Micronesia was colonized by Indo-Malay. Traders of Malay and Arab improved different types of coconut spread west to India, Sri Lanka, and East Africa. During the 16th century, in West Africa, and Caribbean coconuts were introduced along the Atlantic coast of Central America by the European explorers.

Ecological Importance

It serves as an important component in regulating environmental impact. It has huge significance in maintaining the ecosystem. The husk is a huge source of potassium, and is used as mulch but is slow to decompose. In low rainfall areas, these are buried in trenches for conserving water. These can also be used against weed, and are pest tolerant. They serve as a good source of organic matter and hence are used in nursery potting mixes. The roots also protect against wave erosion as they are widespread and dense, and thus stabilize the soil. The dense canopy also provides constant shade to the vegetation that requires less sunlight. It can also allow greater light penetration when planted over wider space. Over the trunks sometimes pepper is also grown. The foliage on the top makes it wind tolerant, and is an excellent windbreak. Potash is formed from burnt husks and used for the better growth of trees. For all these, it has been intercropped with many bowls of cereal, fruits, and vegetables. Many viruses, mycoplasma, and viroids infect the leaves. Some pathogens are associated with living with this tree that derives nutrition to live but potentially does not harm. It is also important for climatic balance; being grown in the coastal region also helps in wind movement (Young et al., 2010). The Hispaniolan woodpecker, bird pests attack the trunk for nesting sites, and damages immature nuts, and the village weaver strips the leaves for nest building. The stem and crown base are invaded by nematode *Rhadinaphelenchus cocophilus* causing red-ring disease (Griffith, 1987).

Global Economy

Coconut has served the purpose of trade dating hundreds of years. In 2016, million tons of coconuts were distributed among different countries. In more than 90 countries, and various territories 59 million tons were produced that was mentioned in the world statistics data of 2016. About more than 72% of total world production was from tropical Asia including Indonesia, the Philippines, and India. It accounts for a large number of both commercial and traditional cultivars. The demand for cultivars has increased due to the global need, and development of new varieties cultivated as per the requirement of the trait. These cultivars are drought-tolerant, improved fruit, and seed variety, pest resistant, and some are even tolerant to cold stress. Few have also been developed with height traits being of dwarf variety but with normal production. Hence the developments of new cultivars were in account with fruit shape, and size, seed quality, copra thickness. Some of these cultivars are Malayan dwarf', 'Jamaican tall', 'West coast tall' (India), 'Hainan Tall' (China), 'Fiji dwarf' (Sri Lanka & India). In

Thailand and Malaysia, the harvesting occurs on large scale for trade purposes and is supplied to the other regions of the world. The queen palm *Syagrus romanzoffiana* used as a substitute for cooler climates not less than USDA Zone 9 for landscaping was placed in the genus *Cocos* but later reclassified in *Syagrus* as fruits were smaller and similar to coconut. In Madagascar, *Beccariophoenix alfredii* was lately discovered nearly like the coconut and can be grown into some extent cooler climates. In 2010, with gross production of 15 million tons, Indonesia became the world's largest producer of coconuts accounting for 64% of the global production. The Philippines is the second-largest producer of it to combat the steep decline in production due to aging, and typhoon wreckage. The first developed macapuno and nata de coco are two important products produced in the past, and its production plays an important role in the global economy.

In India, it is present along the streets of the states of Kerala, Tamil Nadu, Karnataka, Puducherry, Andhra Pradesh, Goa, Maharashtra, Odisha, West Bengal and, Gujarat, and the islands of Lakshadweep, and Andaman, and Nicobar. Here the coconut is cultivated traditionally. *Cocos nucifera* is present on the coat of armed forces, and is there in the national emblem, being the national tree of the Maldives. In the Middle East, the main producing area is the Dhofar region of Oman that has long trade relations with Burma, Malaysia, Indonesia, East Africa, southern India, and China. In Laccadives it is the chief food even today is also distilled; besides this, it yields vinegar and jaggery. Most of the tall mature trees are found in Bermuda but importation was prohibited.

Other Economic Value

It has been exploited economically across the globe for a variety of use. Each, and every part of the tree serves some purpose or other. For the building of small bridges, and houses the trunk is used due to salt tolerance, and straightness. It could also be used as a hardwood replacement, and old stems are used for fencing, poles, and for making furniture. Timber is used for outdoor chromate with copper arsenate; it has also a specialty to be used as flooring. Trunk and shell are even used for craft purposes, such as kitchen utensils, carvings, handles. The base of the trunk is hollowed, and used for storage tanks, and drums. Wood is also used for making paddles of rafts. Shell is dried and turned into charcoal for cooking. Even other plant parts such as husks, spathes are also burnt. Mature green fronds are used to weave and make baskets, trays, fans, mats, thatch, and plaited wires. Coir is fined, and spun into ropes, strings, cordages, and even used to make brushes. Nutshells are used as ornaments as brooches, earrings, neckpieces, and even buttons. Coconut oil is mixed with dye and used to color clothes. Bark oil is also used as a fragrance. Lauric oils are extracted from coconut kernel, and used in soaps, and cosmetics. To light lamps and torches seed oil is also used.

Medicinal, and Food Value

It is imbued with many medicinal qualities since prehistoric times and was known as Arogya Vaidhak which enhances health. Milk of coconut is a diuretic also the roots. It's frequently used as a laxative, and antidiarrheal is used to treat fish poisoning (Yartey et al., 1993). Roots are also anti-pyretic (Brondegaard, 1973). Skin diseases are treated with oil as well as it is applied to teeth. A paste is made out of young leaves and applied over the cuts to stop bleeding. Young nuts contain water with sugar, and other nutrients that are sterile and fresh fed to infants suffering from diarrhea. Seed oil is cytotoxic, emetic, hypotensive, and purgative rubbed onto stiff joints to treat rheumatism and back pains. It is used as an ointment to maintain smooth, soft skin. Along with turmeric used to treat sick infants and women who have just given birth. Coconut oil is massaged on a pregnant mother's abdomen to place the baby from breech back to normal position. Juice is taken to treat kidney problems (Singh, 1986). The root is employed in treating stomachache, and blood in the urine, and boiled in combination with *Ruellia tuberosa* root, and used for bladder ailments, and as an aphrodisiac (Holdsworth, and Wamoi, 1982). A bandage made from the apical bud was applied externally to treat ulcers. It has germicidal property. The dry spongy kernel was used to stop hemorrhage.

Coconut is a staple food with high-quality protein, fat content. It is also rich in vitamin sources such as Vit E, Vit B vit C, and minerals such as calcium, iron, phosphorus. Per 100-gram 354 calories are being served. The overall saturated fat content of raw coconut meat is high (33 grams), moderate content of carbohydrates (15 grams), and protein (3 grams). More than 10% of the Daily Value includes significant content of micronutrients in the form of dietary minerals, manganese, copper, iron, selenium, and zinc. It is used in different forms either for direct uptake or in cooking purposes. Oil is extracted from the dried kernel, copra, and used in cooking. Coconut water is directly taken up as a refreshing drink that is highly nutritious. Varieties of desserts are also made from it. The young tender shoot is also used as salad. Fresh sap from inflorescence is used as toddy as an alcoholic beverage that is further refined for jaggery production. Roots are also roasted and used as a substitute for coffee. The kernel is pressed, and cream is skimmed off, and used in confectionery.

Cultural Significance

In the Indian culture coconut tree is regarded as 'Kalpavrikshya: a tree that grants all blessings'. Even the fruit is the luster of Hinduism. Every pious religious occasion is believed to be an auspicious fruit that is offered to deities. In Sanskrit it is known as Sriphala, the fruit of prosperity as every part is being used for some purpose. It is also symbolic of lord Ganesh serving good luck, and prosperity. Three eyes resemble the eyes of Shiva hence used on holy occasions. It is also broken before venturing to a new house, car, or inaugurating any working place, and even before starting any holy events that remove negativity and bring goodness. It is also placed upon an earthen or copper pot with mango leaves, and placed at the entrance of temples or even on religious occasions at both sides of the main entrance as a symbol of prosperity, and welcoming the goddess of wealth, Lakshmi. It also plays symbolic importance signifying the rough outer part as a proud heart, and inside a sweet, and tender soul. Puja, the holy religious event of Hindu uses coconut as an element either in form of nariyal or Kalash that represents the consciousness that connects to spirit, and in return we receive blessings. Even while performing havan it is offered as sacrificial fire. It is also distributed as Prasad after offering to the god. In mid-July-August, there is a festival called AADI where it is broken over the head of goddess Amman for blessing. During wedding ceremonies, flowers of coconut are placed over rice as a ritual in Kerala. Even it's very much essential during a birth ceremony to bestow the child. It is also offered during traditional abhisheka rituals for the enhancement of spiritual growth. Even the coir is also extracted from dried fruit, and used as incense by lighting it, and offered to god. In Buddhist weddings, it plays an important role. It is also offered along with a shawl to elderly people as a symbol of respect to honor them. In the Hindu month of Shravan, a day called nariyal Purnima is being celebrated. Hence, coconut is omnipresent in every ritual and the sacrament of Indian Culture.

Story, Myth, and Belief

According to Hindu mythology, there was a powerful sage Vishwamitra who created the coconut tree to help king Satyabrata enter heaven who was not allowed by God as he was thrown out with his mortal body and showed gratitude towards him. It is also believed that there is a legend associated with coconut eyes as it looked like Lord Shiva's third eye. that was gifted by him to Ganesha as he was attracted by it, and was given to play with. It is also believed to be obtained during churning of the cosmic ocean by god and observed as a symbol of poornakumbham, a pot full of nectar. It is also believed to be offered as a piece of sacrifice that has been replaced by animals that were earlier offered to god by sages. As it resembles the head of Brahma, and he being the creator of the universe it is considered the same. It is also believed to be symbolic of Ganesha and used before any work for its completion. It is also considered a good omen to be gifted. It is also a symbol of the human ego which is sacrificed by breaking it before starting any ritual and surrendering oneself to god. In Maluku, a girl emerges from the blossom of a coconut tree. In Maldivian folklore, one of the main myths of origin reflects the dependence of the Maldivians on the coconut tree. According to urban legend, more deaths are caused by falling coconuts than by sharks annually.

It is also believed to be associated with the human fertility cult and hence used in wedding ceremonies. Also, pregnant ladies are not allowed to break coconut as the vibration is thought to be fatal to the fetus, and as nuts represent life forms they are not allowed to break. It is also placed over the pot in marriages symbolizing the womb to bestow the couple with a life of fertility. In Gujarat, it is offered by the bride to the groom who needs to be preserved for his whole life. It's also said that if you're impacted by Rahu's nefarious effects, place it near your head on a Wednesday night, and on the next morning offer it to Ganesha. Once a man was going on a long journey before leaving home his mother, and wife wished him good luck by doing tilak and offered him a coconut to carry along with him for a prosperous journey.

There is a popular childhood story of 'the eel, and the coconut tree'. There was a little girl named Tanaiya who lived near the lake in a beautiful hut. She used to swim in the lake daily. One day she noticed a creature moving towards her seeing which she frightened, and ran out of the lake to home. The next morning when she went swimming she saw that creature moving towards her. She gathered the courage to move toward it, and to her surprise it was an eel, seeing which she smiled thinking it to be a wonderful creature. She took it in her hand gazing at it, and wondered how beautiful patterns were drawn on the body, and gently patted. One day after swimming Tanaiya came out of the water and sat on the bank eel also came out to her utter surprise. Soon after that eel transformed into a human, and told he is lord of eel Ambu. He told he liked her very much, and always wanted to be near her, and said the next day when she would come for swimming she would take the eel, and cut its head, and put it inside the soil. According to his advice, the next day she did the same but she was utterly very hurt. Every day she used to sit near that for hours. After many months she observed a sapling growing from beneath the soil that soon grew into a coconut tree. Seeing this she became very happy as the tree grew it offered everything to the little girl. She was very happy and used to dance around it, and used to say it's the best gift of god to her.

Tourism

In Singapore, there is a 106 years old coconut tree that is out to be sold. In Kolkata, there is a 125-year-old female double coconut tree planted by the British and is the lone tree surviving to date which the botanists are trying to save as it was attacked by fungal pathogens. The yield of coconut is high in this tree as it can live up to 1200 years, and bear the largest fruit, about 25kg. So the botanist and the director of the Botanical Survey of India are trying their utmost to make the tree live. In Kerala, a coconut break tour can be done, especially the Kannur beach which has enormous trees grown along the shore. This contributes to the beach's attractiveness, and thousands of tourists are brought every year to capture the beauty. Even every south Indian state has a tremendous coconut tree blooming out that attracts the tourist, not only the tree but also very delicious dishes are famous throughout the world being made out of the coconut.

Urban Forest

It is widely grown even in home gardens as its most part finds use in the home. Urban cultivation is preferred due to its compact rooting habit, non-invasive growth, and limited spread of the crown. The dwarf varieties are specially cultivated to be grown in nursery, and home purpose. This feature of colored fruit, small stature provides an alternative for the urban forest. It has also got some ornamental values serving as a universal icon of the tropic environment. Even the soft tapping of leaves is soothing to the ear. It also attracts a lot of pollinators, and hence many birds can be seen. It has also got a wider life span and does not require much maintenance. In optimal condition, it grows, and fruit throughout the year. It also provides shade to other plants grown in gardens and is used as intercropping. It also maintains the soil pH.

Conservation

The demand for coconut production has increased tremendously due to its versatile uses. Being a crop with unique features its production has reached a premier position in the world. Although we can't completely restrict it from exploitation we can judiciously use it, and follow measures to conserve it. There have been several improvised germplasm conservation done in laboratories, and gene banks that have adopted various ways to conserve it for future use. The seeds have no definite dormancy period and are hence not allowed to preserve for long, so it is better to go for other parts in terms of conservation. Pollens are also cryopreserved even in embryos in mediums that later develop into whole plants. The best germination occurs in 30-35! with 10% sucrose and 30% gelatine. Many cultivars and botanical varieties are being developed for this purpose to meet the growing global need.

References

Amirthalingam, M., & Reddy, P. S.(2013) *Plant and Animal Diversity in Valmiki's Ramayana*- CPR Environmental Education Centre.

Berry, E. W. (1926) Cocos and Phymatocaryon in the Pliocene of the New Zealand.

Brondegaard VJ. Contraceptive plant drugs Planta Med 1973; 23: 167–172

Chan E, Elevitch CR, 2006 Cocos nucifera (coconut), ver. 2.1. Species profiles for Pacific Island agroforestry [ed. by Elevitch, C. R.]. Honolulu, Hawaii, USA: Permanent Agriculture Resources (PAR).

Dendy DAV, Grimwood BE, 1972 Coconut processing for the production of oil and coconut protein food and feed products Vienna, Austria: UNIDO.

Duke JA, 1983 Handbook of Energy Crop Unpublished. Purdue University, West Lafayette, Indiana, USA: Centre for New Crops, and Plant Products.

Flora of China Editorial Committee, 2014 Flora of China., St. Louis, Missouri, and Cambridge, Massachusetts, USA: Missouri Botanical Garden, and Harvard University Herbaria.

Foale-MA, 1992 Coconut genetic diversity: present knowledge, and future research needs. International Crop Network Series No. 892:46-58.

Gallego VC, San Juan NC, Gallego CE, Concibido EC, Aterrado ED, 1987 The survey and Evaluation of Coconut Pest, and Disease Incidence in the Philippines. PCA-ARDB Annual Report, 77-78.

Govaerts R, Dransfield J, Zona SF, Hodel DR, Henderson A, 2014 World Checklist of Arecaceae. In: World Checklist of Arecaceae, London, UK: Royal Botanic Gardens, Kew.

Green AH, 1991 Coconut production: present status, and priorities for research. World Bank Technical Paper No 136, 150 pp

Griffith, R (1987) Red ring disease of the coconut palm *Plant Dis*, *71*(2), 193-196

Grimwood EB. 1975. Coconut tree products. FAO, Rome.

Gunn, B. F., Baudouin, L., & Olsen, K. M.(2011) Independent origins of cultivated coconut (Cocos nucifera L.) in the old world tropics *Plos one*, *6*(6).

Gupta, M Shakti, Plant myths, and tradition in India

Harries HC, 1978 the evolution, dissemination, and classification of Cocos nucifera L. The Botanical Review, 44(3):265-319.

Henderson A, Galeano G, Bernal R, 1995 Field guide to the palms of the Americas. Princeton, New Jersey, USA: Princeton University Press.

Hocher, V, Verdeil, J. L, & Malaurie, B 4.1 Cocos nucifera Coconut *General Editor: Gabrielle J. Persley, the Doyle Foundation, Glasgow, Scotland*, 90.

Holdsworth D, Wamoi B. Medicinal plants of the Admiralty Islands, Papua New Guinea. Part I Int J Crude Drug Res 1982; 20: 169–181.

Holdsworth D. Medicinal plants of the Gazelle peninsula, New Britain Island, Papua New Guinea, Part I. Int J Pharmacog 1992; 30: 185–190

India Biodiversity, 2014 Online Portal of India Biodiversity.

Jay, S. C (1974) Nectar, and pollen collection by honeybees from coconut flowers *Bee World*, *55*(3), 105-111

Lima, E. B. C., Sousa, C. N. S., Meneses, L. N., Ximenes, N. C., Júnior, S., Vasconcelos, G. S., ... & Vasconcelos, S. M. M. (2015).Cocos nucifera (L.)(Arecaceae): A phytochemical and pharmacological review. *Brazilian Journal of Medical, and Biological Research*, *48*(11), 953-964.

Menon KPV, Pandalai KM, 1958. The Coconut Palm A monograph. Errakulam, India: Indian Central Coconut Committee

Moistero AP, 1978. Utilization of coconut palm timber: its economic significance in some countries in Tropics. Forpride Digest, 7:44-57.

Ohler JG, 1984 Coconut- tree of life FAO Plant Production, and Protection Paper No 57 Rome, Italy: FAO.

Ohler JG. 1984. Coconut, tree of life. Plant Production and Protection Paper No.57 FAO, Rome

Orwa C, Mutua A, Kindt R, Jamnadass R, Simons A, 2009. Agroforestry Database: a treereference and selection guide version 4.

Pannetier, C & Buffard-Morel, J (2012) 13 Coconut palm (Cocos nucifera L.) *Trees I*, *1*, 430.

Perera, P. I., Hocher, V., Weerakoon, L. K., Yakandawala, D. M. D., Fernando, S. C., &Verdeil, J. L. (2010). Early inflorescence and floral development in Cocos nucifera L. (Arecaceae: Arecoideae). *South African Journal of Botany*, *76*(3), 482-492.

Singh YN. Traditional medicine in Fiji: some herbal folk cures used by Fiji Indians. J Ethnopharmacol 1986; 15: 57–88

USDA-ARS, 2014 Germplasm Resources Information Network (GRIN). Online Database Beltsville, Maryland, USA: National Germplasm Resources Laboratory.

Werth, E. (1933). Distribution, Origin, and Cultivation of t the Coconut Coconut tree *Ber. Deutschen Bot. Ges.*, vol 51, pp. 301–304. (Article translated into English by Dr. R. Child, Director, Coconut Research Scheme, and Lunuwila, Sri Lanka)

Yartey J, Harisson EK, Brakohiapa LA, Nkrumah FK. Carbohydrate and electrolyte content of some home-available fluids used for oral rehydration in Ghana. J Trop Pediatr 1993; 39: 234–237

Young HS, Raab TK, McCauley DJ, Briggs AA, Dirzo R, 2010. The coconut palm, Cocos nucifera, impacts forest composition and soil characteristics at Palmyra Atoll, Central Pacific. Journal of Vegetation Science, 21(6):1058-1068

Trees of Ramayana (2022): 51-60
Editor: Felix Bast
Today & Tomorrow's Printers and Publishers (India)

Chapter-5

Hintala Tree (*Cycads*)

Abida Khatoon

ताम् रात्रिम् उषितास् तत्र सुवेले हरि पुम्गवाः |
लन्कायाम् ददृशुर् वीरा वनान्य् उपवनानि च || ६-३९-१

सम सौम्यानि रम्याणि विशालान्य् आयतानि च |
दृष्टि रम्याणि ते दृष्ट्वा बभूवुर् जात विस्मयाः || ६-३९-२

चम्पकअशोकपुन्नागसालतालसमाकुला |
तमालवनसंचन्नानागमालासमावृता || ६-३९-३

हिन्तालैर्अर्जुनैर्नीपैःसप्तपर्णैश्चपुष्पितैः |
तिलकैःकर्णिकारैश्चपटालैश्चसमन्ततः || ६-३९-४

शुशुभेपुष्पितअग्रैश्चलतापरिगतैर्द्रुमैः |
लन्काबहुविधैर्दिव्यैर्यथाइन्द्रस्यअमरावती || ६-३९-५

विचित्रकुसुमउपेतैरक्तकोमलपल्लवैः |
शाद्वलैश्चतथानीलैश्चित्राभिर्वनराजिभिः || ६-३९-

गन्ध आढ्यान्य् अभिरम्याणि पुष्पाणि च फलानि च |
धारयन्त्य् अगमास् तत्र भूषणानि इव मानवाः || ६-३९-७

नित्य मत्त विहम्गानि भ्रमर आचरितानि च |
कोकिल आकुल षण्डानि विहग अभिरुतानि च || ६-३९-१०

In Ramayana, Kanda 6; Sarga 39; Shloka 1-10, Valmiki describes that Rama and monkeys see the beautiful and charming gardens from the top of the Suvela mountain. Some monkeys, thrilled with the beauty of gardens while others went towards Lanka, located on Trikuta Mountain where they see the city with a large mansion of Ravana. The courageous chief of monkeys stayed in Suvela Mountain and saw that garden and grooves in Lanka. In that garden, thick Champaka, Ashoka, Vakula Sala, and palmyra trees and enclosed with grooves of Tamala and Panasa trees were grown, Lanka looked very impressive on all sides like the city of Amaravati rule by the god of celestials (Indra), Kanda 6; Sarga 39; Shloka 3, with green lawns and multicolored avenues and with stunning trees of various kinds like Hintala, Arjuna and many more.

Figure: Male plant (*Cycas circinalis*). Photo clicked from the campus of University of Jammu. © Abida Khatoon

Introduction

In an amazing Indian epic, The Ramayana many trees and plants are described which were written thousands of years ago by Valmiki. When Shri Ram and Lakshmana come across "kabandha" In search of Sita, they reached Pampa Sarovar (lake) lies to the West of Rishyamukha hill and east of the Matanga hill, beyond that hilly forest another vana (woodland) which was described very beautifully, the celestial garden of INDRA and KUBERA. After the abduction of Sita by Raven, the two-princess wandered in the forest near the lake where they met Hanuman. The view of the forest is described with so many attractive fruit trees like Jambu (rose apple) Priyala (Almondette) Tilika, Ketaki along *Hintala* (*Cycus*), etc. These sceneries of forest are considered in Ramayana as luxurious vana (forest) which means it resembles heaven. The geographical location of all the plants that he described all over India is more or less accurate. There are around 182 different plants mentioned in the Ramayana. In this lesson, we are going to discuss one of the trees namely *Hintala (Cycas circinalis)*. Our area of focusses is to compile all the information available related to Cycas species, for example, geographical distribution, morphology and anatomy of the tree, evolutionary and taxonomic status, ecological importance, aesthetic values, traditional values, mythological values, etc.

Taxonomic Status

Kingdom: Plantae

Clade: Tracheophytes

Division: Cycadophyta

Class: Cycadopsida

Order: Cycadales

Suborder: Cycadineae

Family: Cycadaceae

Genus: Cycas

Hill and Stenberg (2009) describe the systematic position of Cycas species. The genus was first recorded by Linnaeus in 1753

External Morphology

The tree is evergreen Palm like, also known as Queen Sago is dioecious. The tree is sporophyte (spore-producing and is well distinguished into true stem, leaves, and root). The length of the plant reaches 8-14 feet. The stem is thick, woody, and erect bearing a crown of leaves at the top. Female plants are without branches, male plants sometimes possess branches in rare cases that are sympodial due to the presence of male cones (for pollen production). Stem armor is present throughout the trunk as a result of leaf base persistence (both foliar and scale leaf). These occur in an alternate band. The larger leaf base is foliage while the smaller is scaly in males whereas in females these are scaly and megasporophyll. Leaves; In Cycas leaves are dimorphic (Two distinct leaves) & evergreen Assimilatory fronds. These are large photosynthetic pinnately compound leaves, which form a crown-like on the top of the trunk. The leaves grow in a circular layer and a new layer of leaves grows on the inner side. If we talk about individual compound leaves, it has a central strong rachis single midrib) on which two rows of pinnae (leaflets) grow on either side either alternate or opposite. The length of individual compound leaves reaches up to 1.5 meters. Many pinnae differ from species to species and reach as many as a hundred pairs in a mature leaf. In the young stage, the leaflets have shown circinate vernation (pinnae are coiled). The leaflets are covered by a hair-like minute structure called remental hairs

Scaly leaves or Cataphylls

These are small brown-colored, somewhat triangular leaves. They are found on the apex of the stem. They are protective in function and mainly cove the megasporophyll and young foliage leaf primordia. If we talk about roots in *Cycas* there are two types- Taproot and coralloid root. It is assumed that the taproot system present was initially soon replaced by an adventitious root. The normal tap root is positively geotropic and is responsible for mineral and water absorption and for fixing the plant. On the other hand, coralloid roots grow as a lateral branch from the main tap root system and are negatively geotropic (means they grow towards the upward surface) and grow near the ground surface. The uniqueness of these roots is that they are infected with some bacteria, fungi, and algae, mainly invasion of algae is there and this association is considered as symbiotic interaction. Another peculiar character of coralloid is that the root is dichotomously branched. They divide so repeatedly to form big bunches of greenish or brownish structures, which gives a coral-like appearance, so is named after coral. The coralloid roots have antiviral potential/activities especially against the few viruses of tomato plants (Bissa et al. 2008). The coralloid root of *C. revoluta* is normally adapted to grow on rocky shores. The extraction of methanoic from coralloid root induced differentiation of the long motile filamentous cell of *Nostoc* species called hormogonia which is the center for nitrogen fixation.

Anatomy of internal structure;

Normal root; in the young stage, the root shows a circular outline. The outer epiblema which is also known as Exodermis is an elongated cell arranged tangentially, which is surrounding the cortex. Thin root hairs arise from epiblema. In the cortex region, intercellular space is present which is filled with tannins or starch and sometimes with mucilage. Inner to cortex single-layer barrel-shaped endodermis is present in which Casparian thickening is present. Next to it is a multilayer pericycle. The vascular bundles which are present in roots are arranged radially. Roots are diarch but sometimes no. of protoxylem strands range from 3 to 8. Vessels are absent. Protoxylem contains a spiral tracheid while metaxylem consists of a scalariform tracheid. Pith is not present. The normal older roots undergo secondary growth due to cambium (layer of actively dividing cells). The cambium gives secondary phloem outside towards the cortex and secondary xylem towards the inner side. At the same time, the cells of the outer cortex region start to function as cork cambium which gives cork (dead cells filled with suberin) outside and secondary cortex inner side. As a result of cork development, the epiblema ruptures and there are no root hairs in older roots. Coralloid Root though the internal structure of coralloid is almost similar to normal root except some under mentioned differences. In such a root the secondary structure may be poorly developed or may be completely absent. Cortex is wide. The algal zone is present in the middle of the cortex. The algal zone consists of radially elongated, large, thin-walled cells having large space occupied by algae. Important members participate include Anabaena Cycadae, Nostoc punctiforme, Azotobacter, etc. Because of the presence of blue-green algae and bacteria which fix nitrogen, the function of coralloid is fixing nitrogen. Stem Anatomy like the internal structure of the root, the stem also has the same basic features, with some differences. The stem outline is not circular, rather it has ridges and furrows due to the presence of leaf base persistence. The epidermis is thick-walled. Cortex is wide and thin wall parenchymatous cells fill densely with starch grains, which is the source of **'sago'.** Therefore it is known as Queen Sago palm. Endodermis and pericycle are not well demarcated. Many vascular bundles are arranged in the form of rings. Each vascular bundle is collateral, conjoint, endarch, and open. Pith is largely present. It contains many mucilaginous canals. Secondary growth is similar to that of the root where cambium activity gives secondary phloem and xylem, on the outer side and inner side respectively.

Anatomy of leaves

T.S of rachis shows some structure. The outer epidermis is covered by cuticles and also poses a sunken type of stomata (xerophytic features). Below the epidermis, the hypodermis is differentiated into two regions, outer collenchyma followed by sclerenchyma. The conducting is conjoint (both xylem and phloem are on the same radius), collateral (xylem inner side while phloem outside), and open. In the ground tissue of the rachis mucilaginous canal is also present. Now let's move ahead to see the anatomy of leaflets. Again, the cuticle and sunken stomata are there on the upper portion of both the upper and lower epidermis. Below hypodermis palisade tissues are there which contain chlorophyll. But the palisade tissue is absent on the inner side of the lower epidermis. Spongy tissue is also there. The transmission of food materials from the margin of the leaflet to the central vascular bundle is aided by special cells called transfusion tissue, which is again the characteristic feature of *Cycas* leaflets (Singh, Pande, and Jain 2014).

Reproduction in Cycas

Cycas can reproduce by two modes; sexual and vegetative methods. The plant is strictly dioecious (male and female reproductive structures are borne on separate plants) and reproduction is by seeds produced on open seed-bearing leaves. Sexual Reproduction, male reproductive structure: Male plants are rare. Male strobilus or cone borne strictly on the apex of the trunk, the size of cone is around 50 cm in length. The cone is formed due to the compaction of microsporophyll-producing microspore or pollen grains. Female reproductive structure: Female plant is devoid of the cone; rather a whorl of spirally arranged megasporophyll arises around the shoot apex. Each megasporophyll resembles the foliage leaf and is approximately 10-23 cm long. The lower petiolar part bears the naked ovules on the margins. The ovule of Cycas circinalis is the largest among other species. In Cycas pollination is carried out by wind (anemophily) and caught by pollination drop secreted by ovule. Once pollens reach inside the pollen chamber it rests for some time. Germination takes place after that embryo starts to develop. The mature seed is large 2.5-5cm. If we look at the seed coat it has four- layered consisting of sarcotesta, sclerotesta, a thick layer of spongy tissue, and a thin membranous layer enclosing female gametophyte tissue. The spongy layer aids in the seed dispersion as they cause floatation of seed in water during the rainy season (Singh, Pande, and Jain 2014).

Geographical Distribution

Cycas is distributed in Australia, Japan, Indonesia, China, India, Mauritius, Africa, Nepal, Bangladesh, Sri Lanka, and Myanmar. The genus can also be found in Malaysia and south –East Asia, also extended to Polynesia, Micronesia, and East African, and constituted one of the oldest living fossils of plants. In India, Cycas wells grow naturally in Odisha, Assam, Meghalaya, Tamil Nadu, Karnataka, Andaman, and Nicobar Island. Overall 100 species are widely distributed of which eight species are found in India, chiefly Indo-Chinese (around 40 species) and Australian (27 species). The only living species, *Cycas taitungensis,* has two threatened populations mainly occurring along the Eastern coast of Taiwan (Chiang et al.,2004). Species found in India and their distribution include *Cycas indica* (Mysore, Triputhii), *Cycas revoluta, Cycas rumphii, Cycas annaikalensis* (Kerala, Palghat, Annaikal hills), *Cycas spherica* (Odisha, Bihar), *Cycas pectinata* (west Bengal, Chittagong), *Cycas beddomei* (Cuddapah hills, Andhra Pradesh) and *Cycas circinalis* (Tamil Nadu, Kerala, Karnataka).In Ramayana Hintala refers to *Cycas circinalis*, which is known to endemic in India, restricted to the Western Ghats. Typically occur as dry shrub woodlands in the hilly areas of Kerala, Maharashtra, and Karnataka.

Cycas Cultivation:

Cycas is propagated either by seeds or bulbils. It is developed in the crevices of scale leaves and leaf base at the basal part of an old stem, cut ends of bulbils are treated with fungicides and also with rooting hormones before planted. For seed, it is placed horizontally in moist soil. Once it germinated, placed into the deep pot (Raju, A.J.S& N.G. Rao 2011).

Viral disease in *Cycas: Cycas* plants are sometimes attacked but certain viruses belong to the Nepovirus group. There are various ways by which viruses invade or transmit. One of the ways is by mechanical inoculation to various chenopodium species. Another way of transmission is through the seed of these species (Hanade et al. 1986, Han et al. 2002).

Extraction of starch and preparation of Sago

We already discussed that the Cycas plant is used as a source of carbohydrates. In Tonga Island (a small archipelago in the South Pacific Ocean*) C. circinalis* is cultivated as a food plant. In Japanese culture, they have been using the plant not only for starch extraction but also for alcoholic drinks. In the history of Japan, during the famine period, the stem of *Cycas* has served as living food stock. In-plant part starch is found mainly in the pith and cortex, but the endosperm of the seed also contains a significant amount of starch. Now we are going to look at the general method of sago processing. The first step is peeling off the outer layer/ skin of the trunk and after slicing it into rounded disk-like or small bits. After that, let the slicing pieces dry under the sun to dehydrate. Once they become crispy, grind them and convert them into powder. Then mixed well with excess water in a vessel and stirred for a while & allowed the liquid mixture to stand. A white precipitate (starch) finally settles down at the bottom of the vessel. By decantation method, the upper supernatant liquid is drained off and the remaining starch deposit is washed in water. Now the freshly washed precipitate is rolled between boards, until the moment it turns into spherical pellets called 'Sago'.

Ecological importance

As we already discussed that the pollination is anemophilous, but some latest research shows that beetles like weevils and bees give their contribution to the transfer of pollen. For example, pollination of the Australian cycad *Cycas ophiolitic* (in which there is a limited role of wind pollination rather than beetle pollinator mutualism. Apart from this, another important feature of Cycas includes its seed color, bright-colored like red, orange, purple, and yellow seeds are more common. These colorful seeds attract many birds and mammals which disperse the seed. The next ecological importance of Cycas is the novel interaction with photosynthetic bacteria like *Anabaena*, *Pseudomonas,* etc. These cyanobacteria take shelter in the specialized coralloid root. The *Cycas* provide appropriate & stable habitats; in return, the cycads acquire nitrogen nutrients from the bacteria. Canopy, today cycads are found in every continent except Europe and Antarctica but are restricted to specific areas of tropics and subtropics. *Cycas* is found as a component of forest and occasionally contributes to the canopy.

Economic Importance

Cycas is an ancient group of seed-bearing trees that originated during the Permo-Carboniferous period, some 280MYA. They flourished in the Jurassic period. *Cycas* has a long history of use. *Cycas* trees are used for ornamental purposes; the leaves are used during many religious functions and other auspicious ceremonies along with leaves of *Cocos nucifera.* Male cones of *Cycas* are used in cowshed as mosquito repellents. Ovules and seeds of *Cycas* are consumed where it occurs naturally. The kernels or endosperm are separately dried in sun making kernel flour and used in preparing varieties of cuisine such as Idli and Pitha (Radha & Singh 2008). In terms of economic importance, Cycas contributing in many ways;

Used as food; considered as the source of food materials, such as sago and seed starch, young leaves of *C. circinalis, C. rumphii, C. revolute* are cooked and used as a vegetable various places across the world, such as Malaysia, Indonesia, Philippines, and Japan. Gums extracted from the injured petiole, stem, or megasporophyll of *C. rumphii, C. revoluta* are used in adhesive, antidote, and malignant ulcer. Oil: *Cycas* seeds yield orange color oil which is used in cosmetics. Aesthetics and decorative purpose;

Cycas plants are used as ornamental plants mainly growing in public parks, colleges, and even private areas. Ryukyu Island and some other countries like Japan, Taiwan cut and dried leaves by the special method are for decorative purposes.

Conservation

Today the cycads are in danger of getting extinct because they grow in restricted habitats and due to a slow rate of growth and reproduce so infrequently. Several species are already extinct in the wild; many are listed as threatened due to habitat destruction. Various breeding programs have been initiated by various institutions to conserve. To protect natural populations, five genera are now covered by international law, prohibiting trade of their seeds collection in the wild. Today FAIRCHILD BOTANICAL GARDEN Florida maintains different collections of cycads as the rest of the world. Though the garden was severely hit by 1992, hurricane Andrew damaged or killed most of the cycads. Under the IUCN red list or red data list (IUCN red list further divided into nine groups), one of them is DD (Data Deficient)- where those organisms are placed for which not enough data are available to assess its risk of extension. Many Cycas species are included in the DD category; example includes *C. annakailensis, C. circinalis* (Varghese et al. 2009) C. indica, *C. spherica*. As per the report of Cycad Species Group (SSC/IUCN) almost 53% of all the Cycas are under threat & are fall into one of the categories of the IUCN Red Data List (Donaldson 2003). Threats are due to habitat loss/ destruction due to the clearing of forest-agriculture. In eastern Ghats (Odisha and Cuddapah hills of Andhra Pradesh) the well natural forest of Cycads have suffered degradation and even expect in near future too, due to uncontrolled explosion of human population and their anthropogenic activities like mining, conversion of forest into agricultural lands, deliberated setting of forest fires.

Medicinal importance

Leaves of Cycas served as a source of pharmaceutical products and other known drugs. In addition to angiosperm gymnosperm also contributed to the important medicinal flora. Within a decade, many scientists investigate the presence of hydro-alcoholic and chloroform extract from the *C. revoluta* leaves, which are used to prepare antimicrobial and antioxidant against many microorganisms such as *E. coli*, *Klebsiella pneumoniae,* and *Saccharomyces cerevisiae*. But at the same time, many organisms are resistant to this hydro-alcohol and chloroform extract such as *Aspergillus niger*, *Candida albicans*, Streptococcus pyogenes, etc. In addition to this, cycads also contain other compounds such as methyl azoxymethanol, Beta-methylamino-L-alanine, Beta-alanine-L-oxalyl amino, and cycasin, which might be responsible for the production of neurotoxic effects. Some studies suggested that consuming *Cycas* and their derivatives are associated with certain neurological disorders such as Parkinsonism dementia complex/sclerosis (E Rivadenetra-Dominguez et al. Neurologia. 2014). So, no matter how natural the product is, chances are there that it may pose health risk factors depending upon the composition of chemical compounds.

References

Aluri, R.J. Solomon., (2011). Taxonomic aspect & conning ecology of *Cycas circinalis L. (Cycadaceae: Cycadaceae),* threatened species of India. DOI: 10.11609/joTT.o2372.1425-31

Jain, Pande, Singh. (2014) A textbook of Botany 5th edition (3rd reprint); 2019-2020, Meerut, RASTOGI PUBLICATION

Lindstrom, A. J. (2007) The genus Cycas (Cycadaceae) in India. Doi: 10.7751/telopea20075745 (https://www.researchgate.net/publication/255662496Thegenus_Cycas_Cycadaceae_in_Indi)

Mathur, A. (2011). Leaves of *Cycas revoluta:* Potent antimicrobial and antioxidant agent. World Journal of Science and Technology 1(10): 11-20 ISSN: 2231-2587

Singh, Rita, Singh, J.K. (2011). The importance of Odisha Cycas in India, Biodiversity, 12:1, 21-27, DIO: 10.1080/14888386.2011.574424

Singh,V.P., (2007), Economic Importance of gymnosperm in India. International Journal of Plant Science, Vol.2 No.1 pp.236-238 ref.15

Trees of Ramayana (2022): 61-73
Editor: Felix Bast
Today & Tomorrow's Printers and Publishers (India)

Chapter-6

Indian Rosewood *(Dalbergia sissoo)*

Rashmita Luha

ततः सा वक्र केश अन्ता सुकेशी केश सम्वृतम् ॥ ५-३१-१७
उन्नम्य वदनम् भीरुः शिंशपा वृक्षम् ऐक्षत ।

The above *shloka* from the Sundarakanda, volume 2, chapter 31 in Valmiki's Ramayana published by Gita Press captures a still where Hanuman (hiding on a Shimshapa tree from the Rakshasa guarding Sita in Ashoka Vatika) narrates the story of Lord Rama commencing from his birth and ending with himself espying Sita, who was abducted by Raavan and caged in Lanka. Upon hearing these words, Sita gets startled and with extreme joy, casts her eyes all around in search of the source. Finally, she catches a glimpse of Hanuman hiding and preaching on a bough of the Shimshapa tree beneath which she stood. In Ramayana, the Shimshapa tree is beautifully described as scenic beauty. Shimshapa tree is not native to Sri Lanka. So how come it was there in Ahsoka Vatika? Intriguing! Is it possible that Raavan brought it to his botanical garden from India?

Figure: *Dalbergia sissoo* at fruiting stage (April-May); © Saini, K.C., Senior Research Fellow at the Central University of Punjab [Location- Central University of Punjab, City Campus, Mansa Road, Bathinda, Punjab, India. Date – April 21st, 2020]

Introduction

The genus *Dalbergia* includes as much as nearly 300 species distributed throughout the tropics and subtropics, out of which about 25 species are found in our country. The generic name, '*Dalbergia*' honors the Swedish Botanist, Nicholas Dalberg, and his brother Carl Gustav Dalberg, and the specific epithet; *"sissoo"* is taken from the Bengali vernacular name during the 18th century. The specialty of this genus is that it includes decorative and aromatic woody trees (Saurabh. A, Shekher A.M, Gupta. S.2012). Shisham *(Dalbergia sissoo)*, a deciduous tree, Punjab, Haryana, and other regions of India, Pakistan, and Nepal are home to this plant. Traditionally people use it as timber and fuelwood, besides; it turns out to be a cost-effective method of land protection and reclamation for the farmers. For centuries their importance in medicinal, insecticidal, and harboring honey bees was notable. Dalbergia sissoo is also the State Tree of Punjab vide Govt. notification No. 34/13/Ft. IV-83/6052 dated 15.3.1989 and the provincial tree of Pakistan's Punjab province. Dalbergia sissoo is also made available in Periyar Wildlife Sanctuary, Bandipur National Park, Sariska Tiger Reserve, and Rajaji tiger reserves which come under deciduous forests in India.

If you have the opportunity to visit any of these places, you can certainly find Dalbergia sissoo growing along fertile river banks below 900 m elevations, ranging naturally up to 1300 m. The temperature in which the plant grows naturally ranges from 10-40 °C and it can tolerate average annual rainfall up to 2000 mm.

Common name — शिंशपा (Sanskrit Names), Shisham शीशम (Hindi), Indian rosewood (English Name), Sissu (Manipuri), Sitral (Bengali), Birade (Kannada), Iruvil (Malayalam), काळारुख /शिसव (Marathi), ಬೀಟೆ Beete (Kannada), Karivittti/കരിവിട്ടി Viitti/വിട്ടി Iitti (Malayalam), நூக்கம் Nukkam/ தோதகத்தி' Totakatti (Tamil), ఇరుగుడుచెట్టు Iruguducetu (Telugu)

Taxonomical classification

Kingdom: **Plantae**

Division: **Magnoliophyta**

Class: **Magnoliopsida**

Order: **Fabales**

Family: **Fabaceae**

Sub Family: **Faboideae**

Genus: **Dalbergia**

Species: ***D. sissoo***

Scientific Name: *Dalbergia sissoo*

Chromosome number: 2n = 20

Trade name: Sissoo, Shisham

The genus *Dalbergia* belongs to the legume family Fabaceae, other plants of this family are pea, acacia, bean, chickpea, clove, peanut, silk tree, sunn hemp, tamarind, etc. What do you see common in these family members? To distinguish members of this family checklist 4 things – first - Pea flowers, second - Nodules on the roots, third - Pinnate leaves, and fourth- Seeds in pods like peas or beans. The fact that they are classified as silviculturally and commercially significant is a distinguishing trait of this genus.

Morphological Characteristics

D. sissoo is a large deciduous, perennial, seed propagated, semi-canopy woody tree (Figure 1(a)). It reaches up to 30 m - nearly equals to 20 five-foot-tall people standing straight one over another- at maturity, at a rate of 2 feet each year. The tree has a girth of up to 2.4 m and is often crooked in the trunk region. In the Rawalpindi district of Pakistan at a height of around 1500 m, it is observed to occur in a bush form. The bark is characteristically thick and grey colored with numerous irregular longitudinal grooves and ridges (Luna, 1996). The heartwood varies in color from golden to brown color and the sapwood pale white. The leaves are compound, imparipinnate, and alternate with 3.5-8 cm long rachis which is swollen at base. There are generally 3-5 leaflets, which are alternate, ovate with tapered apex and rounded base. These leaflets are succulent at a young age and with maturity become glabrous. (Figure 1 b). The terminal leaflet is significantly bigger than the others (Parker, 1956; Luna, 1996). They turn from dark green to brown in the autumn and fall off between Januarys to February. Flowering occurs in March and the inflorescence is an axillary panicle with yellowish-white small flowers with a characteristic fragrance. At the onset of April—May, the tree starts fruiting with Pods, reticulate against the seeds, and usually not more than 5 seeded (Figure1 (c)). By the end of November, the pods get matured. Seeds are brown to brownish-black colored - kidney-shaped (Parker, 1956; Singh, 1989; Luna, 1996). *D. sissoo* has a long taproot that may persist upon maturity along with numerous lateral ramifying roots (Hocking, 1993) which form an excellent root system owing to *Dalbergia sissoo* as a soil erosion species.

Geographic Distribution

Studies suggest that the *Dalbergia* genus has a pantropical geographical distribution. It is native to the sub-Himalayan areas ranging from Kabul River (Afghanistan) and passing through northern Pakistan and India, entire Nepal, Bhutan, and major parts of Assam. Due to its high adaptive potentiality, it easily adapts itself to the newly introduced environment. Human cultivation has sky rocketed its distribution and now the species is a worldwide sensation, successfully introduced to countries like Africa, Oceania, Australia, America, the Caribbean, southern USA, and Europe, CABI, 2013. *D. sissoo* is enlisted in the Global Invasive Species Database, GISD, 2017, besides this it is regarded as invasive species in Kenya and Tanzania, BioNET-EAFRINET, 2017. The Florida Exotic Pest Plant Council enlisted *Dalbergia sissoo* as a category II pest on the Invasive Plant List, FLEPPC, 2017. It is also considered as a potential environmental weed in parts of Australia as a result of which is prohibited in Western Australia, (Weeds of Australia, 2016). Meanwhile the economic and agronomic importance counterbalance risks of invasion in many developing countries like India, CABI, 2013.

Habitat

Dalbergia sissoo is naturally found along the riverine at an altitude ranging from 900 meters to 1,300 m or even beyond. It nurtures well in its native place where the average temperature persists from 10–40 °C. There is a variety of soil types in which the plant is capable of growth ranging from pure sand or gravel to rich alluvium of river banks supplemented with profuse moisture and well drainage facility. *Dalbergia sissoo* is observed to grow healthy at a pH of 5.0 to 7.7 and tolerates some degree of salinity, but growth is remarkably hampered on heavy clay soils. It can easily survive periodic flooding of rivers but poorly under waterlogged conditions are catastrophic for the plant. In a study, when newly planted sissoo trees were treated with temperatures below 28 F (-2 C) for a duration the plants die meanwhile older trees can sustain some serious damage at freezing temperatures.

Evolution

The phylogenetic analyses performed on over 64 *Dalbergia* species each representative of its entire geographic range suggests that *Dalbergia* is a monophyletic clade and that it perhaps originated in the New World. From the previous studies, it is evident that there is no relation between geography and the monophyletic clade phylogeny. The *Dalbergia* stem and crown clades estimation is found to be 40.4–43.3 mya and 3.8–12.7 mya, respectively. This concluded various long-distance events of dispersals had caused the pantropical distribution of the genus.

Genetic biodiversity

Wind-dispersed *Dalbergia sissoo* Roxb is widely distributed in the zone ranging from the foothills of the Himalayas from eastern Afghanistan through Pakistan to India and Nepal (Sagta and Nautiyal, 2001; Ashraf et al., 2010). Due to its high economic value, the species is planted worldwide as an exotic species, and possibly Raavan followed the same trend years ago and planted *Dalbergia sissoo* in Ashoka Vatika (Sri Lanka).

Studies on *D. sissoo* in regards to its genetic diversity and pattern of natural populations revealed that there is a relatively high level of genetic diversity, both at the species level and the population level along with a relatively low degree of differentiation among populations (Wang, B. Y.t al.,2011) The unique biological features and global plantation results in the high level of genetic diversity, low degree of differentiation, strong gene flow, and weak correlation between genetic and geographic distances. This Genetic diversity and natural distribution pattern are very helpful for the introduction and conservation of *D. sissoo*.

Ecology

Dalbergia sissoo seeds are dispersed naturally by wind and water. In the dry seasons, they remain in a dormant form in the soil, rapidly germinating on the onset of monsoon which begins in June or July in most of the species native range. After around 19-21 years of age, the Shimshapa tree reaches maturity. (Sangha & Jalota, 2005)

Natural regeneration is also common on-site like abandoned farmland, embankments, landslides, overgrazed areas, etc. Apart from seed, another mode of regeneration from root suckers and stump sprouts is commonly seen in this tree. Unfortunately, under a forest canopy, Dalbergia sissoo cannot establish. For successful natural regeneration abundant soil moisture and a lack of vegetative competition are key factors and when these factors are associated with soil rich in heavy metals, help reduce the risk of Dalbergia sissoo becoming a weed.

Ecological services

Dalbergia sissoo provides numerous services to the environment as well as to the agroforestry, from providing windbreak to shelterbelt and being as a natural shade tree in intercropping of many trees like mango and tea plantations. The well-developed taproot along with its lateral root system checks periodical soil erosion and also helps soil stabilization along banks of rivers and streams. It is widely used for fixing nitrogen in the soil as well as for reforestation. Municipal cooperation, nowadays, to boost go green campaign, are found planting it along the roadside as an avenue tree and in gardens as an ornamental plant due to its fragrant flowers and shade. *Dalbergia sissoo* is crowned as the best phytoremediation species attributing to its high biomass, rapid growth, climate tolerance, economic value, etc. (Saqib ul Kalam et al.,2019) and shows healthy growth in even metal contaminated soil. It is the best pioneer species for land restoration that is degraded with poor soil conditions.

Symbiotic association

Shisham, like its other members of the Leguminosae family, can fix nitrogen and can accumulate a considerable quantity of nitrogen-rich biomass which on decomposition improves the organic content and nutrient status of the soil. This feature nominates it among the most promising tree species commonly preferred for afforestation of degraded land. Particularly it forms a symbiotic association with *Rhizobium spp*- the root nodule forming bacteria and vesicular arbuscular fungi (VAM). It is found that the increased productivity of the plant is attributed to *Rhizobium spp* for nitrogen and improved uptake of immobilizing elements like P, Zn, Cu, and other essential nutrients due to VAM fungi. The scented flowers are pollinated by honey bees, beetles, butterflies. *D. Sissoo* leaves are the larval food of many insects especially for the butterfly, black rajah (*Charaxes solon*). In open forests, D. sissoo is not isolated; it is commonly associated with *Pinus roxburghii* and *Acacia catechu* and in transitional periods with *Shorea robusta*. It is also a vital component of grass savannas on drier sites.

Social impact

D. sissoo is a multi-utility tree with great economic goods and services. We are very well versed with the whooping numbers of products from providing timber, fuelwood, fodder, other minor products (e.g. honey) to thus providing socio-economic stability to rural areas, now have a glance at its ecological services. Ever tried standing under a tree for rest after a breath-taking game? Yes! Of course, the reviving microclimate is attributed wholly to the tree. It not only controls soil erosion but also helps soil regaining its fertility. It is a Farmers' preference for its ease of propagation whether through seed or root suckers. They also associate Sisso with life insurance which can be used in a great financial crisis. The advanced root suckers and runners' systems favor its use as a barrier for soil erosion, as a result, it is planted in eroding gullies. In many n countries like Mediterranea, *D. sissoo* is valued as an ornamental tree along with all associated benefits (Ruskin, 1983).

Invasion

Dalbergia sissoo has been widely introduced around the globe especially in Africa and Asia. Adapting and regenerating extensively on newly-transferred sites by seed and suckers as a sequential consequence Florida, USA, and the Northern Territories, Australia classified it as an invasive species. However, its use in timber and non-timber products manufacturing may overcome any unforeseen danger of invasion in developing countries like India. Sissoo trees (*Dalbergia sissoo*) are large, attractive landscape trees making them suitable for medium to large landscapes. The scenic beauty is attributed to the light green leaves and light-colored bark that stands out from other plants. The U.S. grows it as a landscape tree. The trees are suitable for USDA plant hardiness zones 10 and 11.

How to Grow a Sissoo Tree in a field?

Keep the seeds under full sun or partial shade with well-drained soil. Be cautious seedlings are intolerant of shade. Timely deep irrigation is preferred as it can cause a dense canopy. Treat the soil with iron chelate and magnesium sulfate fertilizers it will lock down iron chlorosis that is the appearance of dark green veins along with the development of yellow leaves which is due to lack of iron uptake in alkaline soils or else Citrus fertilizer will be sufficient.

Economic importance

Sissoo wood is widely used in the making of furniture and cabinets owing to its great strength, durability, and elasticity and in constructional, general utility timber, for making railway sleeper, musical instruments, wheels, small boats, and laminated skis. For ages, it has been used as fuelwood and is eminently appropriate for making charcoal. In ancient scripts, the Sisso tree is mentioned in *Jnatadharmakathanga Sutra*. The Sisso tree has been attributed as a multi-utility tree for producing various wood products as is described in *VaGa-Kamma*, similarly in the production of charcoal in Ingala-Kamma, occupation related to preparing charcoal from firewood.

Leaves are preferred as fodder for many domesticated animals like cow, goat, buffaloes, etc. and when shedding off, provide a good source of humus in the soil. It is a great Nectar source and a range of other natural products such as fibers, alkaloids, tannins, and resins.

You might be thinking that sissoo products will cost a lot more penny, but perhaps there are need and price dependent quality products in the market, we have two types of Sheesham wood timber – heartwood and sapwood. Furniture of Shisham heartwood is stronger long-lasting and among the finest timbers found in every single South Asian house, commonly used for high-grade furniture and marine-grade plywood but a bit expensive whilst that made up of sapwood is cheaper but not durable.

The trees generally provide timber at the end of a 20- to 25-year rotation. The tree branches and leaves provide fodder with estimated dry-matter content of 32.46% and crude protein 2.7- 24.1%. A useful source of honey although the flowers bloom period lasts for not much time. It provides high calorific values of 4.9 and 5.2 kcal/g respectively. Aqueous extracts from the leaves can be used as a pesticide; the pod contains 2% of tannins and can be used in dyestuff. The oil (5.35%) extracted from the heartwood is used as a lubricant for heavy machinery. Fruits liberate ethanolic extract which exhibits molluscicide effect against *Biomphalaria pfeifferi* snail's eggs.

Medicinal importance

In South Asia, *Dalbergia sissoo* is known as folklore -medicinal plant. *D. sissoo* is a folk remedy for several ailments, for instance, for treating skin diseases, excoriation, and gonorrhea (Duke and Wain, 1981). *D. sissoo* leaf extract contains an alcoholic compound which marks antipyretic and moderate analgesic activities (Hajare et al., 2000). Rural people in India and Nepal use leaves for treating non-specific diarrhea in animals. Leaf extract has been used for ages to treat throat problems, heart problems, gonorrhea, etc. (Al-Quran, 2008). Studies showed that the antioxidant activity of leaves extract is twice as high as other commonly used antioxidants like Selenium and vitamin E. This extract also contains flavonoid insignificant amounts and can be used to treat colorectal cancer along with other conventional treatments with chemotherapeutic agents. Current Research is directing toward the anti-cancerous properties attributing to its flavonoids. *D. sissoo* bark has antioxidant properties and can be used for inflammatory disorders (Kumari and Kakkar, 2008). The Bastar region (India) practitioners used it as a potent blood purifier and in Leprosy treatment. Tectoridin (a kind of flavonoid) and astringent present in the roots are used to treat inflammations and infections like abdominal pain, gonorrhea, as well as abortion. In an experiment to investigate the effects of heartwood ethanolic extract (HEE) of Dalbergia sissoo on healing bone fracture and on pathological bone loss in ovariectomized (ovx) rats due to estrogen deficiency, it was found that Oral administration of HEE incite fracture healing and shows osteoprotective effect perhaps due to osteoblast function. (Karvande A et al., 2017). Traditionally *D. sissoo* oil from the seed treats burning and scabies and a decoction of the leaves is prescribed for the acute stage of gonorrhea and to cure boils and pimples. People in many parts of our country still use it to make a toothbrush from its branches.

Injuries, diseases, and pest

According to TOI, 2003 newspaper report the trees in Punjab were drying out for some unidentified reasons, local experts cited viral and fungus infection, waterlogging, climate change, smog, and fog as possible culprits behind the cause.

Dalbergia sissoo is affected by various physical and biological factors. Injuries to the plant are caused by drought, wind storms, and periodic erosion of riverine sites. Weeds, tall grass, climbers, and parasitic plants compete for survival with the tree and challenge its effective adaptability. Seedlings are more prone to being browsed by animals and insects like Leaf defoliator (*Plecoptera reflexa*, *Dichomeris eridantis, Ascotis selenaria*), Leaf miner (*Leucoptera sphemograpts*), Leaf roller (*Apoderus sissu*), Sap sucking bug – (*Drosicha mangifera*). Fungi of the genus *Fusarium, Ganoderma lucidum*, and *Phellinus gilvus* cause foliage diseases, all of which attack the root and vascular system and are the reason for the high proportion of mortality of Indian Rosewood (Sharma, et al, 2000). The roots of dying trees were also tested for pathogenicity due to *Fusarium solani* in *Dalbergia sissoo*.

Conservation record

Until yet, the IUCN has not assessed the species due to its abundance population in the Indian subcontinent above critical level but on 2nd January 2017 and on 4th February 2017, Dalbergia *sissoo* was listed in CITES Appendix II and Annex B of the EU Wildlife Trade Regulations respectively with all the species under the genus '*Dalbergia*'. Let's see behind-the-story facts. The Down To Earth report in January 2019 says 'India demands rosewood out of CITES', India's proposal document says that *Dalbergia sissoo* is a fast-growing species capable of acclimatizing beyond the boundaries of its native region and is no close to its extinction. The trade regulation is of little need concerning the current status of the tree and should be removed from the International Trade in Endangered Species of Wild Fauna and Flora (CITES), an organization aimed to protect endangered plants and animals. CITES put the entire genus *Dalbergia* on looks- alike- criteria because of the difficulty to distinguish the threatened species from the other non-threatened species of the same genus. The considerable rise in demand for *Dalbergia* wood in the international markets fuelling the illegal trade which is decimating *Dalbergia* population is the concern of the multilateral treaty and hence to protect the individual species which need urgent attention, the entire genus was enrolled by CITES.

Nevertheless, the Indian proposal firmly supporting how the trade restriction has devastating consequences on the handicraft makers in India despite the potentiality of the species to invade and maintain its count, the proposal also illuminates the transferring of international- trade- threatened small-clawed otters (*Aonyx cinereus*), smooth-coated otters (*Lutrogale *perspicillata*), Indian Star Tortoise (*Geochelone elegans*) from Appendix II to Appendix I, thereby giving more protection to the targeted species.

Economic importance

In India Shisham (Dalbergia sissoo) stood second only after teak in economic values. India's international trade in Shisham products is estimated at Rs 617 crore while the full potential is Rs 1,000 crore, data from Export Promotion Council for Handicrafts 2017-2018. On account of increased control on trade, only INR 6.17 billion was possible against INR 10 billion or more of the potential export of handicraft items made from sissoo trees, in the year 2017-18. The government report claimed, "*Around INR 5 billion of wooden handicraft exports declined last year by over 10 pc*".

Rituals, folklore, and legends

In ancient Indian manuscripts, particular trees were mentioned among which Shisham is one, which is especially given the status of "trees for image-making for purposes of worship". The sculptures sanction trees and only those trees need to be given importance in terms of worshipping deities. Take, for instance, the images for worship by the Brahmanas are made from Syandana (*Dalbergia sissoo*). The Natyashastra (theatrics and dramaturgy statue) believe to have one of the Hands indicating Trees—Shimshapa, the Ardha-Candra hands crossed. Sissoo tree has been described throughout Ayurveda literature such as the *Caraka-samhita* and the *Susruta-samhita*. In *Dharmashastra,* a King was directed to plant such domestic plants in and near villages, he should nourish them by the stool of goats, sheep, and cows, water as well as meat. A detailed ancient Indian recipe for such nourishment of trees is incorporated in *Sukraniti*. We can also trace remnants of the tree described in Shaktism (Shakta philosophy), Shimshapa was found in Manidvipa (Devi Sakti's abode), according to the Devi-Bhagavata-puraGa. The tree has been shown as the main entity holding different species of birds, beetles due to its fragmented flowers, and rivers are seen flowing through their forests carrying many juicy liquids from the tree.

According to Indian history and geography, the tree "Shimshapa" was mentioned by Somadeva in Kathasarit Sagara dates from the 10th century A.D. Somadeva's writing described the forests and lifestyle of Northern Indians society during the 11th century. His Kathasarit Sagara 'ocean of streams of the story', featuring Shimshapa, is considered as a known Sanskrit epic story that describes the quest and struggles of Prince Naravahanadatta to become the emperor of the *Vidyadharas* (celestial beings) in his life.

Conclusion

D. sissoo is denoted by many botanists as a "living bank account" for security against future economic needs due to the innumerable goods and services provided by the plant to humans and back to nature. The need for the hour is to stress the biological and anthropogenic factors that threaten its survival. *Dalbergia sissoo* is one among the keystone species of the northern plains with high economic values which put it in the center of exploitation. No matter how fast the plant can grow, if not taken care of, we may lose a precious species. Research should be oriented towards the pathogen attacking the tree. climate change also sheds its impact on the rate of growth and development and also governs its therapeutic substances content indirectly. *Dalbergia sissoo* is a very common but lesser-known tree. Who knows what miracle is surreptitiously hidden in it waiting for its discovery?

References

Amitthalingam, M. Plant Diversity in the Valmiki Ramayana, Bhattacharya, M., Singh, A., & Ramrakhyani, C. (2014). Dalbergia sissoo-an important medical plant. *Journal of Medicinal Plants*, *2*(2), 76-82.

Bisht, R., Chaturvedi, S., Srivastava, R., Sharma, A. K., & Johri, B. N. (2009). Effect of arbuscular mycorrhizal fungi, Pseudomonas fluorescens, and Rhizobium leguminosarum on the growth and nutrient status of Dalbergia sissoo Roxb. *Tropical Ecology*, *50*(2), 231.

Carroll, Jackie. Sissoo Tree Information: Learn About Dalbergia Sissoo Trees [Available at: https://www.gardeningknowhow.com/ornamental/trees/sissoo/sissoo-tree information.htm [assessed April 20th, 2020]

Chiavarini, M., Naldini, G., & Fabiani, R. (2020). The role of diet in osteoporotic fracture healing: A systematic review. *Current osteoporosis reports*, *18*(3), 138-147.

Devagiri, G. M., Dhiman, R. C., Singh, Y. P., & Patil, S. K. (2001). Seed source dependent variation in mycorrhizal colonization and nutrient uptake in Dalbergia sissoo seedlings. *Journal of Tropical Forest Science*, 246-257.

Edward F. Gilman, Dennis G. Watson, Ryan W. Klein, Andrew K. Koeser, Deborah R. Hilbert, and Drew C. McLean2 *Dalbergia sissoo: Indian Rosewood*

Gupta, S. M. (1971). *Plant Myths and traditions in India*. Brill Archive.

Karvande, A., Khedgikar, V., Kushwaha, P., Ahmad, N., Kothari, P., Verma, A., ... & Trivedi, R. (2017). Heartwood extract from Dalbergia sissoo promotes fracture healing and its application in ovariectomy induced osteoporotic rats. *Journal of Pharmacy and Pharmacology,* 69(10), 1381-1397.

Kalam, S. U., Naushin, F., Khan, F. A., & Rajakaruna, N. (2019). Long-term phytoremediating abilities of Dalbergia sissoo Roxb. (Fabaceae). SN *Applied Sciences,* 1(5), 501

Koeser, A., Hasing, G., Andreu, M. G., & Friedman, M. H. (2016). How to Use a Dichotomous Key: A Tutorial Featuring 10 Common Shade Trees of the Tampa Bay Area. *EDIS*, *2016*(6), 12-12.

Mali, M. S. Silviculture of Dalbergia sissoo Manas Ranjan Debta, Debasmitra Dutta Pramanick & S.K. Srivastava Northern Regional Centre, Botanical Survey of India, Dehradun.

Murthy, K.M.K., Sundara Kanda (book V) - Book Of Beauty, Chapter [Sarga] 31Verses converted to UTF-8, Nov 09, [Available at: https://www.valmikiramayan.net/utf8/sundara/sarga31/sundara_31_frame.htm] [assessed April 11th ,2020]

Poussio, G. B., Kazmi, M. R., Akem, C., & Fateh, F. S. (2010). First record of Ceratocystis fimbriata associated with shisham (Dalbergia sissoo) decline in Pakistan. *Australasian Plant Disease Notes*, *5*(1), 63-65.

Shah, M. H., Mukhtar, I., & Khan, S. N. (2010). Medicinal importance and association of pathological constraints with Dalbergia sissoo. *Pak J Phytopathol*, *22*(2), 135-138.

Snel, F. A., Braga, J. W., da Silva, D., Wiedenhoeft, A. C., Costa, A., Soares, R., ... & Pastore, T. C. (2018). Potential field-deployable NIRS identification of seven Dalbergia species listed by CITES. *Wood Science and Technology*, 52(5), 1411-1427.

Tewari, D. N. (1994). *A monograph on Dalbergia sissoo Roxb*. International Book Distributors UNEP-WCMC. 2017. Review of selected Dalbergia species and Guibourtia demeusei. UNEP-WCMC, Cambridge

Vatanparast, M., Klitgård, B. B., Adema, F. A., Pennington, R. T., Yahara, T., & Kajita, T. (2013). First molecular phylogeny of the pantropical genus Dalbergia: implications for infrageneric circumscription and biogeography. *South African Journal of Botany,* 89, 143-149.

Wang, B. Y., Shi, L., Ruan, Z. Y., & Deng, J. (2011). Genetic diversity and differentiation in Dalbergia sissoo (Fabaceae) as revealed by RAPD. *Genetics and Molecular Research,* 10(1), 114-120.

Trees of Ramayana (2022): 75-86
Editor: Felix Bast
Today & Tomorrow's Printers and Publishers (India)

Chapter-7

Banyan Tree (*Ficus benghalensis*)

Suman Sasmita Dash

ततो न्यग्रोधमासाद्य महान्तं हरितच्छदम्।।2.55.6।।

विवृद्धं बहुभिर्वृक्षै श्श्यामं सिद्धोपसेवितम्।

तस्मै सीताञ्जलिं कृत्वा प्रयुञ्जीताशिषश्शिवाः।।2.55.7।।

Shri Rama with his wife Sita and younger brother Lakshmana obeying his father's word of fourteen-year exile to the forest, sacrificed kingship and the palace. Though he was brought up with royal status, he didn't hesitate to leave Ayodhya and his beloved citizens, in a casual outfit, only with basic requirements for the journey. They reached the hermitage of Rishi Bharadwaj beneath the forest, at the confluence of the river Ganga and Yamuna. The sage offered them warm hospitality and suggested Chitrakoot be the best place for their sojourn. He instructed them on the route for Chitrakoot. He also advised Mata Sita to convey an auspicious prayer to a large banyan tree, named Shyama, after crossing the river Yamuna by a raft. On approaching, Sita offered homage to the tree. Moreover, Shri Rama, Mata Sita, and Lakshmana stayed at Panchavati, a forest comprising five banyan trees during the crucial period of exile, where Sita gets abducted by Ravana, the king of Lanka. Akshaya Vatan, a banyan tree, is blessed by Vaidehi to remain immortal, as the tree did not turn back as the witness of a tribute to her father-in-law, Dasharatha, at his funeral ceremony.

Figure 1: The enlarged view of the arrangement of leaves and fruits on a branch of *Ficus benghalensis*. © Suman Sasmita Dash

Taxonomic Position:

Domain: Eukaryota

Kingdom: Plantae

Subkingdom: Tracheobionta

Superdivision: Spermatophyta

Division: Magnoliophyta

Class: Magnoliopsida

Order: Urticales

Family: Moraceae

Genus: *Ficus*

Species: *Ficus benghalensis*

Botanical Name: *Ficus benghalensis* L.

Vernacular Name: English: Banyan fig, Indian banyan, Weeping Chinese banyan; Hindi: Bargad, Bar; Gujrati: Vad, Vadlo, Bor; Odia: Bara gacha; Urdu: Bihar; Kannada: Aalada, Mara; Malayalam: Peraal, Aalamaram; Marathi: Vada, War, Wad; Bengali: Bat gaach, Bath, Bot; Telugu: Marri chettu; Tamil: Alai.

Sanskrit Name: Vata, Kalpavriksh, Nyagrodha

Introduction

The banyan tree is an important part of the life of the Indian subcontinent. The tree is native to South & East Asia. It is the National tree of India. It is also the state tree of Madhya Pradesh. The banyan tree is the largest in the world in terms of circumference. The name "Banyan" is believed to be derived from the word "Baniya", which means grocer or merchant in the Gujarati language. The trees are described as the offices of the Indian traders. They used to conduct their business under its shade. *Ficus* is the Latin name for the figs and *benghalensis* is given after the place of its origin, Bengal. It is also named Bengal fig. The tree is considered to be sacred in some places of India as well as China. The Banyan tree has marked its place in Indian literature. An excellent example is "The Banyan Tree" by Rabindranath Tagore. Robinson Crusoe, a famous character in the novel by Daniel Defoe, built his home on the branches of a banyan tree.

Morphological Characteristics

The large, fast-growing, perennial, woody, and deciduous epiphyte grows up to an average height of 20m and 200m (700ft) in diameter. The average lifespan of the tree is about 200 years, but it is believed to live thousands of years, as the major trunk is hidden by successive aerial roots. One of the major characteristic features is aerial prop roots, which grow into woody trunks, i.e. indistinguishable from the main trunk. The wood is soft, porous, and water-resistant. Leaves are ovate, obtuse, 3 nerved, entire, coriaceous, 20-40cm long with 4-6 pairs of lateral veins (Joseph et al., 2010). Petioles are ventrally compressed and hairy, containing broad smooth greasy glands at the apex. The arrangement of leaves and fruits is shown in figure.

It is said that the Banyan tree isn't flowerless; it bears fruits, but never blossoms. The uniovulate flowers or florets lie inside, enveloped by a thick layer of fruit flesh. The structure is called a syconium. The receptacle is closed by an ostiole, formed of three basal bracts. The fruit is an achene, stalkless, globose-ellipsoid, and scarlet red when ripe (Kothapalli et al., 2014). Figs occur in pairs in leaf axils and are 1-2cm in diameter. It is monoecious. The male flowers bearing pollen and the female flowers bearing the seeds are lined on the inner side of the fruit. The inflorescence is hypanthium type. Besides, there are neutral flowers or gall flowers, i.e. neither female nor male. Female flowers are sessile, ovary straight, long, eccentric and contain sepals shorter than male flowers. Gall flowers are pedicellate, sepals 4, and carry developing insects. Male flowers are many, lanceolate, sepals 4, stamen 1 and mainly occur near the mouth. Seed figs consist of female flowers with long styles of various lengths; while gall figs consist of gall flowers with a short style and male flowers. Upon pollination, the florets develop into achenes or drupes. It is also named as strangler fig, as it is propagated from rock crevices or on any tree as an epiphyte. The chromosome number of the diploid plant is 26 (Ohri and Khoshoo, 1986).

Habitat & Distribution

Banyan trees grow well in high humidity and wet habitats on well-drained sandy loam soils. Established trees are drought-resistant. They require moderate sunlight. They get easily damaged in frost. Therefore warmer climates are usually preferred. However, it may withstand mild frost (Oudhia, 2004). Annual rainfall of 1000-2500m is preferred, but it may tolerate 500-4000m. It can grow in a range of 300-1300m of altitude and 30°N to 10°S latitude. The pH of 5.5-7 is suitable for its growth, tolerating 4.5-8.5. It grows in an annual daytime temperature of 26-36! but can tolerate up to 9-40!.

The tree is found in tropical and subtropical regions of the world. It is mainly indigenous to Indian subcontinent. The first place where it was introduced as a cultivated plant were Western Africa, North America, the West Indies, Australia, the Middle East, and numerous Pacific islands, but it has since naturalized in many tropical locations throughout the world. In Africa, the species is reported in the Central African Republic, Egypt, Kenya, Morocco, Seychelles, Tanzania (Zanzibar Island), and Uganda. In Asia, the tree is distributed in Afghanistan, India, Bangladesh, Nepal, Pakistan, Maldives, Malaysia, Indonesia, Israel, Chagos Archipelago, Myanmar, Qatar, Singapore, Thailand, Sri Lanka, and Vietnam. It is also found in Bahamas, Jamaica, United States (Florida, Hawaii), Australia, Fiji, American Samoa, Nauru, Samoa, Papua New Guinea, Kiribati, French Polynesia, Northern Mariana Islands, and U.S. minor outlying islands. In Australia, the oldest herbarium collection was recorded in 1899 (Atlas of Living Australia, 2014). In India, it is found in almost all regions, mainly throughout the sub-Himalayan regions and deciduous forests. Lahaina's famed banyan tree, Hawaii, the largest banyan tree of the USA, with a canopy covering an area of 1.94 hectares, was planted by then-mayor William Owen Smith, on April 24, 1873, in memory of the 50th anniversary of the first American Protestant mission. The tree was gifted to the sheriff from the missionaries of India.

Cultural Importance

Ficus benghalensis is described as Kalpavriksh in mythology, because of its ability to fulfill all needs. In Hinduism, it is considered the symbol of immortality. It is worshipped as Lord Brahma, as a symbol of longevity. The tree is usually planted far from the village as it does not allow the growth of any other plant beneath its canopy. Thus, it is described as a hermit, away from materialistic life and represents spiritual aspirations. Rishi Markandeya found shelter under the banyan tree during torrential rain. Lord Shiva, the greatest of hermits, as Dakshinamurthy, is portrayed meditating under the shades of a banyan tree with rishis at his feet. Under its shade, Lord Rishabhanatha, also known as Adinatha, the first Jain Tirthankara, achieved enlightenment through asceticism. Jyotisar, Haryana, India witnessed the sermon of Shrimad Bhagavad Gita delivered by Lord Krishna to Arjuna during Mahabharata under a banyan tree. Krishna is called Vatapatrasayi, Lord of the banyan leaf, as he is believed to rest on a banyan leaf. In India and Nepal, the banyan tree is grown closer to the peepal tree (*Ficus religiosa*) Banyan tree symbolizes Devi Lakshmi and the peepal tree is the symbol of the Lord Vishnu. The tradition of wedding a peepal tree with a banyan tree has been practiced from ancient times. The banyan tree is associated with the Lord of death, Yama. In Vana Parva of Mahabharata, answering the question of Yudhishthira, Rishi Markandeya told a story of a woman, named Savitri, who lost her husband, Satyavan under a banyan tree, followed Lord Yama to the land of death and saved him through her determination. On the eve of Vat Savitri brat, Married women in the Western Indian states of Gujarat, Maharashtra, Goa, and some regions of Uttar Pradesh, worship the banyan tree by tying a knot around it and pray for the well being and long life of their husbands. The tree is worshipped as 15th-century saint Kabir, as a giant banyan tree is said to have grown from teeth cleaning twig or datun used by him. In Buddhism's Pali canon, the banyan (Pali: nigrodha) depicted the sensual desire of human beings. A large banyan tree, called Kalpabata, present in the premises of Puri Jagannath Dham, Odisha, India is worshipped by the devotees and is believed to be 500 years old. Banyan trees are considered sacred by local Dai people in the Xishuangbanna region of China. The Banyan tree is included in the coat of arms of Indonesia, symbolizing the Unity of Indonesia with many far-flung roots and power. The Lam Tsuen Wishing Trees, named for the banyan trees are located near the Tin Hau Temple in Lam Tsuen, Hong Kong. Vetals and pisachas are believed to reside on the branches of banyan trees. Philippine mythology describes a variety of spirits (*diwata* and *engkanto*) and demon-like creatures (among the Visayans, specifically, the *dili ingon nato*, meaning "those not like us"), *Maligno* (evil spirits) to dwell on the banyan trees. In Guam, the Chamorro people believe that *Taotaomona*, the spirits of the ancient Chamorro, guard the banyan trees. "Paradise Lost" written by 17th century English poet John Milton, depicts Eve and Adam using banyan leaves to sew their first clothes (Book 9, 1090-1120). Soeharto utilized it as a logo for his party, the Golongan Karya (Golkar), acknowledging the profoundly established belief of his comrades in the sacred nature of the banyan tree.

Ecological Importance

Ficus species are associated with agaonid wasps (Hymenoptera: Chalcidoidea: Agonidae) and are only pollinated by their associated wasp species. When the female flowers mature, they emit specific volatile compounds that attract fig wasps. Female wasps have functional heads, eyes and are capable to modify head and antenna in response to the shape of inflorescence opening. Female wasps, thus, carry out pollination of figs colonizing new hosts. The head and thorax of female wasps are flattened and elongated. Mandibular appendages are present on the head that bears rows of teeth. This facilitates the entry of female wasps through the bract-lined ostiole at the apex to the florets. The fig wasps deposit pollen on the stigma surface of female flowers or seed figs and direct the viable seed set. These also lay eggs on gall figs by inserting their ovipositors into the styles. Gall figs, in return, provide nutrition to the developing larvae. Fig pollination serves as the example of convolved mutualism and sex ratio evolution. *Eupristina masoni* is the pollinator wasp associated with *Ficus benghalensis* [Weiblen G.D., 2002]. It also homes several species, including frugivorous birds, bats, butterflies, bees, macaques, and even the endangered slender loris. These help in the dispersal of seeds and their propagation. Some of the fruit-eating birds are mynah birds (*Acridotheres tristis tristis*), blue-faced doves (*Geopelia striata*), lace necked doves (*Streptopelia chinensis*), and house sparrows (*Passer domesticus*), etc. Compared with trees in urban areas, the trees, likely to be native to a region, play a critical role in supporting local biodiversity. The massive roots help in soil conservation.

Economic Importance

The plant is considered mainly for its food and medicinal value. Figs are edible but aren't usually preferred by humans. For insects, birds, and mammals, it offers food and forage. The linings of drawers and cabinets, poles, cart yokes, furnishings, and well linings are all made of wood. Wood is also used for paper pulp. The aerial roots are a good source of temporary binding material. The aerial roots and leaves can be used to make ropes and crafts. Several secondary metabolites, including tannins, resins are obtained and are of commercial use. The leaves are used to make plates.

The latex of the tree is used to yield inferior quality rubbers. [Sethi et al , 2003, Kang et al., 2002]

Pharmacological Value

Leaves of *Ficus benghalensis* contain phytochemicals that exhibit anticancer properties, mainly against cervical cancer [Kumaresaran et al., 2018]. The fruit extract of the banyan tree shows anti-tumor activity. The bark and leaves have analgesic and antipyretic properties. A decoction of leaf buds and aerial roots, mixed with honey, can be used to cure the burning sensation. Diabetes is treated using a decoction made from the bark. 3-O-beta-D-galactosyl cellobiose, present in the bark, possesses anti-diabetic action [Sharma et al., 2007]. Alpha-amyrin acetate present in aerial roots shows antihyperglycemic action [Singh A.B. et al., 2009]. Ethanol extracts of fruit, aerial root, and bark produce a significant decrease in blood glucose level. Phyto-constituents present in roots show a potent anthelmintic property [Manoj A. et al., 2008]. The aqueous extract of the aerial root has immunomodulatory potential, by stimulating cell-mediated and antibody-mediated immune responses. It was found to enhance phagocytosis by human neutrophils in vitro. Polar constituents on *F. benghalensis* bark have anti-stress and anti-allergic effects in asthma. The flavonoids, tannins, and phenolic compounds present in the aqueous extract of aerial roots act as antioxidants that protect against oxidative damage due to prolonged stress and prolonged exposure to infection. Methanol extract of leaves also exhibits antioxidant properties. The plant also reveals anti-diarrhoeal properties [Singh et al., 2019]. Diarrhoea and dysentery are treated with the bark. The latex is used to treat hemorrhagic diarrhoea, dysentery, and inflammation. The ethanol extracts of bark from younger plants possess a greater anti-inflammatory effect than that present in the drug Indomethacin. To heal the wounds, A mixture of leaf powder of banyan tree and coconut oil is applied topically on the affected places [Joseph et al., 2010; Kothapalli et al., 2014]. The alcoholic and aqueous extracts of young prop roots have the potential to promote growth [Nidhiya et al., 2009]. It is widely used among the tribes of Western Maharashtra, India. The plant has significant antimicrobial activity. The latex of *Ficus benghalensis* possesses toxicity to *Penicillium citrinum* growth and has been found to suppress citrinin production to a different extent. Plant extracts exhibit toxicity to *Epidermophyton floccosum* (filamentous fungus, Division: *Ascomycota*) and *Microsporum gypsum* (Division: *Ascomycota*). Methanol extracts of fruit have antibacterial action against *E.coli,* while the ether extract of the fruits show toxicity to *E.coli*, *S. typhi,* and *L. acidophilus* and it was found to be highly bactericidal against *L. acidophilus.* The bark extracts show better antibacterial activity against *Actinomyces viscous* (Aswar et al., 2008; Gaherwal, 2013; Shandavi et al. 2010).

Recreation and Tourism

Ficus benghalensis is labeled as a keystone species as a large number of wildlife; birds, insects, bats, etc depend on it for food and shelter. The tree, due to the fast and strangler pattern of growth, spreads over a vast area. The green foliage offers a great respite during summer. It is usually portrayed as the panchayat's meeting place for dispensation of justice, in movies as well as stories. The tree is still honored for its shade. For ages, it has been the beholder of many spades parties, village khatti, and gossip. Kids love to play and spend quality time under its shade. Children as well as adults enjoy swinging to and fro on hanging banyan roots. Intently watching the flurry activities during the fruiting season is fascinating. This entices nature lovers, environmentalists, and ecologists more, especially for recording facts for assignments or books or portraits. City dwellers visit there to catch a glimpse of nature. It offers aesthetic and restorative environments, helps to relieve mental stress, and become physically fit. With increasing urbanization and a stressful modern lifestyle, the demand for eco-tourism and outdoor recreation is increasing. Table 1 describes the largest banyan trees in India according to the canopy cover and crown size (Barness Y.D., 2013). Thimmamma Marrimanu, Andhra Pradesh, India, is the largest banyan tree in the world, in the Guinness Book of World Records in 1989, with a canopy cover of 19,107 square meters (4.721 acres) and 4000 prop roots. Kabirvad, a banyan tree named after saint Kabir, is located on the river island of Narmada, Gujarat. The area of its canopy is 17,520 square meters (4.33 acres) with a perimeter of 641m (2103ft). Pillalamarri, Telangana, India, spread over an area of 4 acres is the third-largest banyan tree according to an archeological survey of India and is approximately 800years old. A 450 years old giant banyan tree is present on the grounds of Theosophical Society headquarters, Chennai, Tamil Nadu, under which people attended disclosure of dignitaries, like J. Krishnamurti, Annie Besant, and Maria Montessori. Dodda Aloda Mara, also called the big banyan tree, at Bengaluru, Karnataka has spread across an area of 3 acres and is 400 years old. A thousand-year-old banyan tree, spread in 50,000 sq. ft. is located at Chausath Yogini temple, Madhya Pradesh. A three-hundred years old banyan tree, spread over 3.5 acres, at Cholti Kheri, Fatehgarh, Punjab is the first biodiversity heritage site of Punjab, India. Banyan trees were planted by celebrities near downtown Hilo, Hawaii during the 20th-century form Banyan drive. Ta Prohm in the Angkor complex comprises gigantic roots of banyan tree over stones, probing walls, and terrace. The UNESCO

World Heritage status attracts more tourists to the complex. This contributes significantly to the economic output. The government is now encouraging the development and promotion of such tranquil scenic places. The beauty holy banyan tree at Jyotisar tirth has been enhanced with a marble chariot depicting Krishna delivering the sermon of Bhagavad Gita to Arjuna, a mango-shaped lake with a covered bathing facility for ladies, cemented parapet and enclosures, guest house, and restaurants for pilgrims. The government has constructed a 5 themed amusement park with a meditation hall and regular light and music show on the site.

Role as Urban forest

Banyan tree is fast-growing and is considered as the period of leaf fall is not conspicuous. The large sprawling tree spread its wide canopy over a vast area. A single banyan tree can be designated as a micro forest. However, these are easily handled as ornamental trees in very minimal space. Due to the complex network of roots and extensive branching, the tree is employed in penjing and bonsai. The oldest living bonsai is in Tainan, Taiwan, and is 240 years old. It can be grown indoors or in gardens, provided with moderately moist soil, moderately bright light, and an indoor temperature of 21! during summer and 10-18! in winter. Urban forests perform many ecosystem services, including reduction of air pollution, improving air quality, carbon sequestration, reduction of stormwater runoff, alleviate the intensity of heat island, cooling the air temperature, and providing aesthetic beauty to the urban landscape. Banyan trees are mainly dominant in terms of biomass and carbon storage value. Urban forests modify the microscale climates through direct shading or Evapotranspiration or reduction of wind speed. The 300 years old large banyan tree on the campus of Gujarat State Fertilizer Corporation Ltd, with a canopy cover of 4000m, accounts for carbon stock of about 1.55 tonnes and the yearly rate of sequestration by increasing stock is around 5900 tonnes [Status of Tree Cover in Urban areas of Gujarat (2012), Forest Department of Gujarat].

Conservation of the Tree

Being stuck between two major cyclones in 1864 and 1867, the 51ft wide main trunk of the Great Banyan, Kolkata, India, got infected by a fungus and was cut off to save the rest of the tree successfully, in 1925 (Allison Meier, 2013). Several such trees are uprooted due to natural disasters. Excessive loss of branches and aerial roots and setting up concrete structures to restrict the growth of aerial roots or several pruning practices has become a threat to the giant tree. However, Religion and cultural practices serve as boons to the conservation of the tree and biodiversity. In ancient India, the practice of conservation has emerged by maintaining the woodlands as sacred. Banyan tree is one among the heritage trees of India, because of its majestic look, historical aspects, and old age, according to Indian National Trust for Art and Cultural Heritage (INTACH), a non-profit organization in 2008-09. Special protection measures, along with 20 times replantation (standard: 10 times) plans, are implemented to ensure its existence. The heritage tree is provided with a template, describing its name, age, size of canopy coverage, and importance to mankind and biodiversity (Barness Y.D., 2013). Herbicides and pesticides should always be used with proper caution. Thimmakka, a 107-year-old Environmentalist from Karnataka, along a 4-kilometer stretch of roadway between Hulikal and Kudur, India has planted and cultivated 385 banyan trees, now being designated as National Highway 48 (April 14, 2019- The Hindu). She has received more than 50 awards and honors for her environmental work including the National Citizens Award (1996) and the Godfrey Phillips Award (2006). Her contribution to nature made its way to BBC's 100 Women 2016 list of the world's most powerful and inspiring women. She also bagged the prestigious Padmashree award for this on Mar 16, 2019. She is dearly called Saalumarada, which means rows of trees.

Related Species

Ficus is a flowering plant, formerly discussed under the order Urticales, Family Moraceae. The family is also known as the mulberry or fig family. The family includes about 40 genera and 1000 species. According to APG 3, It is placed in the order Rosales as the sister family of Urticaceae (Berg et al., 2001). Some of the closely related species are *Ficus religiosa* (Peepal tree), *Ficus carica* (Common fig), *Ficus elastica* (Indian rubber plant), *Ficus benjamina* (Weeping fig), etc.

Conclusion

Secretly, we all desire to have wild animals or birds as pets in our homes. But has anybody ever thought of planting the National tree of India at home? While there lies a lot of issues with capturing National birds or animals at home, planting such a large tree will gain appreciation. Such a practice will surely help to improve the urban climate.

References

Joseph B., Raj S.J (2010) Phytopharamacological and phytochemical Properties of Three *Ficus* Species, *International Journal of Pharma and Bio Sciences*, vol 1.

Kothapalli P.K., Jagadeesh, Sanganal S., Shridhar N.B. (2014) Phytopharmacology of *Ficus bengalensis* - A Review, *Asian J. Pharm. Res.*

4(4): Page 201-204.

CABI, Undated: CABI Compendium: Status as determined by CABI editor. Wallingford, UK: CABI https://www.cabi.org/isc/datasheet/24066#toreferences

Sharma S., Chaturvedi M., Edwin E., Shukla S., Sahrawat H. (2007), Evaluation of the phytochemicals and antidiabetic activity of *Ficus benghalensis*, *Int. J. Diabetes. Dev. Ctries.*, 27(2).

Singh A.B., Yadav D.K., Maurya R., Srivastava A.K. (2009), Antihyperglycaemic activity of α-amyrin acetate in rats and db/db mice, *Nat. Prod. Res.*, 23(9).

Manoj A., Urmila, A., Bhagyashri, W., Meenakshi, V., Akshaya, W., Kishore, N.G. (2008). Anthelmintic activity of *Ficus benghalensis*, *Int. J. Green Pharm.*, 2(3).

Aswar M., Aswar U., Wagh A., Watkar B., Vyas M., Gujar K. (2008), Antimicrobial activity of *Ficus benghalensis*, *Pharmacologyonline* 2: 715-725.

Gaherwal S. (2013) Antibacterial Activity of *Ficus benghalensis* (Banyan) Fruit Extract Against Different Bacteria, *International Journal of Microbiological Research* 4, 177-179 DOI: 10.5829/idosi.ijmr.2013.4.2.7450

Shandavi C.B., Vikas V.P., Vijay R.P. (2010), Antibacterial Activity of *Ficus benghalensis* barks on *Actinomyces viscosus*, *Int. J. Pharm. Sci.*, 2(1).

Kumaresan S., Ramasamy R., Jayachandran P. (2018), Antioxidant and cytotoxic activity of combined extracts prepared using *Ficus Religiosa* & *Ficus benghalensis* leaves against Cervical cancer cell line (HELA) *Asian Journal of Pharmaceutical and Clinical Research*, Vol. 11, no. 12, pp. 407-10. doi:10.22159/ajpcr.2018.v11i12. 26948.

Weiblen G.D (2002), How to be a Fig Wasp, *Annu. Rev. Entomol.* 47 :299-330, http://arjournals.annualreviews.org/doi/abs/10.1146/annurev.ento.47.091201.145213?cookieSet=1&journalCode=ento.

Oudhia P (2004), Bar or Bargad *Ficus benghalensis L* https://www.hort.purdue.edu/newcrop/CropFactSheets/ficus.html

Status of Tree Cover in Urban areas of Gujarat (2012), Forest Department of Gujarat

Atlas of Living Australia, 2014. Atlas of Living Australia. http://www.ala.org.au

Barness Y.D. (2013), Conservation of Indian Heritage trees, https://tasmaniangeographic.com/wpcontent/uploads/2017/10/ConservationofIndian HeritageTreesMonograph-JournalofHeritageStudies.pdf

Seth M.K., (2003) Trees and their economic importance, *Botanical Review*, Vol. 69, No. 4 pp. 321-376.

Kang H., Kim Y.S., Chung G.C. (2002) Characterization of Natural Rubber biosynthesis in *Ficus benghalensis, Plant Physiology & Biochemistry*, Vol 38(12), pp 979- 987.

Meier A., (2013), Curious Fact of the week: The tree that is a forest https://www.atlasobscura.com/articles/curious-fact-of-the-week-great-banyan-tree

Staff Reporter (2019, April 14), Nature enthusiasts get green lessons from Saalumarada

Thimmakka,*TheHindu*,https://www.thehindu.com/news/cities/Coimbatore/nature-enthusiasts-get-green-lessons-from-saalumarada-thimmakka/article26837299.ece

Ohri, D., Khoshoo, T.N. 1986. Plant DNA contents and systematics. In: S. K. Dutta, edsDNA systematics, Vol II. Plants, CRC Press, Florida, pp. 2-19.

Berg, C.C. 2001. Moreae, Artocarpeae, and Dorstenia (Moraceae). With introductions to the family and *Ficus* and with additions and corrections to Flora Neotropica Monograph 7. Flora Neotropica Monograph 83. *The New York Botanical Garden*, New York. p. 347.

Singh A.K, Tripathi R., Kumar A., Kumar S, Prakash S, Singh A.K., (2019), *Ficus benghalensis* Linn.: A tribal medicine with vast commercial potential, *Indian Journal of Agriculture and Allied Sciences*, Vol 1 (3).

Nidhiya I.S.R., Rao C.M., Pai K.S.R. (2009), Growth promoting potential of *Ficus bengalensis* root extracts in immature female rats, *Pharmaceutical Biology*, 47:4 https://doi.org/10.1080/13880200902746522.

Trees of Ramayana (2022): 87-100
Editor: Felix Bast
Today & Tomorrow's Printers and Publishers (India)

Chapter-8

Sacred Fig (*Ficus religiosa*)

Deepak Das

Shlokas where mentioned

Sacred fig is mentioned in Ramayana in various slokas of different kandas and sargas. Mainly it is depicted in Ayodhya Kanda (Book 2) and Aranya Kanda (Book 3)

बिल्वा मार्दङ्गिका आसन् शम्याग्राहा विभीतकाः।

अश्वत्था नर्तकाश्चासन्भरद्वाजस्य शासनात्।।2.91.49।।

Meaning: On Bharadwaja's command, bael trees acted as drummers, palm trees as cymbalists, and the peepal trees as dancers.

स्थलप्राये वनोद्देशे पिप्पलीवनशोभिते।।3.11.39।।

बहुपुष्पफले रम्ये नानाशकुनिनादिते।

Meaning: This plain land in the beautiful forest track is adorned with fig trees, filled with flowers, fruits, and delightful sounds of different birds.

Figure 1: Ficus religiosa tree (Sacred fig), Date of capture: 21/04/2020, GPS coordinates: 18°48'54.77"N 82°42'51.52"E Locality: Court Lane, Koraput, Odisha, India. Photo courtesy: Deepak Das ©

Taxonomy/ Botanical classification

Domain: Eukaryota

Kingdom: Plantae

Subkingdom: Viridaeplantae

Division: Spermatophyta

Subdivision: Angiospremae

Class: Dicotyledonae

Order: Urticales

Family: Moraceae

Genus: *Ficus*

Specific epithet: *religiosa* L.

Synonyms

Ficus peepul (Griff.)

Ficus superstitiosa (Link)

Ficus caudata (Stokes)

Urostigma religiosum (L.) Gasp

Vernacular names

Common name: Peepal, Holy fig, Sacred Fig, Peepul, **Assamese** – Ahot, Pippol, **Bengali** – Asbattha, **Gujarati** – Asvattha, Piplo, **Hindi** – Aswattha, Peepal, **Kannada** – Aralimara, Asvatthamara, **Malayalam** – Arayal, Pippalam, **Manipuri** – Sana khongnang, **Marathi** – Aswattha, Pimpala, **Mizo** – Hmawng, **Nepali** – Pipal, **Odia** – Awattha, Osta, **Punjabi** - Pīpala dā rukha, **Sanskrit** – Aswattha, Pippala, Bodhivrikshya, Plaksha, Chaitya, **Tamil** – Aracamaram, Pippalam, **Telugu** – Pippalamu, ravichettu, **Urdu** - Pipal

Morphological Characteristics

The sacred fig is a dicot plant that belongs to the Moraceae (mulberry) family. It is commonly noticed growing on walls and abandoned lands. It is a broad-leafed, perennial tree. The average lifespan of the tree is 900 to 1500 years. It is seen that some peepal trees can live up to 3000 years. It attains a height of about 20 – 25 m on average. But some very old trees can grow up to 30 meters and more. It can be propagated through seeds as well as vegetative means. Most of the tree parts are woody. The roots of the tree penetrate deeper and can spread to a large area.

Canopy: The peepal tree has a huge trunk with dense canopies. The canopies of some old trees are spread to 500 m^2. The aerial parts of the tree require adequate sunlight, that is why they spread in such a large area. The trunk of old trees is generally fluted. The canopies provide shelter to different animals including humans. It also forms a habitat for insects, birds, mammals such as squirrels, bats, and monkeys.

Bark: The bark of this tree is commonly grey-colored. It is smooth and not so rough. The bark is exfoliating in rounded flakes with age in an irregular pattern. When the bark is cut down it excludes milk which contains many secondary metabolites. This is the reason herbivores do not eat the plant parts when it is young.

Leaves: The leaves of Peepal are ovate type. The shape is heart-shaped and it has a leathery texture. It can be as long as 20 cm long. The petioles of the leaves are long and it has an extremely long and caudate apex which is a characteristic feature. (Flora of Nicaragua, 2014). The colour of the young leaves is reddish-pink which turns out into copper and when matures converts to green.

Flowers: The flowers of the sacred fig tree are minute and they are within fleshy receptacles which are referred to as fig. The flowers are within the fruit which is held by a specialized structure called syconium (Syconium is an urn-shaped receptacle that bears up to 7000 highly simplified uniovulate flowers). The syconium of the sacred fig tree is monoecious which contains both male and female flowers as well as gall flowers (It is a form of female flower which is modified and has a short style working as hosts to pollinators) within the receptacle. The male flowers present are a few numbers near the apical pore and are sessile. The calyx is 2/3 lobed with a single stamen and a short filament. The female flower is also sessile which contains 4 lobed calyces, thin style, and narrow stigma. The gall flowers are pedicellate with ¾ lobed calyx, short style, and enlarged stigma with 2 lobes (Flora of China Editorial Committee, 2014). After pollination, the flowers from seeds and the florets develop into drupes or achenes.

Fruit: The fruit comes on the tree during March-May, but in many cases, fruits can be found at other times also. These are formed as solitary or paired. The texture of the fruits is soft and smooth and the shape is round. It is green when young and changes into orange-reddish when it matures. The fruit of the plant is an accessory (The part of the fruit comes from the parts other than ovary, here fruit comes from receptacle) and multiple fruits (fruit comes from multiple flowers). They are present at the axil of the leaves and are sessile. These have a diameter of 1-1.5 cm. The figs' taste is sweet that is why many frugivorous animals feed on the fruits. The fig is an enclosure referred to as drupe and it contains tens to thousands of tiny fruits called achenes. The color of the achenes is brownish and about 1-2 mm in diameter. The fig contains many seeds within it. The seeds are enclosed by an endocarp layer.

Genetics

According to IPCN Chromosome Report, 2014 the plant *Ficus religiosa* has 26 autosomal chromosomes (IPCN Chromosome Reports, 2014). That is the haploid number of chromosomes in *F. religiosa* is 13.

Habitat

It is a dry season deciduous, evergreen tree. It is mainly found in sub-montane forests. It is found widely in plane areas as well as uplands. It can be seen from 10 m to 1520 m altitude. It is tolerant to a wide variety of soils as well as different concentrations of rainfall. Whatever the soil type, the plant needs well drainage of water to grow. It grows in areas from 500 mm to 5000 mm rainfall. In India and South Asia notably in Buddhist countries it is grown wild as well as cultivated. It is planted at Hindu temples, Buddhist monasteries, Jain temples, Villages, and roadsides (Madulid, 1995; Flora of Nicaragua, 2014). As this tree is believed to be sacred people also grow this in their gardens. It is used as an ornamental tree which can be seen in parks too. Often the tree can be seen growing on the walls of the houses or other trees.

Geographical Distribution

This tree can be seen worldwide but it is native to Indo-China, the Indian subcontinent (India, Pakistan, Bangladesh, Sri Lanka, Nepal, Bhutan), and tropical Asia up to Thailand and Vietnam (Rojo et al., 1999; Orwa et al., 2009; Flora of Pakistan, 2014). Now it is introduced to many islands as well as other tropical continents including the Caribbean islands. It is also introduced to the African subcontinent, North America and South America. It is widely planted in hot countries like Hawaii, South Africa, Florida, etc. but it is not neutralized like in the Indian subcontinent (Starr et al., 2003; Strohecker, 2013). The reason for this is the absence of its pollinator fig wasp *Blastophaga quadriceps.* In Israel, this tree is planted and it attained neutralization because the fig wasp has been successfully introduced

(Galil and Eisikowitch, 1968; Orwa et al., 2009).

In India, the peepal tree is native to many states in northern and eastern India. The tree is introduced to the north-eastern states successfully. It is native to states like Delhi, Punjab, Haryana, Rajasthan, Gujarat, Maharashtra, Madhya Pradesh, Uttar Pradesh, Odisha, West Bengal, Tamil Nadu. It is planted in Andaman and Nicobar Islands, Arunachal Pradesh, Assam, Andhra Pradesh, and Kerala. In India, the fig wasp is present almost in every state, so the tree obtained neutralization at all the locations. In Haryana and Odisha, the sacred fig tree is taken as the State tree.

Origin and History

There is no such evidence for the origin of the *Ficus* genus. Even not any unambiguous fossil of the genus is known to date. However, according to the current molecular clock, it is estimated that *Ficus* is relatively an ancient genus being at least 60 million years old (Khan et al., 2011). The species' radiation occurred 20 to 40 million years ago. There are some legends about it. It is the first known depicted tree in history. There are descriptions about the *F. religiosa* in Mohenjodaro, an Indus valley civilization of about 3000 to 1700 B.C. (Choubey et al., 2015). It is believed that the tree originated in the northern and eastern parts of India.

Ecological significance

Initially the tree grows as an epiphyte on other trees (Rojo et al., 1999; Mabberly, 2008). It does not grow as a parasite but only for anchorage. When it matures it either splits the host plant or strangles it. This tree has no aerial root like the banyan tree (*Ficus benghalensis*).

There are particular fig wasps for each fig species. The wasp lays its eggs on the fig and in the process, it pollinates the flower. Both the fig plant and the fig wasp cannot complete their life cycle without each other. The fig wasps are mainly of order 'Agaonidae'. After they lay their eggs the larvae develop on the fruit. The fig wasp species related to *Ficus religiosa* is *Blastophaga quadriceps* (Ramirez, 1969). The fig trees and the fig wasps show co-evolution. The wasps are obligatory mutualist of figs, are selected to adapt the morphology of fig's flowers and inflorescence whereas the figs also adapt to the morphology of the wasp. This brings a change in physiology and reproductive strategy in both individuals. Non-pollinating wasps are also present but they do not show less speciation and do not co-evolve with the related species than the pollinating wasps. But in pollinators coevolution is very common.

The figs produced on the plants serve as food for many frugivores. As they visit to eat and rest under the tree, they disperse other seeds to this area and help in forest generations. We can say that the figs are responsible for the generation of the forests by frugivores. The tree is also home to different birds, insects, and mammals; it increases the biodiversity around and plays a major role in biodiversity conservation. It is also host to different lac insects (Orwa et al., 2009).

Another major contribution of *F. religiosa* to the ecosystem is, it releases oxygen all the time during the day and even during night (Singh et al., 2016). Most of the plants release oxygen during the daytime only and take oxygen for their respiration during the night. But the peepal tree can perform CAM pathway during the night and it releases oxygen. When the tree is in the early stages, it lives as an epiphyte; it performs its photosynthesis in the CAM pathway (Tiwari et al., 2019). When it matures and transfers into the soil it changes into the C3 pathway.

In some areas where these trees grow on the walls, it damages the buildings. They destroy the buildings by the ability of their penetrative power and strength of the roots.

Economic significance

The different parts of the tree are being used for a wide variety of purposes and thus account for an incredible economy. A secondary metabolite called tannin is present in the bark that is often used as a dye for the cloth. Paper is also obtained from the bark due to its fibrous nature (Bircher and Bircher, 2000). From the plant exudates called latex, the varnish is made. From the resins and gums of the tree, a sticky substance called wax is obtained often used for sealing. It is also used for cavity filling of ornaments as artificial. The wood is soft and durable used for making matchsticks and even exploited as packing material. Low weight and low-quality wood are also used as fuel and for burning. Its leaves are dried and painted with acrylic colors for home decoration purposes. Many people in India also collect them and frame them for keeping at home for worshipping. Leaves are also used as animal fodders for feeding camels and elephants. It is often grown for ornamental purposes.

***F. religiosa* as food**

Generally, the parts of the plant are not eaten although the fruits and leaf buds are edible. These do not taste good and are mainly used as famine food (= any food that is inexpensive and used for nourishment when nothing better is available or in times of starvation). Still, in some places in

India people take these. In Rajasthan and Madras presidency, the ripe fruit is eaten. The people at the Garhwal Himalaya mountain range take raw fruit as food (Gupta, 1962). In the Balrampur region of Uttar Pradesh, the bark of the tree is pounded and flour is prepared from it for bread.

But the parts of the tree have a greater value as forage and fodder. It is chiefly used to feed elephants, goats, and cattle (Rojo et al., 1999). It can be used as food for invertebrates like lac insects and wax insects. It can also be used as food for silkworms (USDA-ARS, 2014).

Phytochemical constituents of the plant

Constituents of bark: Lots of active phytochemical contents are found in the bark of this tree. The bark of the tree contains around 8.7% of total tannin. Phytosterols like lanosterol, stigmasterol, bergapten, etc are isolated from the alcoholic extract of the bark (Rutuja et al., 2015). Phenolic compounds and saponins have been found in the inner bark. The bark also contains alkaloids and glycosides and flavonoids. Wax is also found on the bark.

Constituents of fruit: The fruits of *F. religiosa* contain significant amounts of flavonoids like kaempferol, myricetin, quercetin, and other phenolic compounds (Rutuja et al., 2015). The fruit pulp contains asparagine and tyrosine amino acids in an abundant amount. Different terpenoids are also present in the fruits.

Constituents of leaves: The leaves of the plant contain secondary metabolites like campesterol, stigmasterol, isofucosterol, tannic acid, etc. Among the amino acids which are present in abundant amounts are arginine, alanine, proline, tyrosine, methionine, tryptophan, valine, leucine, and isoleucine (Rutuja et al., 2015). Some flavonoids and terpenoids are also present.

Constituents of seeds: The seeds which are present in a thousand in a fig contain phytosterolin, β-sitosterol, and different glycosides, glycosylates, albuminoids, flavonoids, and coloring matter. It also contains 0.7-5.1% of caoutchoue (Rutuja et al., 2015).

Constituents of roots: Roots of the tree contain secondary metabolites like tannins, saponin, alkaloids, β-sitosterol-D-glucoside (Kumar et al., 2018).

Constituent of latex: The latex contains alkaloids, glycosides, flavonoids, tannins, and different amino acids (Kumar et al., 2018).

Medicinal activities

Analgesic activity: The methanolic extract of stem bark of the *F. religiosa* was used on mice to treat acetic acid-induced writhing. It reduces the pain by 71.56 and 65.93% respectively when given in concentrations of 250mg/kg and 500mg/kg (Rutuja et al., 2015). This activity suggests that the extract of the bark has analgesic property probably by inhibitory action on prostaglandins.

Anti-inflammatory activity: The methanolic extract of the bark was tested for anti-inflammatory activities in Wistar albino rats. A very effective drug was prepared by using its carrageenan-inducing and indomethacin activity. The extract also has anti-lipid peroxidation effects.

Antioxidant activity: Oxidative stress is the major cause of type-2 diabetes. The free radicals are generated during oxidative stress and these cause damage to the insulin receptors inducing diabetes as there will be fewer sites available for insulin function. The aqueous extract of *F. religiosa* was screened for its antioxidant properties in streptozotocin-induced diabetic rats. The extract contains tannin, flavonoids, and polyphenols. Doses of the aqueous extract at 100mg/kg and 200 mg/kg to the diabetic rats resulted in decreasing the level of fasting blood glucose and increasing body weight (Rutuja et al., 2015). The aqueous extract also restored the erythrocyte GSH in the rats.

Antimicrobial activity: Using the ethanolic extract of *F. religiosa* leaves the antimicrobial property was investigated using the agar well diffusion method. Four bacteria species were taken for the testing i.e. *Bacillus subtilis, Staphylococcus aureus, Escherichia coli, Pseudomonas aeruginosa* and two fungi taken were *Candida albicans and Aspergillus niger*. It resulted that the concentration of 25mg/ml was active against all the bacteria species but was very less effective against the fungi species (Rutuja et al., 2015). The methanol extract, petroleum extract, and hexane extract also were tested for antimicrobial activity. The antibacterial activities of the extracts were compared with other available antibiotics. The methanol extracts showed much more activity in comparison to aqueous and chloroform extract. The hexane and petroleum ether extract did not show any antimicrobial activity. The chloroform extracts showed strong inhibitory activity against the bacteria like *Salmonella typhi, S. typhimurium,* and *Proteus vulgar.*

Wound healing activity: An ointment was prepared from the aqueous leaf extract of *F. religiosa* and tested for possible wound healing activity on the Wistar albino strain rats. And it helped in the wound healing process. The tannin content present in the extract possesses the ability to increase the collagen content on the wounded area which promotes the healing of the wound.

Proteolytic activity: The latex of the different *Ficus* species has significant proteolytic activities. A comparison was done among the 46 species of *Ficus* species for the electrophoretic and chromatographic properties of the proteins. *F. religiosa* showed the highest proteolytic activity.

Anti-ulcer activity: The ethanol extract of stem bark of the tree was tested against indomethacin and cold-induced gastric ulcer and pylorus ligation assays. The extract reduced the ulcer index in all the assays used during the investigation. But it was observed that the extract decreased the number of gastric juices and increased its pH (Rutuja et al., 2015).

Ethnomedicinal uses

All the plant parts of *F. religiosa* are used in Ayurveda since ancient times. There are a lot of descriptions about it being a wholesome medicinal plant.

Bark: The bark of the tree is used to treat astringent, cooling, gonorrhea, diarrhoea, dysentery, aphrodisiac, hemorrhoids, and gastrohelcosis, and burns.

Leaves: The leaves and tender shoots of *F. religiosa* are widely being used in purgative, skin diseases and to heal wounds. The juice of the leaves is very much effective in treating Asthma, cough, STDs, haematuria, toothache, migraine, gastric problems, and scabies.

Fruit: The raw fruit is used to treat Asthma, digestive disorders, and laxative disorders. While the dry fruit is used for the treatment of tuberculosis, fever, paralysis, and hemorrhoids.

Seeds: For refrigerant problems and laxative disorders the dried seeds are being used.

Latex: The latex derived from the tree is being used as medicine for neuralgia, inflammations, and hemorrhages.

Cultural significance

The scientific name of the sacred fig tree is derived from the religious views it. As the tree is believed to be sacred in Hinduism and

Buddhism and planted in the premises of temples and monasteries, the name "religiosa" is given (Flora of Pakistan, 2014). Except for Ramayana, there are descriptions in Veda, Upanishads, Puranas, Arthashastra, Mahabharata, Shrimad Bhagavadgita, Buddhist literature, and Jain religious books about the peepal tree. It is also called the Bodhi tree. 'Bo' means 'Supreme knowledge'. The Hindus worship the tree as well as Buddhists. Buddhists believe that they can achieve supreme knowledge by meditating under the Bodhi tree.

Stories, Myths, and Legends:

About Hindu and Buddhist mythology the peepal tree or *F. religiosa* is believed to be sacred as there are descriptions and mentions about this tree in many holy books.

In Shrimad Bhagavad Gita, the most famous and best known Hindu literature, there are many mentions of the sacred fig tree. It is mentioned in the 15th chapter, 1st verse, and 10th chapter, 26th verse of the epic tale. The shlokas read:

ऊर्ध्वमूलमध:शाखमश्वत्थं प्राहुरव्ययम् ।

छन्दांसि यस्य पर्णानि यस्तं वेद स वेदवित् ।। 1।।

Here Shree Krishna tells Arjuna that there is an immortal Aswattha tree that has its roots upwards and downwards. The one who will know about this will be the knower of the Vedas.

अश्वत्थ: सर्ववृक्षाणां देवर्षीणां च नारद: ।

गन्धर्वाणां चित्ररथ: सिद्धानां कपिलो मुनि: ।। 26।।

In this shloka Shree Krishna tells that of all trees he is the sacred fig tree, Aswattha and among all sages he is Narada. Of all Gandharvas (Singers of God) he is Chitraratha and among all the perfect beings he is Kapila sage.

According to Buddhist holy books and beliefs, the 'Mahabodhi' (the sacred *F. religiosa)* at Bodhgaya is the most sacred tree. It is believed that Siddhartha Gautama, who later became known as Gautama Buddha, attained enlightenment under this tree (Rojo et al., 1999). It is believed that he sat and meditated under this tree for seven weeks without moving. The Bodhi tree present today at the Bodhgaya is known as the descendant of the Mahabodhi. The other holy bodhi trees which are famous are present at Sravasti (Anandabodhi tree), at Anuradhapura, Sri Lanka (Bodhi tree). The Bodhi tree in Sri Lanka is believed to be planted in 288 BC during the reign of King Ashoka. All the *F. religiosa* is not taken to be a Bodhi tree. The plant is a descendent of a previous Bodhi tree.

There is a myth in Brahma Purana that there were two demons named Aswattha and Peepala. Aswattha would take the form of a tree and Peepala would take the form of a Brahmin and they harassed and killed people in the disguised form. Later Shani deva killed both the demons and that is why people worship the Peepal tree on Saturdays.

According to Skanda Purana Lord Vishnu was born under a peepal tree. Also, the peepal tree is considered as Trinath (Brahma, Vishnu, and Shiva). The root is believed to be Brahma, the trunk as Vishnu, and the branches as Shiva. There is also the description in Skanda Purana about the Saraswati river originating from a water pot and flows through an Aswattha tree on the Himalayas. There is also a myth regarding Lord Shree Krishna being killed by an archer under a sacred fig tree.

Generally, people do not cut a peepal tree as they believe cutting down a peepal tree is equivalent to killing a Brahmin. The sacred fig tree is often worshipped as 'Kalpabriksha' which completes the desires of people. According to Skanda Purana, one can take a peepal tree as his/her son. If he has no son then their family race is believed to continue till the tree lives. Often the peepal tree (*F. religiosa*) is planted near a banyan tree (*F. benghalensis*) because the banyan tree is thought to be the husband of the peepal tree.

Tourism

Being a sacred tree, in Hindu and Buddhism religious places it is planted and it attracts a large number of pilgrims which serve as tourist places. Also, like a tree with a larger size and a very long lifespan, it lives many centuries and is being used as a tourist attraction.

The Mahabodhi tree in Sri Lanka is a major tourist attraction for Buddhists worldwide. The *F. religiosa* plant is believed to be more than 2000 years old. The Foster Botanical garden in Honolulu, Hawaii is one of the oldest botanical gardens in the world. It also consists of a Sacred fig (*F. religiosa*), which is a close descendant of the Mahabodhi tree under which Gautama Buddha attained enlightenment. It is also a famous tourist attraction for Buddhist pilgrims.

In India, the sacred fig tree is planted in many famous temples and Buddha monasteries. The most famous among all is the Mahabodhi tree at Bodhgaya. At the city palace near Udaipur lake, Rajasthan there is a hollow and strangely twisted peepal tree. Many people visit the place to watch the wonder of nature. At the Pushkar lake in Ajmer, Rajasthan a sacred peepal tree is signposted as a mausoleum of Panchasantha vir. It is named 1008 Panchasantha vir tree. In Ludhiana, Punjab a clock tower is made on an old sacred peepal tree. At the main gate of Kaziranga National Park, Assam there is an *F. religiosa* near the single-horned rhino statue. So, this famous tree is named the Rhino gate tree. At the famous hill station Mount Abu, Rajasthan there is a giant, venerable and tall peepal tree named Kamala Nehru Giant Bodhi Tree situated near a heritage site on a rocky hill.

Urban forest

It is often planted as an avenue tree in home gardens. Due to its ornamental features, the saplings are grown in the nursery. Being the religious sacred fig, it is also grown as bonsai in a pot in eastern Asia countries (Kumar et al., 2011). According to traditional Hindu Vaastu shastra, the bonsai are bought and kept in homes. As it is a fast-growing plant and gives large amounts of oxygen it is generally planted roadside in villages and cities. It is quite easy to grow the plants as they can be propagated through seeds and by vegetative means. Naturally, the seeds do not propagate on their own. When the fruits are being eaten by the birds and frugivores, they digest the hard coat of the seeds and disperse those and then the plants germinate.

Conservation

The conservation status of the tree is still not evaluated. It is not in the book of the IUCN Red List of endangered species. Still, due to urbanization and growing lifestyle, The trees have been depleted on large scales. Why out of bloom it becomes a need to conserve the tree? Along with Neem (*Azadirachta indica*) and Tulsi (*Ocimum sanctum*) the *F. religiosa* plant provides oxygen to the atmosphere. This tree plays an important role in preventing ozone layer depletion. It generates O_2 during the night also. It also contains a lot of medicinal properties and other economically important products. It also gives us shade; shelter and it contains cultural significance. So, it is important to conserve the holy tree. As it needs little care to grow, we can plant the tree in gardens, parks, institutions, and public places.

References

Bircher, A. G., & Bircher, W. H. (2000). Encyclopedia of fruit trees and edible flowering plants in Egypt and the subtropics. *American University in Cairo Press. 596.*

Choubey, J., & Yadav, R. A. (2015). Multifarious medicinal value of "peepal" - a review. *Indian Journal of Life Sciences*, *5*(1), 100.

Flora of China Editorial Committee, 2014. Flora of China. St. Louis, Missouri and Cambridge, Massachusetts, USA: Missouri Botanical Garden and Harvard University Herbaria.

Flora of Nicaragua, 2014. Flora of Nicaragua, Tropicos website. St. Louis, Missouri and Cambridge, Massachusetts, USA: Missouri Botanical Garden and Harvard University Herbaria.

Flora of Pakistan, 2014. Flora of Pakistan/Pakistan Plant Database (PPD). Tropicos website St. Louis, Missouri and Cambridge, Massachusetts, USA: Missouri Botanical Garden and Harvard University Herbaria.

Galil, J., & Eisikowitch, D. (1968). On the pollination ecology of Ficus religiosa in Israel. *Phytomorphology*, 18(3), 356-363.

Galil, J., & Snitzer Pasternak, Y. (1970). Pollination in Ficus religiosa L. as connected with the structure and mode of action of the pollen pockets of Blastophaga quadraticeps Mayr. *New Phytologist*, 69(3), 775-784.

Galil, J. (1984). Ficus religiosa L.–the tree-splitter. *Botanical journal of the Linnean Society*, *88*(3), 185-203.

Gupta, R. (1962). Some unusual and interesting food plants of the Garhwal Himalayas. *Journal d'agriculture traditionnelle et de botanique appliquée*, *9*(11), 532-535.

IPCN Chromosome Reports, 2014. Index to Plant Chromosome Numbers (IPCN), Tropicos website. St. Louis, Missouri, USA: Missouri Botanical Garden.

Kapoor, L. D. (1990). Handbook of Ayurvedic Medicinal Plants, CRC press. *Inc., Boca Ration, Florida, USA.*

Khan, K. Y., Khan, M. A., Shah, G. M., & Hussain, I. (2011). Ethnomedicinal uses of Genus Ficus L. in Pakistan.

Khanom, F., Kayahara, H., & Tadasa, K. (2000). Superoxide-scavenging and prolyl endopeptidase inhibitory activities of Bangladeshi indigenous medicinal plants. *Bioscience, biotechnology, and biochemistry*, *64*(4), 837-840.

Kumar, A., Sandeep, D., Tomer, V., Gat, Y., & Kumar, V. (2018). Ficus religiosa: A wholesome medicinal tree. *Journal of Pharmacognosy and Phytochemistry*, *7*(4), 32-37.

Kumar, P., & Dwivedi, P. (2011). Bonsai: symbol of culture, ideals, money and beauty. *International Journal of Agriculture, Environment and Biotechnology*, *4*(2), 115-118.

Mabberly, D. J., (2008). Mabberley's Plant-book: A Portable Dictionary of Plants, their Classifications, and Uses. *Third edition. Cambridge, UK: Cambridge University Press.*

Madulid, D. A. (1995). *pictorial cyclopedia of Philippine ornamental plants*. Bookmark. 214-217.

Orwa, C., Mutua, A., Kindt, R., Jamnadass, R., & Simons, A. (2009). Agroforestree Database: a tree reference and selection guide. Version 4. *Agroforestree Database: a tree reference and selection guide. Version 4.*

PIER, 2014. Pacific Islands Ecosystems at Risk., Honolulu, USA: HEAR, University of Hawaii.

Ramírez, W. (1969). Fig wasps: mechanism of pollen transfer. *Science*, *163*(3867), 580-581.

De Padua, L. S., Bunyapraphatsara, N., & Lemmens, R. H. M. J. (1999). Plants resources of South East Asia (Prosea), medicinal and poisonous plants. *Prosea Bogor*, *12*(1), 277-289.

Rutuja, R. S., Shivsharan, U., & Shruti, A. M. (2015). Ficus religiosa (Peepal): A Phytochemical and pharmacological review. *International Journal of Pharmaceutical and Chemical Sciences*, *4*, 360-370.

Singh, D., Singh, B., & Goel, R. K. (2011). Traditional uses, phytochemistry, and pharmacology of Ficus religiosa: A review. *Journal of ethnopharmacology*, *134*(3), 565-583.

Singh, S., & Jaiswal, S. (2014). Therapeutic properties of Ficus religiosa. *Int J Eng Res Gen Sci*, *2*(5), 149-158.

Singh, S., Jain, S., Alok, S., Chanchal, D., Rashi, S., & Pradesh, U. (2016). A review on Ficus religiosa-An important medicinal plant. *Int J Life Sci Rev (IJLSR)*, *2*(1), 1-11.

Tree, B., Starr, F., Starr, K., & Loope, L. (2003). Ficus religiosa.

Strohecker, L. F. (2013). With the arrival of pollinator wasp, both trees can reproduce. Maui News.

Tiwari, P., Ansari, V. A., Mahmood, T., & Ahsan, F. (2019). A Review on Taxonomic Classification, Phytochemical Constituents and Therapeutic Potential of Ficus religiosa (Peepal). *Research Journal of Pharmacy and Technology*, *12*(11), 5614-5620.

USDA-ARS, 2014. Germplasm Resources Information Network (GRIN). Online Database. Beltsville, Maryland, USA: National Germplasm Resources Laboratory.

Warrier, P. K. (1993). *Indian medicinal plants: a compendium of 500 species* (Vol. 5). Orient Blackswan. 38-39

Trees of Ramayana (2022): 101-110
Editor: Felix Bast
Today & Tomorrow's Printers and Publishers (India)

Chapter-9

Indian Bael (*Aegle marmelos*)

Bibhuprasad Behera

धवाश्वकर्णककुभैर्बिल्वतिन्दुकपाटलैः।

सङ्कीर्णं बदरीभिश्च किन्न्वेतद्दारुणं वनम्।।1.24.15।।

(This forest packed with dhava, kakubha, ashvakarna, patala, bilva, tinduka, and badari trees, how furious this forest could be)

आम्रजम्ब्वसनैर्लोध्रैः प्रियालैः पनसैर्धवैः।

अङ्कोलैर्भव्यतिनिशैर्बिल्वतिन्दुक वेणुभिः।।2.94.8।।

This mountain is filled over with a diversity of flowering trees and trees laden with fruits, shady and enchanting, asanas, mango, rose apples, lodhras, priyalas, ankolas, jackfruit trees, dhavas, lovely tinisas, bilva trees.

स्निग्धपल्लवसङ्काशा पीतकौशेयवासिनी।

शंसस्व यदि वा दृष्टा बिल्व बिल्वोपमस्तनी।।3.60.13।।

He! Bilva tree, have you seen a lady precious like your tender leaf, dressed in yellow silk, a lady whose breasts are round like Bilva fruits.

Figure: *Aegle marmelos* tree in village Bamajhatipatana, Odisha. ©Bibhuprasad Behera

Bilva tree (Devnagari, Sanskrit), a holy tree which is importantly mentioned in Valmiki Ramayana which has the botanical name *Aegle marmelos L.*, generally called as Indian bael. It is not only limited to this but also known for Bel(Hindi), Bengal quinche, golden apple, Japanese bitter orange, stone apple, or wood apple. In Ramayana, this tree has been used for edible purposes or some construction work. Maharsi Valmiki has also written on his Ramayana that, emotional Lord Ram asked about his wife to this plant, when he was searching his missing wife Devi Sita and also compared her with some parts of the tree for giving clues. It is famous as a holy plant in India and somewhere it is also worshipped by people. It consists of several ecological and economical importance and its chemical nature of leaves, fruits, bark, etc is a blessing to the Ayurvedic world. There are also several myths, social and cultural activities are linked with this plant. Economically it is used for human food, materials (resin and gum), and medicine.

Taxonomic position

Aegle marmelos L. belongs to the Rutaceae family commonly known as the rue or citrus family, which are usually placed in the order of Sapindales. Its taxonomical hierarchy is

Kingdom: Plantae

Subkingdom: Tracheobionta

Division: Magnoliophyta

Class: Magnoliopsida

Subclass: Rosidae

Order: Sapindales

Family: Rutaceae

Genus: Aegle

Species: marmelos

Morphological Characteristics

Aegle marmelos is a deciduous, slow-growing, medium-sized tree having a length up to 12 - 15 meter long with a short, soft, and thick trunk, flaking bark and sometimes spiny branches are also observed. Bael is a perennial plant (lives more than 2 years). The bark is flaking, pale brown or greyish, armed with long spines of 1.2 - 2.5 cm in singly or pairs. A gummy sap, resembling gum arabic secreting out and hangs down in a long strand from wounded branches and becoming solid gradually. It is sweet at first, but after irritation to the throat.

The trifoliate leaves are alternately oriented, with each leaflet measuring 5 to 14 cm long and 2 to 6 cm broad, with a pointed tip, rounded base, shallowly toothed leaflets, and a long petiole. It is finely hairy, pale green, and pinkish maroon in young while mature it is dark green and completely smooth. Every leaf consists of 4 - 12 pairs of side veins that are joined at the margin.

Flowers usually appear with young leaves having length up to 1.5 - 2 cm, greenish-white or yellowish, and sweetly scented. In short, flowers are clustered at the end of the twig and leaf axils. Flatten calyx with 4(5) small teeth, calyx consists of four to five petals of 6 - 8 mm overlap in the bud. Anthers consist of stamens having pale brown, short filaments, and short style. The bright green ovary with an inconspicuous disc is also observed.

The bael fruit is globose or slightly pear-shaped, having a diameter 5-12 cm, with a thick, hard shell, and doesn't split upon ripening. In young, this woody shell is smooth and green and when it turns ripe it is yellow, grey, and hard. Inside the fruit, there are 8 - 15 or 20 sections filled with yellowish soft, pasty, sweet, fragrant, and resinous pulp. Nearly 6 to 10 small (nearly 1 cm in length), hard, flattened-oblong seeds are present inside each section (although seed numbers vary from plant to plant). Each seed bears woolly hairs and is enclosed in a sac of adhesive. It takes about 11 - 12 months to ripen on the tree. This juicy yellow, fibrous pulp is very aromatic, testing marmalade and smelling like roses.

Habitat, origin, and distribution

The terrestrial *Aegle marmelos* plant is subtropical and grows altitude from sea level to 1200 m altitude. It grows well in plain areas or dry forests on hilly areas. Although *Aegle marmelos* is native to India it is widely distributed and majorly found in the Indian subcontinent and southeast Asia like Ceylon, China, Pakistan, Nepal, Myanmar, Bangladesh, Vietnam, Laos, Cambodia, Indonesia, Tibet, Java, Thailand, Philippines, Fiji, and Sri Lanka. In India this plant is growing well in northeast India, Indo-Gangetic, plains up to 500 m of the sub-Himalayan tract, and dry, deciduous forest of central and southern India. In India, it is mostly cultivated in Andhra Pradesh, Bihar, Chhattisgarh, Haryana, Himachal Pradesh, Maharashtra, Odisha, Punjab, Rajasthan, Tamil Nadu, Uttar Pradesh, Uttarakhand, West Bengal, and also seen in the Andaman Islands.

Taxonomically related plant

The genus which is belongs to the family Rutaceae, in the major group of angiosperms. Although there are five species listed under the genus Eagle, out of these, only two species are accepted excluding *Aegle marmelos.* These are *Aegle devandra, Aegle glutinosa.* Although there is less description about this species, a similar plant *Swingla glutinosa* which is a subtropical plant and used as an ornamental plant in Mexico. One difference is noticed from *Aegle marmelos* is fruits are not edible. *Aegle devandra* is native to the Philippines.

Cultural practices

Soil and climate

Although bael is a subtropical fruit crop, it has got diverse adaptability and can grow well equally in tropical, arid, and semi-arid regions. *Aegle marmelos* not only grow best on rich, well-drained soil but also have grown and performed well on oolitic limestone of southern Florida as well as fruited well in swampy, stony, or alkaline soils having ph range 5-8. This tree requires a dry season to give fruits.

Planting

Despite the fact that planting is best done during the rainy season, spring also can be suitable for planting, or irrigation facilities are available. Before one month of onset monsoon, dig a planting pit of 1m length X 1m wide X 1m height. Keep the pit open for 20-25 days. After that fill the pit with humus-rich topsoil and FYM (10-15). Then irrigation is necessary to settle the soil. Put the saplings at the center and fill the pit with soil to support the plant. Make a basket around it and irrigate gently. Young plants need to irrigate regularly to avoid water scarcity in summer. It is importantly needed to be watered at the time of the emergence of new leaves.

Harvesting and yield

Seedlings produce fruits after 8 to 10 years of planting, whereas they are budded and grafted after 4-5 years of planting. After the fruit set, Bael trees need 8 to 10 months to mature and 10 to 12 months to ripening. Mature fruit can be judged by the greyish color skull and in the ripening stage; it turns slightly yellowish-green or yellowish-grey. Fruit should be harvested with a 5 cm fruit stalk. Under good management, the average yield is 300-400 per tree.

Chemical constituents and food value

They are lots of investigation, researches have been carried out with different part of the *Aegle marmelos* and as a result verities of a chemical compound like alkaloids, terpenoids, carotenoids, tannins, fatty acids, and coumarins are isolated from the different parts. The aromatic leaves of the Bael tree consist of flavones, gamma-sitosterol, beta-sitosterol, glycoside, aegelin, lupeol, rutin, marmeline, phenyl ethyl, etc.

Alkaloids

The new forms of alkaloids like halforidino, ethylcinnamamide, and marmeline were isolated from leaves of *Aegle marmelos*. In recent 2009, series of phenyl ethyl cinnamates including anhydro marmeline, aegelinoside A, and B are also reported in leaves of *Aegle marmelos*.

Terpenoids

Since 1950 several workers have been working on the essential oils of *Aegle marmelos* in India. They found out the alpha phellandrene is the most common constituent of the essential oil from twigs, leaves, and fruits. Limonene (82.4%), alpha phellandrene (56%), and p cymer (17%) were reported as the main constituents of leaves. Main constituent Limonene is used as a marker to identify *Aegle marmelos* oil samples.

Carotenoids

Carotenoids cause pale color in fruits; major constituents like marmelosin, skimmianine are therapeutically active principles of *Aegle marmelos*. Minor constituents like sitosterol, ascorbic acid, alpha amyrin, tannins, crude fibers, and crude proteins are also available.

Tannins

In wild varieties, there are 9% of tannins where less are present in cultivated type. Tannins like skimmianine are present in leaves which are known for 4, 7, 8- trimethoxyfuroquinoline.

Food value

Table:1 Nutritional value of *Aegle marmelos* (% per 100g), (Source: Purohit, 2004, Shankar, 1969 and Paricha, 2004)

Components	Value	Components	Value
Water	64.2	Potassium	0.6
Protein	1.8	Iron	0.3
Fat	0.2	Vitamin A(IU)	186
Mineral	1.5	Vitamin B	0.001
Fibre	2.2	Nicotinic acid	0.9
Carbohydrate	30.6	Riboflavin	1.2
Calcium	0.09	Vitamin C	0.01
Phosphorus	0.05	Caloric value	129

Believes, myths, and story

In Hindu culture, Lord Shiva is believed as the god of the destroyer of the world among the Hindu trinity Brahma, Vishnu, and Maheshwar. And according to Hindu beliefs Bilva trifoliate leaves are offered to Lord Shiva to fulfill their wishes. It is also believed that trifoliate leaves are symbols of three functions of creation, preservation, and destruction. It also symbolizes the trident held by Lord Shiva in his right hand and some people compare it with 3 Gunas of Sattva, Tamas, and Rajas and with Lord Shiva's three eyes.

There are beautiful myths about the origin of the bilva plant that is the tree was born from the sweat drop of Devi Parvati. Once Devi Paravati planned to visit the most excellent mountain Mandaranchal with her companions Jaya, Vijaya, Jayanti and Mangalaruna. After reaching there Parvati and her friends stepped down on the mountain to survey the beautiful scenery of Mandara. In this time of journey, a Drop of sweat fall on land from the forehead of the Devi Parvati. When the Sweatdrop fell on a rocky mountain, it transformed into a tree of trifoliate leaves and was named as Bilva tree by Devi Parvati. The companion of Parvati, Jaya, Vijaya, Jayanti, and Mangalaruna also was found to see Saktis emanating from Paravati and entering into this trifoliate tree.

According to Hindu mythology 9 Shaktis they are; Dakshayani is present in the main axis, Aparna in the Inner stem, Maheshwari is present in the branches, Paravati in leaves, Gouri in the outer Bark, Katyayani in fruits, Durga in flowers, Uma in twigs and Bhavani occupied the place in its thorns for protection of devotees from difficulties. So during Durga Pooja, priests come near to the bilva tree, to invite and worship all the nine Shaktis in the form of Devi Durga. This procedure is done on the sixth day of the 10 days festival.

Ecological importance

Every tree means several ecological importances. Although less specific significance is reported in species *Aegle marmelos*, it plays an important role in climate. This species is known for being a climate purifier by absorbing toxic gas from the atmosphere. The root of the mature plant is deeply entered into the soil which helps in the prevention of soil erosion. Besides these, it provides oxygen to sink carbon dioxide and creates a habitat for many organisms like the leaves of this plant are larval food for two Indian butterflies *Papilio demoleus* and *Papilio polytes* (swallowtail butterflies).

Economical importance and Uses

Aegle marmelos have great economical importance, used as medicine in some traditional ways because of pharmaceutical properties, and fruits are used as juice, toffee, slab, fruit squash, and also for medicine.

Traditional uses

The products obtained from Bael are highly therapeutic and nutritive. Fruits work well against viral and intestinal practices. Bael leaves are also used for the treatment of jaundice and wounds in earlier times. The leaf extracts are also useful for the treatment of deafness and leucorrhoea. Fruit gives energy and feelings of freshness. It is very useful for thyroid-related disorders. Other uses reported in the treatment of swollen joints, comma, and typhoid.

Pharmaceutical Uses

Antifungal and antimicrobial activity

The presence of coumarin in the leaves of *Aegle marmelos* and alkaloids, saponins, and flavonoids in the root of *Vitex negundo* shows antifilarial effects against Brugia malayi microfilariae. Essential oils extracted from the leaves of Bael show antifungal activity, which is observed by using spore germination assay. It shows the 100% inhibition of spore germination against several fungi.

Immune enhancing activity

It is successfully tested that methanolic extract of *Aegle marmelos* fruits is useful for modulating the immune system. In an experiment, it is concluded that, when some animals were treated with both methanolic extracts of *Aegle marmelos* fruits and extract of *Oscimum sanctum*, it increases circulating antibodies significantly in indirect haemagglutination test.

Wound healing activities

Uses of methanolic extract of *Aegle marmelos* injection and ointment are observed in both incision and excision wound models. And as conclusion, it responds well in both types of wound models. In the excision model, faster epithelialization and a higher rate of wound contraction are evaluated as compared to wound control.

Other products from the Bilva tree

Candy

Little pieces of its fruit pulp are impregnated with sugar or glucose syrup. The total sugar content should be up to 75 percent to prevent fermentation. After that, it is free up the syrup, and the bael candy is dried in open sunlight or 55-60° C for 8-10 hours in an oven.

Bael fruit squash

A good bael fruit squash was composed of 50° Brix, 50 percent extracted pulp, and 1% of acidity. After that 300 ppm, So2 is added to chemically preserve it. Fruit beverages are commercially composed of at least 25 percent of fruit pulp, 40-50 percent of TSS, one percent of acid and other preservatives like sodium metabisulphite, sodium benzoate (1g/liter).

Toffee

Because of its fantastic nutritional and medicinal properties, it is far better than other ordinary coffee. A bael toffee is composed of 100 parts of the extracted pulp, 40 parts of cane sugar, 4.5 parts of glucose, 10 parts of milk powder, and six parts of hydrogenated fat.

Slab

Ripen fruits are used for the preparation of the slab. Wash the ripened fruits, isolate the fruit pulp by breaking the shell and remove its hard skull. Mix well the 1kg of fruit pulp with 200-300 ml water and heat it to 800° C. Collect pastry fruit pulp free from seeds and fibers through string heated mass. Then add citric acid, sugar, potassium meta-bisulfate to this treated pulp. Boil treated fruit pulp and spread around the aluminum trays with smeared butter. To preserve the moisture content of 14.5%, it needs to be dry at 55-60° C for 15-16 hrs. Cut the slab and wrap it in butter paper and pack in aluminum foil.

Conservation

An endangered tree *Aegle marmelos is both* economically and ecologically important to mankind as well as the environment, so it must need to be conserved for the future. Nowadays seed germination in the cultivation of medicinal plants is a very important problem. Several studies show that there are highly significant effects of hydro priming on seedlings' vigor, germination percentages.

Conclusion

The holy plants *Aegle marmelos* have allrounder activities like medicinal, ecological, economic, nutritional, and as well as mythological significance. We discussed all the features, cultivation, chemical constituents, uses, and some beliefs related to this plant. After all, we should notice one thing, how great are our culture and our holy books. We are taught to worship this plant since childhood and it is justified. This tree is doing a better job than our worshipped God. To take the trifoliate leaves of the bilva tree we should remember three practices; Care for the Bilva tree, Conserve the Bilva tree, and blessed by the Bilva tree.

References

B. Venudevan, P. Srimathi (2013), Conservation of endangered medicinal tree bael (Aegle marmelos) through seed priming, Biology.

Jaswant, Akilandeswari, V. Loganathan, S. Manimaran and Ruckmani, (2001). "Wound healing activity of Aegle marmelos". Indian J. Pharm.

Neeraj, Vinita Bisht, and Vishal Johar. 2017. Bael (Aegle marmelos) Extraordinary Species of India: A Review. Int.J.Curr.Microbiol.App. Sci.

Parichha Saswati (2004). Bael (Aegle Marmelos): Nature's Most Natural Medicinal Fruit". Orissa Review.

Patel P, Mohammed S, Asdaq B (2010)."Immunomodulatory activity of methanolic fruit extract of Aegle marmelos in experimental animals" Saudi Pharmaceutical Journal.

Roy SK, Singh RN (1979). Bael fruit (Aegle marmelos) a potential fruit for processing. Econ Bot.

Sahare KN, Anandhraman V, Meshram VG, Meshram SU, Reddy MV, Tumane PM, (2008) "Anti-microfilarial activity of methanolic extract of Vitex negundo and Aegle marmelos and their phytochemical analysis." Indian Journal of Experimental Biology.

Taxon: Aegle marmelos (L.) Corrêa". GRIN Global, National Plant Germplasm System, US Department of Agriculture. 19 September 2017.

The Astrological Magazine, Volume 92. Raman Publications. 2003. p. 48.

Yadav NP, Chanotia CS. (2009). Phytochemical and pharmacological profile of leaves of Aegle marmelos. The pharma Review.

Trees of Ramayana (2022): 111-119
Editor: Felix Bast
Today & Tomorrow's Printers and Publishers (India)

Chapter-10

Jujube Tree (*Ziziphus jujube*)

Rashmi Pratap Singh

मयातुविविधंवन्यंसञ्चितंपुरुषर्षभ।
तवार्थेपुरुषव्याघ्रपम्पायास्तीरसम्भवम्।।3.74.17।।

According to Srimad Valmiki Ramayana book which consists of a total of 10 volumes. Book 3 Valmiki Ramayana Aranyakanda in prose (Chapter) sarga 74, above lines are said by Shabri. It is said Shabri collected the sweetest fruit for Ram and his brother Lakshman and offered them while they visited the hermitage. "Oh best one among men Rama thus I was told by those highly providential sages, Oh best one among men, oh manly tiger, and I have collected various forest fruits (Jujube) that occur on the moorlands of Pampa lake for your sake"

According to Ramayana, there was a young woman called Shabri, who was the daughter of a hunter, went to a teacher named Mathanga and asked her to be his disciple and teach her true wisdom. She stayed with Mathanga in his ashram and engaged herself in the service of the community there. She used to keep the ashram clean all the time and was greatly devoted to her teacher and was rendering him a selfless servicc with full dedication.

One day when sage Mathanga had to leave this world by seeing this Shabri said she would also be left this world with him. But the sage said your good deeds are still unpaid to you so she has to wait there for Rama and Laxmana to come in search of Mata Sita and bless her for her good deeds so she waits for them in the ashram. Shabri was waiting for Rama as instructed by the sage. She gathered the wild red date for Rama which she offered him with great devotion. To serve the best ones, she would bite them and check before offering them to the lord. Her innocent devotion pleased the lord who granted her liberation before leaving the place.

Figure: Jujube Tree (*Ziziphus jujube*). © Rashmi Pratap Singh

Introduction:

Ziziphus jujube, also known as Chinese date, is a well known species from the genus Ziziphus. Not only they are being eaten fresh, it is also dried, baked and being consumed as herbal medicine because of its numerous health benefits. It belongs to the buckthorn family (Rhamnaceae)

Taxonomy

Domain: Eukaryota

Kingdom: Plantae

Phylum: Spermatophyta

Class: Dicotyledons

Family: Rhamnaceae

Genus: Ziziphus

Species: Ziziphus jujube

Morphological Characteristics

Ziziphus jujube called jujube is sometimes a small droopy branched shrub or somewhat large spiny deciduous tree that is native from south-eastern Europe to China. It typically matures over time and reaches a height of 15-30metres tall (Morton 1987). Fruit is round to elongate drupe of varying size (cherry to plum) along with a single stone within. When maturing from green to red each smoothed skinned fruit has a sweet crisp flesh somewhat reminiscent of an apple. After maturation, its colour changes red-brown the fruits get wrinkled and take the appearance of date hence the common name of Chinese date for this plant.

Origin and Distribution:-

The origin of jujube was first documented in the Classic of Poetry around (1046-771BC). Today, jujube is found in various parts of the world but it is native to southern china. In an ancient Chinese book called *Huangdi Neijing* (475-221 BC) which is mainly based on herbal medicine, one of China's five most significant fruits, jujube, has been described as such. Jujube is indigenous to Chinese culture (Morton, 1987). It not only taste good but this fruit has important medicinal properties nitrify blood, improves the quality of sleep, and regulates digestive systems.

Ziziphus jujube M. Philip Miller was an English botanist of Scottish descent was first named *Rhamnus Ziziphus* in his species *Plantarum* later Philip named it *Ziziphus jujube* using Linnaeus species name for the genus. Vegetative propagation of high yield variety is seen in some parts of India Arabians believe that jujube and lotus are closely related and are mentioned in Quran. Although it is unknown to most westerners, the jujube is one of the world's major fruit crops and is cultivated in India, Russia, the Middle East, southern Europe, and especially China.

Climate: Wild trees are found up to an elevation of 5400ft but commercial cultivation extends only up to 3280 ft. Jujube can tolerate temperature between 37 to 43degree Celsius (Morton 1987). The tree requires a good annual rainfall of 150 to 225cm.

Soil: In India, the tree can be grown in variety of soil but it grows best in sandy or slightly alkaline soil, laterite medium black soils with good irrigation. Even moderately saline soils are permitted. The tree is quite exceptional in its ability to tolerate waterlogging as well as drought stress.

Propagation: The Indian jujube is mainly grown from its seeds. The viability of persists for 2-3years. The rate of germination, however, decreases with age. High quality or superior plants are selected for grafting or budded onto seedlings of the wild types.

For the selection of seeds for growing rootstocks, the stones must be taken from fruits that are fully ripened on the tree itself. They are put into a 17-18% salt solution and all that floats are discarded. The stones that sink are dipped in 500ppm thiourea for 4hrs then cracked and the separated seeds will germinate in 7days. Seeds in uncracked stones require 21 to 28days. If seeds are sown in springs the seedlings will be ready for budding in 4months. Proper handling of the taproots and care is necessary while transplanting nursery stock to the field. Therefore, the rootstock may be raised directly in the field and budding did in situ. Ring budding shield budding grafting techniques are also practiced. It is seen that grafted plants are less thorny than seedlings.

Season and Harvesting: Some varieties ripen in early October others mid-February to mid-march. In India Two to Three pickings are done by hand from ladders, a worker is capable of manually harvesting about 110 lbs (50kg) per day. The remaining fruits present on the tree are shaken down without breaking its branches (Scholey et al., 2017). After wrapping in white cloth the fruit is put into paper lines burlap bags holding 110lbs for transporting to distant places.

Yield: Trees carry 5000-10000 small fruits per year in India. Trees grown by a selection of Superior plants and then grafted may yield as many as 30,000 fruits. In India, the highest; production is, normally ranging from 30 to 50lb yields 175lbs annually. Special cultural treatment increases fruit size and yield as well.

Keeping quality: In Indian jujube manages the transportation handling shipment and marketing very well. Storage experiments very well. Storage experiment in India showed that slightly under-ripe fruits. Rinse and keep for 8days under wheat straw, 7days under leaves, and 4 days in carbide (50 to 60kg).

Fruit: The fruit of wild trees is 1.5 – 2 cm in length while cultivated reaches a length of 4-6cm. They may be oval round or oblong. The skin of the fruit is smooth or rough glossy thin but tough, it is initially light green further turns to yellow then red-brown. At first, the aroma is apple-like and pleasant but it becomes peculiarly musky as the fruit ages. When it's light green it tastes sour which is the under-ripe stage when turns red it tastes sweet and soft.

Ripe fruits are mostly preferred to consumed raw moderately unripe fruits are dried and sweetened sometimes salted and consumed. In some parts of India it is immersed in a salt solution and then cooked in sugar syrup with citric acid stored for 1 to 3 months. People of Southeast Asia eat the unripe fruits with salt. With ripe fruits crushed in water- a very popular cold drink is prepared. Ripe fruits are after sun-drying crushed to powder is prepared. The dried and fermented pulp is a common component in African cakes (Morton, 1989).

In Indonesia young leaves of jujube are cooked and consumed. Jujube liquor is made and sold as crema de ponsigue in Venezuela. The fruits are an important source for birds which eat the whole fruit along with the seed. The fruits can be either deciduous or evergreen

Fruit content

Water: 0%

Protein: 7.3g, fat: 1.2g, Carbohydrate: 84g

Fibre: 49, Ash: 3g

Minerals: calcium; 130mg; phosphorus: 168mg; Iron; 3.5mg Magnesium-0mg Sodium: 12mg, potassium: 150mg, Zinc: 0mg

Vitamins; a-125mg; Thiamine (B1):0.1mg; Riboflavin (B2): 0.18mg; Niacin:2.8mg; B6:0mg; C ;300mg

3 jujubes roughly contains

1. Protein 1gram
2. Carbohydrate: 20grams
3. Fibre:10grams
4. Vitamin C:77%
5. Potassium:5% of the DV

Leaves: The leaves may be ovate, oblong, or elliptic. They are glossy green with finely toothed margins; each leaf has two sharp stipules which are modified to spines. The leaves being nutritious are consumed eaten by camels, cattle, and goats and are considered nutritious. They contain cetyl alcohol and alkaloids like protopine and berberine. The leaves are also collected for food for silkworms.

Flowers: The flower consists of five petals which are yellow in colour and small in size. No showy white to yellow-green flowers. Not more than three fragrant flowers are found in the leaf axils. Flowers blossom in the leaf axils during late spring.

Varieties: In India, more than 90 varieties are found which differ in their habit, leaf types, fruit shape, size, keeping quality, and fruiting season. Amongst the important cultivators, around eleven of them are mentioned in the encyclopaedic wealth of India- Banaras, pewandi, dandan, kaithli, Muriamahrara, narikelee, nazuksanauri 1 sanauri 5 thornless and umran.

A report published by Haryana Agricultural University according to which 70 cultivators collected from all jujube growing areas of northern India and set out in an Experimental orchard in 1967 and four were singled out as the most promising cultivars.

Culture:

Trees that are not trimmed regularly must be spaced at 36 to 40ft (11-12m), but the regularly pruned trees can be set at 23 to 26ft. Trimming should be done during the first year of growth to maintain the plant to one healthy shoot and branches. The plant should be pruned from the top once in year. During the 2nd and 3rd years the trees are fully shaped. Therefore pruning is done immediately after harvesting at the beginning of the dormancy period and It's possible to erase half of the preceding year's development. Sometimes a second round of pruning is done just during the onset of flowering. This will lead to a great development in quality, size, shape, and number of fruits in the upcoming season.

In India, it has been tradition to apply manure and ash fertilizer but now days each tree has been given annual treatments of 22lbs mannurewith1.1lbs ammonium sulphate for every year of age up to the fifth year. Some cultivators use only commercial fertilizer containing (NPK) in large amounts twice annually. During summer when the temperature remain higher the period of fruit development starts, irrigation is highly beneficial. Water stress will cause immature fruit drop. In India irrigation is done around 3o times during the winter season. Zinc and boron are sometimes applied to enhance the shininess of fruits.

Pest and Diseases:

The greatest enemies of jujube in India are fruit flies, *Carpomyia vesuviana,* and *Carpomyia incomplete*. Some plants are found to be more susceptible than others due to which and the flies and insects attack the large, sweet fruits, while if you see the neighbouring tree, bearing a smaller, less sweet fruit is slightly affected. Regular pesticide spraying can successfully manage pests and diseases. A leaf-eating caterpillar called Porthmologaparaclina, and the green slug caterpillar, *Thosea sp*. feed on the young and tender leaves. A mite, *Laracarus transitions*, form scales like galls on twigs retarding growth and reducing the fruit crop.

The tree is subjected to shrouding by a parasitic vine (*Cucuta spp).Oidium sp.* Powdery mildew causes defoliation and fruit drop. An Ascomycete fungus called (Cladosporiumzizyphi) causes defoilation. Leaf spot results from the infestation by *Cercospora spp* (Scholey et al, 2017). In 1973 a case was reported from Poona University saying witches broom diseases caused by mycoplasma-like organisms were found in jujube plants. Leaf rust, caused by phagophore *Zizyphus Vulgaris,* ranges from mild to severe on all commercial cultivars in Punjab.

Toxicity: In Abyssinia, the fruits are used to catch fish by tranquilizing them in. The leaves contain saponin hence they are known to produce lather when rubbed in water(Scholey et al, 2017). If one is taking the antidepressant medication venlafaxine or other serotonin-norepinephrine reuptake inhibitors (SSNRIs). Jujube should be avoided else it may interact with those drugs.

Wood: The wood is somewhat reddish in colour with fine-textured and high durability. It has a wide range of applications, including well liner, legs for bedsteads, farm tools, and house polls; tool handles, gunstocks, saddle trees, slippers; golf clubs, household appliances, being a good source of charcoal and activated carbon it is also used as firewood. In many regions of tropical Africa, the branches are wrapped around conical thatched roofs and to keep animals contained, rope was used to create thorny corral walls.

Nectar

Indian jujube hosts insect *kerrialacca* which extracts the juice from the leaves and covers it with a reddish-orange resinous substance. The lac was used for dyeing but nowadays the purified resin is used as the shellac at the commercial level. Low-quality shellac is made into sealing wax and varnish whereas higher quality shellac is used for fine lacquer work and lithographic ink. The trees are intentionally grown in October and November around huts every year, so that resin can be collected in April and May. Regular pruning is done to provide sufficient number of young shoots for inoculation.

Preferred scientific name: *Ziziphus jujube.*

Preferred common name: common jujube

International common names:-

English-Chinese date tree, Chinese jujube tree, jujube.Spanish: azufaifo, jinjolero, French; gingeolier, guindanlier, jujubier common

Local common names

Afghanistan: ber, borjelachi, kabuliber, pewandiberregu, seober, yellandri.

Germany; Acofeifeira; brustbeerbaum, chinesische, judendron,jujube, kahiblaettrigerjujubenstrauch

India; Ber, Bor, jelachi, regu, yellandri

Italy: gluggiolo, sisifo

Myanmar; Zi

Netherland; Jujubenboom

Pakistan: ber, bor, jelachi, regu, yellandri

Trade name: ber

Medicinal Use:-

Traditionally, one of the main uses of jujube is found in herbal medicine, it helps to calm down the mind and improves the quality of sleep. Jujube possesses neuroprotective activities, by protecting the neuronal cells against neurotoxin stress, stimulating neural differentiation, increasing expression of neurotrophic factors, and promotes memorizing and learning. Jujubes are a repository of vitamins and antioxidants mainly vitamin C which helps in rejuvenating skin, produces free radicals, and strengthens our immunity system. It also prevents early signs of aging and helps in brightening and clearing out the dull skin (Scholey et al, 2017).

Jujube has low salt content and high potassium content, and both of these qualities about the fruit ensure the blood pressure levels are in control (Tripathi, 2014). Potassium helps in keeping the blood vessels relaxed and blood pressure under control. Jujube is loaded with calcium, phosphorus, and iron which help to keep our bones strong. People having osteoporosis are advice to eat sweet jujube to reverse the effect and make the health condition better.

According to Chinese medicinal research, jujube is regarded a medicinal herb that calms the mind and relieves mental tension. A hydroalcoholic extract of Z. Jujube has been shown to possess antiepileptic effects against induced seizures in rodents. Triterpenic acid is considered an active ingredient for the effect on anti-inflammatory and anticancer activities. It is also used for the treatment of Anxiety, asthma, diarrhoea, fatigue, and fever (Tripathi, 2014). Jujube is also said to increase strength, stimulate appetite and improve liver health. A report published in nature around 2013 says *Ziziphus mucronata* tends to have anti-diabetic properties.

Other Uses

Gun powder (Dog-wood) is made from the wood of *Zizyphus mauritiana* and also of Rhamnus and Frangula. Some recently published articles say phytochemical and pharmacological tests suggest that flavonoid polysaccharide and triterpenic acid are the main active ingredients within jujube. In addition to betulinic acid and jujuboside B, they contain some active components that show beneficial effects on the cardiovascular system (Tripathi, 2014).

Some therapist advice to consume jujube either as a herb or in tranquilizing recipe by combining it with other herbal medicines for the treatment of insomnia and amnesia. The fruit is used in dyeing silk in Burma .The bark yields a nonfading cinnamon-colour dye in Kenya.

Ecological importance:

Ziziphus trees and shrubs grow well in arid climatic conditions almost on every continent due to their versatile nature in being able to adapt to almost all abiotic stress for this reason they plays an essential role in the soil conservation with the help of their strong and long roots. In many regions, it is grown as a hedge with its spines creating effective fencing for grazing animals. In addition to fruits, seeds, leaves, roots, and bark of Ziziphus trees are used in various traditional medicines.

Reference:-

Morton, J.,(1987) "In Fruits of warm climates" Indian jujube p. 275-275

Scholey, A., Benson, S., Gibbs, A., Perry, N., Sarris, J., Murray, G.(2017). Exploring the effects of Lactium and zizyphus complex on sleep quality: A double- Blind, Randomized Placeb- controlled Trial. *Nutrients* 9(2), 154.

Tripathi, S. (2014). Ziziphus jujuba: a phytopharmacological review. *International Journal of Research and Development in Pharmacy & Life Sciences*, *3*(3), 959-966.

Tahergorabi, Z., Abedini, M. R., Mitra, M., Fard, M. H., & Beydokhti, H. (2015). "Ziziphus jujuba": A red fruit with promising anticancer activities. *Pharmacognosy reviews*, *9*(18), 99.

https://www. Bhagavatamkatha .com/ramayan story lord rama, meeting shabari

https://www.speakingtree.in/allslides/story of Rama and Shabri

Trees of Ramayana (2022): 121-133
Editor: Felix Bast
Today & Tomorrow's Printers and Publishers (India)

Chapter-11

Champak Tree (*Magnolia champaca*)

Baisakhi Mahala

सालैः तालैः तमालैः च खर्जूरैः पनसैः द्रुमैः |

नीवारैः तिनिशैः चैव पुन्नागैः च उपशोभिताः || ३-१५-१६

चूतैर् अशोकैः तिलकैः केतकैर् अपि चंपकैः |

पुष्प गुल्म लता उपेतैः तैः तैः तरुभिर् आवृताः || ३-१५-१७

स्यन्दनैः चंदनैः नीपैः पर्णासैः लकुचैः अपि |

धव अश्वकर्ण खदिरैः शमी किंशुक पाटलैः || ३-१५-१८

The above reference meant to the mountains of Panchavati forest when Lord Rama, Devi Sita, and Lakshmana on being banished from Ayodhya by traveling by foot had reached the forest. They were enthralled by nature's peaceful splendor. The mountains were brightened by the beauty of nature which included the Sal trees, Palm trees, Cinnamon trees, Date palms tree, Jackfruit tree, and Calophyllum trees. The mountains also had the taste of sweet mangoes. It had the shade of the great Ashoka tree. The environment on the mountains was lightened by the gorgeous fragrant from the ketaka and the Champaka trees. The sacredness of the mountain was maintained by the mere presence of the Syandana tree which is known as the flower queen (Its significance is also due to its mention in Ramayana during the Kishkinda Kanda and the Aranya Kanda), Sandalwood trees, Dhava tree, and the Ashwakarna trees. The mountain was covered with many more beautiful flowers producing shrubs. The trees there were

शुकबर्हिणसङ्घुष्टं क्रौञ्चहंसरुतायुतम्।।2.10.12।।

वादित्ररवसङ्घुष्टं कुब्जा वामनिकायुतम्।

लतागृहैश्चित्रगृहैश्चम्पकाशोकशोभितैः।।2.10.13।।

दान्तराजतसौवर्णवेदिकाभि स्समायुतम्।

नित्यपुष्पफलैर्वृक्षैर्वापीभिश्चोपशोभितम्।।2.10.14।।

दान्तरजतसौवर्णैस्संवृतं परमासनैः।

विविधैरन्नपानैश्च भक्ष्यैश्च विविधैरपि।।2.10.15।।

उपपन्नं महार्हैश्च भूषितैस्त्रिदिवोपमम्।

तत्प्रविश्य महाराजस्स्वमन्तः पुरमृद्धिमत्।।2.10.16।।

न ददर्श प्रियां राजा कैकेयीं शयनोत्तमे।

entangled with beautiful climbers glorifying the beauty of the mountain and the forest.

It also had been referred to in another reference. In the palace of Ayodhya, when king Dashratha entered the beautiful room of Kaikeyi, he was pleased with the magnificent beauty. The room was filled with the beauty of peacock and parrots. It was filled with the cries of cranes and swans. The room was filled with melodious music from the hunchbacks. The room was decorated with flowers from champaka and Ashoka trees. The room was blown away by the sweet fragrant of the champaka flowers. The bowers in the room looked beautiful due to the entangled creepers. The room also witnessed a beautiful picture gallery which enhanced the beauty of the room. Royal sofas covered with expensive silk, ivory, gold, and silver glorified its beauty more. The presence of pools surrounded by fruits and flower trees enhanced the beauty of the room. The royalty of the room was depicted but the presence of various delicious and luxurious eatables and drinks kept there. With these expensive and glamorous decorations, Kaikeyi's room gave the feel of being in heaven. Despite all these glorifying beauties, the king was not pleased happy at heart as his beloved queen Kaikeyi's presence was being missed from the room.

[Figure: *Magnolia champaca* (champak tree), Date of capture: 20/04/2020, GPS coordinates: N 21°50'41.22204" E 86°56'17.35512" Address: Chitrada, India, Odisha-757018]. © Baishakhi Mahala

Different names of the tree according to different regions:

The tree is denoted by different people all over the world according to different cultures of the people around the world. Some of its vernacular names are mentioned here-

In Bengali it is referred to as champaka, Champa, similarly, in Lao (Sino-Tibetan) it is known by the name Champa, in Burma, it is identified as mawk-sam-lung, in Cantonese, they recognize it by the name of sampige, Indonesian - Cempaka kuning, capaka, cempak

In English it is referred to as golden Champa, yellow Champa, fragrant champaca, orange chempaka French - ilang-ilang, in Sanskrit it is known as champaka, people in Gujarat call it rae-champo, in Hindi they call it chempaka Sinhala – sapu Spanish- champaca Tamil- chambugam, simpangan, chembuga Thai people denote it as Champa pa, Champa Khao, Champa, Odia people call it Champa.

Taxonomy:

Kingdom: Plantae

Class: Angiosperms

Order: Magnoliales

Family: Magnoliaceae

Genus: Magnolia

Species: champaca

Morphological Characteristics

It is an evergreen or semi-deciduous tree. It ranges in its height from small to medium and may reach up to a height of 50m tall. It is usually bole straight and is cylindrical. The diameter is up to 200cm. Its trunk ranges up to 1.92 meters in diameter. The tree often contains a narrow umbelliform crown. The bark's texture is generally smooth and its color ranges from grey to greyish white. The inner bark of the tree is fibrous and ranges in color from yellow to brown. The crown of the tree usually ranges from being conical to cylindrical.

Leaves:

The leaves of the tree are simple, entire, and are arranged spirally. The stipules are joined together or are often free from the petioles. The petiole is 1-3 cm long and is stout and they are arranged in a plano-convex manner in the cross-section. They have elliptic-lanceolate.

Flowers:

Flowers are short and are on axillary brachy blast. They are solitary and rarely occur in pairs. The tepals are usually large and are 6-21 in number. The flowers are arranged in 3-6 subequal whorls. The flowers are white to yellowish in color. There are many stamens and the anthers are usually short to prominently elongated form with the connective gynoecium (Karthikeyan V et al., 2016). They are usually spirally arranged and they have many free or connate carpels containing many ovules. The flowers are usually large cup-shaped lacking petals or sepals. They have tepals that are flower parts resembling the petals. The flowers have strong fragrant and are produced from June to September.

The carpels are obovoid to ellipsoid and produce 2-4 seeds from September to October. The fruiting carpels usually dehisce along the dorsal suture. When they are free or fused, they form a fleshy or woody syncarp. The seeds remain hanging from the funicle.

Hybrids:

There are many different varieties and hybrids of *Magnolia champaca* found:

Magnolia champaca var. *champaca* is found in china and grows up to a height of 30 meters in height. *Magnolia champaca* var. *pubinervia* which grows up to a height of 50 meters is also documented in china. A cross between magnolia and Alba produced a white-flowered hybrid variety.

Fruits:

The fruits are borne spirally in a cluster (6-30 cm long) which hangs downward. Around 6-40 individual fruits are found in each cluster. Each fruit is about 1.5-2 cm long and is woody and is pale brown. It bears large cream-colored lenticels. The fruits on ripening split open to release 2-6 insides. The seed is covered on the outside with red or pink flesh and appears to be hanging freely on a white thread.

They are usually perennial and have a photoautotrophic mode of nutrition.

The trees are capable of producing fruits and flowers throughout the year. The flowers produced are protogynous and are usually pollinated by the beetles. The Beatles during pollination feed on the stigmas, pollen, nectars, and also on the various secretions from the petals. The species can undergo hybridization and produce various wild species.

Root: They are dicot plants and possess a shallow and well-developed tap root system.

Habitat:

They are usually found in scattered form in the primary lowland to montane rain forest region. They are found in altitudes of up to 2100m. they are found at an absolute maximum temperature of about 35-40oC and an absolute minimum temperature of about 3-10oC. It generally grows well in moist, deep, well-drained, fertile, and good quality soil. It requires annual precipitation of 2250-5000 mm or more. It grows well in moist and damp climatic conditions. Rich sandy loam soil helps in better growth of the tree. Some of its biophysical limits are Altitude: 600- 2000 m Mean annual temperature: 7-38oC (Minter, S. “Fragrant Plants.” in Prance, G. and M. Nesbitt; 2005).

Distribution of the species:

It is thought to have originated in India so its native is considered to be India. From India, it spread to the rest part of the world though it is in the form of exotic species in some part of the world like Indonesia, Laos, Malaysia, Myanmar, Nepal, Sri Lanka, Thailand, Vietnam (Jain PP, Suri RK, Deshmukh SK, and Mathur KC; 1987). It is assumed that these trees had probably originated in India and it was then distributed in a region from India to China, Indonesia, peninsular Malaysia, Sumatra, Java, etc. it is now seen to be cultivated throughout the tropics. The Magnoliaceae family are thought to have originated from south Asia and North America but then they were found all over the world due to their beauty.

Other plant species related to this family:

Magnoliaceae is a family of plants that includes numerous plant species -like Champaca, Dugandiodendron, Liriodendron, Magnolia, Manglietia, Michelia, Sphaerostema, and Talauma.

The plant species belonging to this family have several economic importance like they are mostly used for ornamental cultivation and wood is used as a source of timber. The wood is generally lightweight and finely grained and is used as a pipe organ building. In some species, their leaves and large white fragrant flowers have some medicinal values and can be used as a remedy for cramps, nausea, abdominal pain, indigestion, etc. they also are seen to bear antifungal and anti-bacterial properties.

Oldest fossil:

They are perhaps the world's oldest species of plants and have dated back to 130 million years. Most of the primitive living angiosperms belong to this family. Some of the primitive characteristics of these families are that in some species they are seen to bear large flowers with numerous sepals and petals which are together referred to as tepals due to their similar shape and size. It has also been observed in many species that they have numerous stamens that are spirally arranged at the base of the cone-like receptacle containing numerous carpels that are spirally arranged. The family Magnoliaceae contains two subfamilies i.e. Magnoliaceae and Liriodendroideae. It was seen that the late Albian genus Archaeanthus shares many features including the reproductive features of the Magnoliaceae. Endressinia brasiliana is a magnolia fossil ~~and~~ is obtained from the Lower Cretaceous of Brazil.

Conservation of the tree:

Tree Management:

Trees that are propagated from seeds usually take 8-9 years to flower whereas those that were propagated asexually could flower in 2-3 years. The tree demands light and grows well in it but is greatly susceptible to fire.

Germplasm conservation:

Around 10000-25000 seeds per kg have been stored in the germplasm. They follow the orthodox method for seed storage. The seed's viability can be preserved under moist conditions at 5oC for seven months or can also be stored in the pits for 4 months at 13oC.

Cultural significance:

The flower due to its great fragrance and smell is used in temples. They are usually found in temple and village grounds. The essential oils extracted from these flowers are used in the making of incense sticks which are used in temples. They are also used in making flower garlands. They are also used in many other ceremonies that may be marriages, worship, etc.

Myths:

There is a myth in the public in China that the fragrant scent produced from the flowers is used to summon the spirits in many rituals and events to imbibe positivity.

The people in this tradition also believe that the flower helps to detect the virginity of the bride that is if the flower doesn't open or doesn't smell good it denotes that the bride is not a virgin and if it smells good and opens up then the bride is virgin.

Stories and legends related to it:

There is a legend related to the Champa tree. Long before, there lived a king and he had two wives. The older wife was not capable of giving birth to children and so being jealous of the younger wife conspired to kill all the children that were borne by the younger wife. As per for conspiracy she started substituting the babies with monkeys. As years passed by the elder queen did this with seven sons and a daughter of the younger queen. Exchanging them with the monkeys she buried them outside the palace wall. Observing this the king in anger banished the younger queen.

As years passed by outside the palace where the older queen had buried the seven children grew seven handsome and tall trees bearing sweet and fragrant flowers. Along with these seven trees was a small delicate tree. The trees got quite famous in the kingdom due to their beautiful and highly fragrant flowers and also because the flowers from these trees could only be plucked by the banished younger queen. The king on hearing this asked his gardeners to bring some flowers from the trees. As the gardener returned empty-handed the king along with the older queen went to visit the trees. The trees on seeing the older queen stretched their branches and leaves and leaves and the cry of 'murderer' was heard. Shocked with the hearings the king went to the trees and the leaves showed him his face. The king was surprised to have enquired from him the entire matter and to his shock found out the truth from them and the truth regarding their mother. The trees asked the king to get them back their mother, who is the younger queen. The king then banished the older queen for her shameful deeds and reinstated the younger queen. Both the king and queen then looked after the trees as their children. The large tree was Champa and the younger tree was a delicate one.

Another story related to the champaka tree is that once sage Narada was traveling to a Shiva temple in Karnataka. Near the temple, he was greatly moved by the strong fragrance of the champaka flowers. He stood under the tree to take in the fresh smell. Just then he saw a brahmin priest near the tree. On enquiring the priest he found that he was a priest from the nearby village and was drawn by the enchanting smell of the tree. The main motive of the priest was to pluck flowers from the tree but he was refrained from doing it on seeing Sage Narada. Sage Narada then went inside the temple by the time the priest plucked some flowers and hit them in the basket. Sage Narada on returning saw the priest standing there still and felt something was fishy. On asking the priest he said that he was just going to leave for home. After he left Narada asked the champaka tree if anyone had plucked flowers from the tree but the tree denied. Still not convinced by the answers from the tree sage Narada went back to the temple and was shocked on seeing the Shiva linga covered with flowers. He then asked a man sitting nearby as to who had offered the flowers and found out that a brahmin had offered the flowers to the linga and being pleased by his worshipping Shiva had blessed him immensely and the brahmin had become powerful in the king's court. But the Brahmin was very evil towards the poor people and harassed them a lot. Sage Narada then asked Shiv Ji as to why he blessed the Brahmin although he was evil to which Shiva replied that he was pleased by the Brahmin's dedication and worship towards him and so had blessed him. Sage Narada then angry with the champaka tree cursed them that they could never be used for worship of Shiva and cursed the Brahmin to be born as a demon and said that he could only get moksha by getting killed by Lord Rama.

It is also mentioned in Bhagavad Purana (3:21) that next to the Bindu Sarovar lake where the Sage Kardama performed some austerities was surrounded by some spiritually elevated and fragrant trees which included the champaka trees. It is also mentioned in the Shiva Purana that the Kailash was surrounded by many fragrant flower trees which included the champaka trees. In the Bhagavad Gita, it is also said that often the vrajas of Vrindavan would talk and enquire to the champaka trees that if they had seen Lord Krishna pass by the way.

Ecological importance:

Champaka tree is used in reclaiming nature. Some places in Java have been badly eroded; these trees can be used to reforest these areas. The roots of these trees can also be helpful in nitrogen-fixing. The vesicular-arbuscular mycorrhizae are seen on the roots of these trees which play a significant role in nitrogen fixation (Thapar HS, Vijayan AK, Kamla Uniyal, and Uniyal K; 1992). It also works as a soil improver and helps in increasing the fertility of the soil. The soil present under these tree cover has been seen to exhibit a great increase in the soil pH, there is also an increase in the organic soil content in the soil. It also increases the amount of available phosphorus in the soil. It has also been observed that there are many pests associated with the tree which includes some major host like Graphium doson (common jay), it also includes association with some minor host like Kerria lacca (lac insect) it is also seen to have an association with some wild host like Papilio demoleus (chequered swallowtail). The trees largely contribute to oxygen production in the environment. They contribute to the preservation of nature's ecological equilibrium. They are also home to several birds and animals. They are home to several insects and pests. It has also been reported that in the thick Biligiri hill ranges which serves to be the home for the Soliga tribe there stands the oldest champak tree that is estimated to be around 1000-1500 years old. It is known as the mammoth Champa tree or the Dodda Sampige Mara. It is home to many birds like doves, serpent eagles, etc. It serves as a place of tourist interest due to its large branches and strong trunk.

The champ species is a highly threatened species due to its overexploitation and hence is conserved by a program known as USAID's Hariyo Ban Program. It works to promote the conservation of the tree by seedling production, plantation activity, and management. A total of 225,000 seedlings have been planted by the program in 57 community forests.

Urban forest:

In the case of urban areas, the trees are grown with utmost care. Many measures are taken to see if the tree is growing properly and efficiently like the tree shows a moderate growth rate and possesses evergreen broad form. Proper watering is required that is around 15-20 gallons of water per week is done for the first two years. For the next year, 15-20 gallons of water can be provided twice a month. These requirements can greatly vary according to soil, temperature, wind conditions, etc. it has also been reported that the urban forest helps in decreasing the level of pollution. One urban forest of champaca is found in Bangkok (Bejranonda, S. & Attanandana V; 2011).

Economic significance:

As timber:

It is considered to be a timber tree. The wood in the tree is soft and is evenly grained. The sapwood is whitish, whereas the heartwood is pale-brown to olive-brown in color and glossy in appearance. Generally, the heartwood of this species is strong, durable. Evenly grained and capable of taking a high polish. The woods of these species are not very strong but can last for a longer period (Armiyanti Kadir M.A, Kadzimin S., & Panjaitan S.B; 2010). The wood of these species is used for packing cases, carriages, crates, furniture, bentwood articles, toys, pencils, bobbins, tea chests, and plywood in ships and boat buildings.

In India, the species is usually grown and used as ornamental and the leaves, fruits, flowers of the species can be used for making medicines and essential oil. In India, sweetly scented and fragrant flowers are used for hair adornment.

Essential oils:

The oil extracted from champaca is usually derived from sub-tropical trees with deep and fragrant flowers. This extraction has a great range of applications in an aroma lamp, diffusor, bath, inhaler, massage, light bulb ring, mist sprays, and perfumes. This extraction forms one of the most important components of the world's most expensive perfumes. Flowers yielding these essential oils hence have great importance in perfumery. Ana's analyses of the seeds showed low kernel contents but high oil contents (Sushil Kumar, Bhandari RS and Kumar S; 1993). It was most commercially exploited due to its oil production.

Poison:-

The extracts have also been reported to have many toxic effects. The leaf extracts show toxic effects on rice fungus. The fatty oil extracted from the seeds shows antibacterial activity.

Fuels:-

The bark and branches of the trees are often used as fuelwood and their gross energy value is about 21000 kJ/kg.

Fodder:-

Silkworms are fed by the leaves of the tree. It is used as animal feed, fodder, and forage.

Wood products:

The wood produced from the tree champaka can be used in many ways like they can be used to make containers like boxes, tanks, and vats. They can also be used to make different furniture. They can be used to make short fiber pulps. In many places, they are used to make gates, exterior fittings, fences, flooring. They can also be used for both heavy and light construction. Wall paneling is also using these woods. The wood produced can be used to make veneers (Chopra RN. Nayar SL, Chopra IC., 1986). Other wood-based materials like hardboard, fibreboard, plywood, particleboard, laminated wood are also manufactured from these woods. Many woodwares like brushes, cutlery, musical instruments, tool handles, wood carvings, and ferries are also made from these woods. The products manufactured from these woods play an important role in increasing the economy of the country.

Medicinal value:

In some places like Burma, its aromatic bitter bark is used to treat intermittent fever, its flower is used to treat leprosy, and the leaves can be used in the treatment of colic. A decoction obtained from the barks and leaves is also often given after childbirth where the bark is used as a febrifuge. It has also been reported that the plant has beneficial effects on several ailments like high blood pressure, muscle spasm, infertility, epilepsy, etc. It is often also used as a purgative, in the treatment of cough and inflammation.

It also has several other medicinal values like they are used to treat bleeding disorders such as nasal bleeding and heavy periods, they can also help in treating urinary problems like dysuria, urinary retention, it plays a role in making as well as treating poison and thus is involved in toxic conditions and poisoning, on the consumption of excessive sweet small children often undergo worm infestation which can be treated by using the bark of the tree, it has also shown great significance in treating the heart-related problem like a cardiac tonic, congenial for heart, it also aids in treating gout, it eases the pain when the extraction of its leaves are used on burning sensation, its bark also helps in healing ulcers and wounds. The flower buds also show antidiabetic activity (R. Vimala, S. Nagarajan, Muzaffer Alam, T. Susan, S. Joy; 1997).

Reference:

Ananthi T, Chitra M (2013) In vitro Evaluation of Antioxidant Activity of Michelia champaca (L.) Flowers. American Journal of Advanced Drug Delivery 1:734-742.

Ananthi T, Chitra M (2013) Screening of Invitro AntiInflammatory activity of Michelia Champaca Linn. Flowers. Asian J Pharm Clin Res 6:71-72.

Ananthi T, Jasmin Barvin I, Chitra M (2014) Antihyperlipidemic Activity of Michelia champaca L. In Triton WR 1339 Induced Albino Rats. Int J PharmTech Res 6:1368-1373.

Dama G, Bidkar J, Deore S, Jori M, Joshi P. Helmintholytic activity of the methanolic and aqueous extracts of leaves of Michelia champaca. Research Journal of Pharmacology and Pharmacodynamics, 2011; 3(1): 25-6.

Gowdam JVN and Jayanthi R. 1988. Role of rooting cofactors in rooting of Michaelia champaka L. by air layering. Lal Baugh. 30(1): 59-60.

Gupta S. Mehla K, Chauhan D, Nair A. Anti-inflammatory activity of leaves of Michelia champaca investigated on acute inflammation induced rats. Latin American Journal of Pharmacy, 2011; 30(4): 819-22.

Hong TD, Linington S, Ellis RH. 1996. Seed storage behavior: a compendium. Handbooks for Genebanks: No. 4. IPGRI.

Jacobsson U, Vijaya Kumar, and Shantini Saminathan. 1995. Sesquiterpene lactones from Michelia champaca. Phytochemistry. 39(4): 839-843.

Jain PP, Dobhal NP, Rajendra Pal and Ayyar KS. 1988. Chemical studies on oil-seeds of forest origin. Indian Forester. 114(3): 158-162.

Jain PP, Suri RK, Deshmukh SK and Mathur KC. 1987. Fatty oils from oilseeds of forest origin as antibacterial agents. Indian Forester. 113(4): 297-299.

João Henrique GL, Oriana AF, Paulete R (2009) Chemical composition and seasonal variation of the volatile oils from leaves of Michelia champaca L., Magnoliaceae. Braz J Pharmacog 19:880-882.

Laskar S and Datta M. 1992. Tree cover improves soil fertility and water retention. Indian Farming. 41: 10-17.

Luna R K. 1997. Plantation trees. International Book Distributors.

Mullaicharam AR, Surendra Kumar M. Effect of Michelia champaca Linn on pylorous ligated rats. Journal of Applied Pharmaceutical Science, 2011; 1(2): 60-4.

Mullaicharam AR, Surendra kumar M (2011) Effect of Michelia champaca Linn on pylorous ligated rats. Journal of Applied Pharmaceutical Science 01: 60-64.

Surendra Kumar M, Aparna P, Poojitha K, Karishma SK, Astalakshmi N. A comparative study of Michelia champaca L. flower and leaves for anti-ulcer activity. International Journal of Pharmaceuticals Sciences and Research, 2011; 2(6): 1554-8.

Taprial S, Kashyap D, Mehta V, Kumar S, Kumar D. Antifertility effect of hydroalcoholic leaves extract of Michelia champaca L.: An ethnomedicine used by Bhatra women in the Chhattisgarh state of India. J Ethnopharmacol, 2013; 147(3), 671-5.

Taprial S. A review on phytochemical and pharmacological properties of Michelia champaca Linn. Family: Magnoliaceae. International Journal of Pharmacognosy, 2015; 2(9): 430-6.

Umadevi P, Deephi K (2012) Antibacterial and free radical scavenging activity of Michelia champaca Linn flower extracts. Free Radicals and Antioxidants 2:58- 61.

Trees of Ramayana (2022): 135-144
Editor: Felix Bast
Today & Tomorrow's Printers and Publishers (India)

Chapter-12

Mango Tree (*Mangifera indica*)

Sahil Narwal

वधूनाटकसंङ्घैश्च संयुक्तां सर्वतः पुरीम् |

उद्यानाम्रवणोपेतां महतीं सालमेखलाम् ||

The above shloka from Balakanda, chapter 1.5 tells us about the city Ayodhya. According to the shloka, the Ayodhya accommodates groups of danseuses (female ballet dancers) and theatrical personnel. The Ayodhya is surrounded everywhere with the beautiful gardens and brakes of mango trees, and her wide fort-wall which covers Ayodhya is like her cincture ornament.

तस्मिन् बिल्वाः कपित्थाः च पनसा बीज पूरकाः |

आमलक्यो बभूवुः च चूताः च फल भूषणाः ||

The above shloka from Ayodhya Kanda, chapter 2.91 tells us about the plants present there. The major plants present there were, Bilva, Kapittha, Panasa, Citron Amalaki, and Mango Trees laden with fruit.

अमी लक्ष्मण दृश्यन्ते चूताः कुसुम शालिनः |

विभ्रम उत्सिक्त मनसः स अङ्गरागा नरा इव ||

The shloka from Kishkindha Kanda, chapter 4.1 narrates to us about the beauty of mango trees and their similarity with men. The shloka narrates that Lakshmana, these mango trees with greenish-yellow flowers are appearing like men whose hearts are flirtatiously aroused, and who have creamed their bodies with greenish-yellow body cream?

Figure: Mango tree (National Dairy Research Institute campus, Karnal, Haryana, India) © Sahil Narwal

Introduction

The living beings present on this earth, along with the plants, animals, microbes, soil, water, air, etc., along with their genomes and ecosystems make up the biodiversity of the earth.

One of the greatest epic poems of Sanskrit literature is the Valmiki Ramayana. The Ramayana is filled with amazing and enchanting descriptions of nature's grandeur. It has two major events namely Rama's 14-year exile in the forests and the rescue of Sita from the captivity of Ravana in Lanka. In this epic, a wide swathe of territory was covered which in present-day constitutes Uttar Pradesh, Madhya Pradesh, Maharashtra, and Karnataka up to Lanka beyond the sea. Such a large territory would cover a wide range of flora and fauna. An amazing fact about Ramayana is that it is geographically quite accurate despite its time. The various sites visited by Rama can still be identified from the description in the text. Also, the flora and fauna can be found as described in the text. The flora mentioned includes various herbs, shrubs, trees, medicinal plants, ornamental plants, etc. one of the trees mentioned in Ramayana is the mango tree which is the topic of this term paper.

Mangifera indica (mango)

The *Mangifera indica* is a tropical plant. It is also known as mango. It belongs to the plant family Anacardiaceae. In Sanskrit, it is called chuta, Amra. The mango has various names in India and all over the world also. Some of the names of mango in India are aam, ambo, amba, Amra, ghari am, mamadi, mamaram, mamidi, manga, mavena, Mavi, mavu, rasala, etc. similarly there are various names of mango all over the world. The mango belongs to the family Anacardiaceae which includes plants like cashew, hog plum, pepper tree, pistachio, poison ivy, etc. mango is one of the most popular tropical fruits. The name *Mangifera indica* was given by Carl Linnaeus. He also classified the plant. The genus *Mangifera* includes 69 species which are mostly restricted to tropical Asia. Mango is the state tree of Maharashtra and Chandigarh.

Classification of mango

Kingdom Plantae – Plants

Subkingdom- Tracheobionta – Vascular plants

Superdivision- Spermatophyta – Seed plants

Division- Magnoliophyta – Flowering plants

Class- Magnoliopsida – Dicotyledons

Subclass- Rosidae

Order- Sapindales

Family- Anacardiaceae – Sumac family

Genus- Mangifera L. – mango

Species- Mangifera indica L. – mango

Morphological Characteristics

The mango tree is a large tree that has a dense crown and is evergreen. When matured the trees can attain a height of 40 m or more, the trunk can be of 60-120 cm and greyish-brown in color with longitude-fissured bark.

Seeds-Mango seeds are single, big and flat, ovoid oblong, and surrounded by the fibrous endocarp at maturity. The testa is thin and the tegument is papery. Embryos are dicotyledonous. The seeds cannot survive for more than a few days or weeks at ambient temperatures. The seeds are recalcitrant. This is the reason that mango was not dispersed to a large distance by seed until recent times.

Seedlings-The mango seedling (in the case of poly-embryonic seeds it is called seedlings) develops after 2 weeks and grows systematically from the start: a flush brings out the new shoot which extends in about 1 month, after which the buds remain inactive for some time.

Leaves -10-12 new leaves are produced in flushes 1-3 times a year. Leaves are shed from the trees after 4-5 years. Leaf morphology changes according to the cultivar. Leaves are spirally arranged, simple. The young leaves are copper-colored, turning to light then dark shiny green. The petiole is 1-12.5 cm long, with pulvinus at the base. The leaf is a blade variable in size and shape, usually narrowly elliptic to lanceolate, 12-38 x 2-13 cm. The leaves are somewhat leathery, tapering at base, margin often undulating, apex acuminate, nerves 12-30 pairs, elevated on both surfaces.

Roots-The tree roots extend to a considerable depth into the soil. The root system is a long, dynamic taproot and plentiful surface feeder roots, which helps the tree to find the necessary moisture for flowering/ flushing during the dry season.

Flowers-The inflorescence takes 25-30 days for full bloom from the time of initiation. The inflorescence is rigid and erect. It may grow up to 30 cm long and has a lot of branches. Although the terminal branch is invariably cymose, the inflorescence is generally tertiary. It is generally densely flowered, with male or hermaphrodite flowers that are both borne inside a same flower. Depending upon the cultivar it has 300–6000 reddish-pink to greenish-white flowers which are 5-8 mm in diameter. 1 mm long pedicels; 5-lobed calyx; 5 petals (twice as long as the calyx, ovate to ovoid to lanceolate and also thinly pubescent) are present. The pistil is abortive in male flowers, style lateral, stigma simple. When just a tiny fraction of the flowers are pollinated, a good yield of fruit is produced. Environmental and cultural factors strongly affect the ratio of males to perfect flowers. The floral disc is four- or five-lobed, fleshy and large which is located above the base of the petals. There are five large, fleshy stamens, but only one or two of them are fertile. The other stamens are infertile staminodes with a tiny gland on top. Central stamens are present. The anatropous and pendulous ovule is present.

Fruit-The fruit is a large, fleshy drupe, which contains an edible mesocarp of varying thickness. The mesocarp is resinous and can be highly variable concerning shape, size, color, presence of fiber, and flavor. The flavor of mango ranges from turpentine to sweet. A thick and gl[illegible] exocarp is present. The fruit's proximal end is where a characte[illegible] develops laterally. Above the beak a sinus is present. Fruit shape [illegible]y. It could be elongate, oblong, and ovate or intermediate forms involving two of these shapes. Fruit length ranges from 2.5 to 30 cm which depends on the cultivar. The endocarp is thick, woody, and fibrous. Fibers from the endocarp enter the mesocarp also. Chlorophyll, carotenes, anthocyanins, and xanthophylls are also present in the fruit. The color of the skin is generally a mixture of green, red and yellow pigments, although fruit color is genotype-dependent. The fruit ripens after 3-4 months; some late cultivars ripen after 5 months. The period from fruit set to maturity mostly ranges from 10 to 28 weeks which depends upon cultivar and climate.

Distribution of mango

Mangoes were cultivated in South Asia for thousands of years and they reached Southeast Asia between the fifth and fourth centuries B.C. The wild mango is native to the Himalayan slopes of India and Burma. Throughout India and Southeast Asia, perhaps 40 to 60 of such trees still exist. Over the years, mango has spread to many parts of the tropical and subtropical world. Mangoes have been grown since 2000 B.C. Its flavor, size, and texture developed over the years. The travelers who tasted the mango were fascinated with its aromatic qualities and flavor and they introduced the fruit to other tropical countries. As the mango adapted to new areas, new varieties evolved which made it popular and new names were given such as "apple of the tropics, "King of fruit" and "Fruit of the Gods".

Mango was domesticated more than 4000 years ago in India, and traders, explorers, and kings transported it to other subtropical parts of the world to cultivate it. During the 4th and 5th century B.C., Buddhist monks brought mango to the Malaya Peninsula and East Asia. During middle of the 7th Century A.D., The mango was initially brought to China when Chinese adventurer Hwen T sang brought the fruit back from India. Further, the Persians carried it to East Africa (Purseglove, 1969). With the spice trade, the cultivation of mango began moving westward. The Portuguese became the first to start trading mangos when they landed in Calcutta in 1498. The word mango originated from Malayalam "manga" and Tamil "mangai". The Portuguese, fascinated by the fruit on their arrival in Kerala, introduced it to the world as "Mango". The Portuguese were the first to introduce grafting on mango trees and they produced extraordinary varieties like Alphonso. Alphonso is named after de Albuquerque. He was a nobleman and military expert who helped to establish the Portuguese colony in India. In the 1600s the Spanish travelers brought mango to South America and Mexico. The first attempt was made in 1833 to introduce mango into the US in Florida. A very small percentage of fresh mangoes that are available commercially in the US are grown in South Florida and Southern California. The Portuguese took the mango to West Africa and Brazil during the 16th century AD. The mango was first established in Brazil and then the mango was carried to the West Indies being first planted in Barbados in about 1742 and later in the Dominican Republic.

Habitat

The mango trees grow best in lowland tropical forests but can also grow at an altitude of 1200 meters. The mango tree can also thrive where there is a clear distinction between the rainy season and dry season. It grows best in the dry season with sandy soil having a pH of 5.5 to 7.5. Direct sun is also preferred for the growth of fruits.

Evolution

Mango's history begins hundreds of years ago on the Indian subcontinent. According to historians and horticulturists, the cultivated mango has originated in India. Based on the observed degree of genetic variation, Vavilov (1926) proposed the Indo-Burma area as the Mango's source. According to Mukherjee (1951), the origin of the genus *Mangifera* was probably in South – East Asia but the origin of cultivated Mango was in the Assam – Burma region. Scientists at the Birbal Sahni Institute of Palaeobotany in Lucknow have tracked the origination of the genus *Mangifera* back to 60 million-year-old fossilized mango leaves. The fossil was found in the Palaeocene sediments near Damalgiri, West Garo Hills, Meghalaya. The name of the fossil is Eomangiferophyllum damalgiriensis (Mehrotra et al., 1998). From the extensive comparison of the anatomy and morphology of several modern-day species of the genus *Mangifera* with the fossil samples, it can be concluded that North-East India is the Centre of origin of the mango genus, from where it spread into neighboring areas of SouthEast Asia and then slowly to the whole world.

Genome evolution

To investigate the evolutionary history of the mango genome, scientists performed a gene family clustering using mango and 11 other representative angiosperm species, including 2 species in the same order Sapindales (*Citrus sinensis* (sweet orange) and *Dimocarpus longan*

(longan)), 7 in the same Eudicot clade (*Carica papaya*, *Arabidopsis thaliana*, *Theobroma cacao*, *Citrullus lanatus*, *Prunus persica*, *Vitis vinifera*, and *Solanum Lycopersicum*), and 2 outgroup species (*Oryza sativa* and *Amborella trichopoda*). From the result, 248 single-copy families were used for phylogenetic tree construction and species divergence time estimation, which placed mango as a sister species in adjacent with sweet orange and longan, which is consistent with published results. Scientists estimated that mangoes diverged from the ancestor of longan and sweet orange ~ 70 million years ago (MYA).

Ecological importance

Mango is mostly cultivated for its fruit which can be eaten in three different ways, depending largely on the production or yield: unripe (mature green, very popular in Thailand and Philippines), ripe (common way, throughout the world), and processed (at various stages, in the form of chutney, pickles, dried slices, canned slices in syrup, juice, paste, etc.)

Seed kernels can be used as fodder for cattle feed and poultry. In traditional medicines, dried flowers or bark and decoctions of the kernels serve as astringents. Wood may be used for a variety of applications since it is relatively sturdy, durable, and great to work with; but, if used in building, it must be protected with preservatives.

The uses of mango are-

(a) For animal fodder/feed/forage

(b) Can be used in agroforestry, shade and shelter, soil improvement

(c) Fuelwood

(d) Fruits, spices, and culinary herbs

(e) Source of medicines

(f) Industrial and domestic woodware

(g) Plywood

(h) Beams, floorings, heavy construction

How to grow a mango tree in a field?

A mango tree can grow in a wide range of climates, but it shows the best growth in tropical and subtropical climate conditions. During their growth period, they need a good amount of rain, but during the flowering, they need a dry season. Red loamy soil is best suited for mango, although it can grow in any type of soil. In India, they grow in alluvial, clayey, or laterite soil. The pH range should be around 4.5-7.0 for mango cultivation.

Economic importance

Among the world's most mango-producing countries, India ranks first. 50% of the world's mango production is accounted for by India. Apart from India, prominent mango-producing nations include China, Brazil, Thailand, Egypt, Philippines, Pakistan, Indonesia, Nigeria, and Mexico. 52% of world production i.e. 12 million tonnes are shared by India as against the world's production of 23 million tonnes (2002-03). World mango production is averaged at 22 million metric tonnes per year. Worldwide production is mostly concentrated in Asia which accounts for 75% of mango production, followed by South and Northern America with about 10% share. Graph 1&2 depicts the area under cultivation and production trends of mangoes in India during 1997-98 to 2001-02. Major mango-producing States of India are Andhra Pradesh, Bihar, Gujarat, Karnataka, Maharashtra, Orissa, Tamil Nadu, Uttar Pradesh, and West Bengal. The other states include Madhya Pradesh, Kerala, Haryana, Punjab, etc.

Medicinal use

Mango produces various pharmacologically and medicinally important chemicals such as mangiferin, mangiferonic acid, hydroxymangiferin, polyphenols, and carotenoids. These chemicals have various functions such as-

(i) Pharmacological activities

(ii) Antioxidant

(iii) Radioprotective

(iv) Immunomodulatory

(v) Anti-allergic

(vi) Anti-inflammatory

(vii) Antitumor

(viii) Antidiabetic

(ix) Lipolytic

(x) Antibone resorption

(xi) Monoamine oxidase inhibiting

(xii) Antimicrobial

(xiii) Antiparasitic

Insect, pests, and diseases

According to the National Horticulture Mission, Ministry of Agriculture, India they have mentioned some major insects are Hopper, Mealybug, and fruit fly that affect the mango tree. Several other insects affect the mango tree. Also, there are some pests like red tree ants, termites, etc. Some of the diseases of mango trees are powdery mildew, dieback, sooty mold, and many more. The Ministry of Agriculture has released some guidelines on how to identify these insects, pests, and diseases. Also, the Ministry has written measures to control the diseases. The article is mentioned in the reference.

Conservation status

As per International Union for Conservation of Nature's Red List of Endangered Species, the red list criteria and category of mango are data deficient. Also, according to the International Union for Conservation of Nature's (IUCN) Red List of Threatened Species, there is a protected population on the Mysore plateau in a biosphere reserve in India.

Rituals and folklore

In northern India, the mango leaves are tied at the entrance of the house to ward off evil and negative energy. The leaves are tied on special occasions like marriage or during pooja or making a new house so that the occasion occurs without any problem. These leaves are tied to the house entrance until they dry up and then fall themselves.

Conclusion

Mango has been an important part of Indian culture for ages. It was mentioned in ancient Indian books and folklore. Mango was so loved that it got scattered throughout the world. This led to the formation of various new varieties of mango all over the world. Even in India, mango has several varieties like the dusheri, happus, Alphonso, langda, totapuri, etc. the mango was not only loved for its juicy fruit but was also used as a medicinal plant in ancient India. Mango has several names like "the king of fruits".This is why mango was mentioned in Ramayana also. Humans have always been mesmerized by the mango and will continue to do so. Mango is a plant that takes time to grow and hence even in abundance it needs care so that the precious tree doesn't become extinct. Though much has been researched about mango, there is still some information about the mango that is yet to be discovered.

References-

Mehrotra, Rakesh & Dilcher, David & AWASTHI, N.. (1998). A Palaeogene Mangifera - Like leaf fossil from India. Phytomorphology: An International Journal of Plant Morphology. 48.

Mehta, I., History of Mango –King of Fruits. International Journal of Engineering Science Invention (IJESI) 6.7 (2017): 20-24. http://www.ijesi.org/papers/Vol(6)7/Version-3/D0607032024.pdf

National Horticulture Board, Ministry of Agriculture, Government of India http://nhb.gov.in/report_files/mango/mango.htm

National Horticulture Mission, Ministry of Agriculture, Government of India http://midh.gov.in/technology/IPM-Mango-Revised-Sept2011.pdf

Rao, D, H., Murthy, K, M, K. Valmiki Ramayana. 2008 https://valmikiramayan.net/

Shah, K. A., Patel, M. B., Patel, R. J., & Parmar, P. K. (2010). Mangifera indica (mango). Pharmacognosy Reviews, 4(7), 42–48. https://doi.org/10.4103/0973-7847.65325

Wang, P., Luo, Y., Huang, J. et al. The genome evolution and domestication of tropical fruit mango. Genome Biol 21, 60 (2020). https://doi.org/10.1186/s13059-020-01959-8

World Conservation Monitoring Centre. 1998. Mangifera indica. The IUCN Red List of Threatened Species 1998: e.T31389A9624842.

Yadav, D., Singh, S, P. Mango: history origin and distribution. Journal of Pharmacognosy and Phytochemistry 6(6) 2017 http://www.phytojournal.com/archives/2017/vol6issue6/PartR/6-6-82-484.pdf

Trees of Ramayana (2022): 145-152
Editor: Felix Bast
Today & Tomorrow's Printers and Publishers (India)

Chapter-13

Palmyra Palm Tree (*Borassus flabellifer*)

Suman Singh, Avijit Pattnaik

ततस्सरलतालाश्च तिलका नक्तमालकाः।

प्रहृष्टास्तत्र सम्पेतुः कुब्जा भूत्वाऽथ वामनाः।।2.91.50।।

The above Sloka is mentioned in Ayodhyakanda, Sarg- 91 and Sloka 50. This Sloka depicts how different plants took different forms at the order of Bharadwaj. The Sloka means- "Thereafter pine, palmyra, tilaka, and naktamala trees were transformed into hunchbacks and dwarfs and moved about in great delight"

कदल्याढकिसम्बाधं नारिकेलोपशोभितम्।

सालैस्तालैस्तमालैश्च पुष्पितैस्तरुभिर्वृतम्।।3.35.13।।

This Sloka mentioned in the Aranyakanda, Sarg-35 Sloka 13 depicts the beautiful scene of Panchvati forest where Lord Rama stayed. The shloka means- "The place covered with banana plants and coconut trees as well as blossoming sal and Tamala trees was looking extremely beautiful."

Figure: *Borassus flabellifer* in its natural habitat. © Avijit Pattnaik

Common names of the tree

Hindi: (Trinaraaj), (Taada), (Tala), English: Palmyra palm, Sanskrit: Trnam-indrah, or Talah, Tantuniyosah, Tranam-raj, Mahatah, Tranam-ketuh, Urdu: تاڑ Taad, Marathi: Taada, Tamil: தாலம் Talam, Gujarati: તાડ Taad

Taxonomic Position

Kingdom: Plantae

Phylum: Tracheophyta

Class: Liliopsida

Order: Arecales

Family: Arecaceae

Genus: *Borassus*

Species: *flabellifer*

Morphological Characteristics

It is a solitary unbranched (mostly) and erects palm which can grow to a height of 25-30 m with a trunk diameter of about 1m at its base. The trunk is black and is surrounded by a dense mass of long adventitious roots. The older Palmyra palms resemble their wood with that of coconut palms, but Palmyra's wood is much darker in color. The leaves are fan-shaped and 3 m long, with robust black teeth (serrated) on the petiole margins. B. flabellifer is a dioecious plant with male and female flowers on separate individuals.

The size of male flowers is less than 1 cm in length and these form clusters of semicircles, hidden under the scale-like bracts, and overall forming the catkin-like inflorescences. The female flowers are the size of a golf ball and are solitary. After pollination, these flowers develop into fleshy fruits that are 15–25 cm in width; each fruit contains 1-3 seeds. The fruits are dark-colored (black to brown) with sweet, fibrous pulp and each seed is enclosed within a woody endocarp. The fruit is ovoid, measuring 10 cm to 18 cm in diameter, has a black husk, and is borne in clusters. Palmyra trees can live up to 100 years.

Characteristics of the family

Arecaceae- the majestic family of palms includes some of the largest angiosperm leaves (*Raphia* [jupati]), inflorescences (*Corypha*), and seeds (*Lodoicea* [double coconut]). It consists of woody shrubs, vines, or trees comprising about 200 genera and 3000 species. The inflorescence of this family is usually paniculate and is subtended by one or more bracts that may become woody at maturity. The flowers are actinomorphic and may be bisexual or more often unisexual. The stamens are organized into two whorls, each with three stamens, making a total of 6 distinct stamens in each androecium. But sometimes it comprises up to several hundred stamens that could be adnate or connate. The gynoecium may be syncarpous or apocarpous. The fruit is usually a drupe. Some important species belonging to this majestic plant family include edible, commercially significant, ornamental as well as forest species:

Areca Palm-*Areca triandra*, Royal Palm-*Roystonea regia*; Foxtail Palm-*Wodyetia bifurcate*, Fishtail Palm-*Caryota mitis*; Edible Date Palm-*Phoenix dactilifera*; Christmas Palm-*Veitchia merillii*, European Fan Palm-*Chamaerops humilis*, Majestic Palm-*Ravenea rivularis*, Senegal Date Palm-*Phoenix reclinata*, Indian Date Palm-*Phoenix sylvestris*, Bismarck Palm-*Bismarckia nobilis*; Queen Palm-*Syagrus romanzoffiana*, Chinese Fan Palm-*Livistona chinensis*, Coconut Palm-*Cocos nucifera*, Sylvester Palm-*Phoenix sylvestris*; Branched Palm-*Hyphane indica*; *H. dichotoma,* etc.

Origin and distribution of the tree

Borassus flabellifer is distributed in India extending through South-East Asia to New Guinea. It is most commonly found in India, Cambodia, and Myanmar. It is believed that B. flabellifer is a selection from the more diverse *Borassus aethiopum* Mart. of Africa. It got distributed probably with Indian trade routes during prehistoric times. In India, the palm is concentrated within the semi-arid regions of Maharashtra, Tamil Nadu, Odisha, Karnataka, Andhra Pradesh, Bihar, and West Bengal. India has nearly 102 million palms and half of them are in Tamil Nadu only. The Arecaceae is of special interest because of having the most extensive and longest fossil records of any family among monocots, extending some 80 million years ago to the **Late Cretaceous Period.**

Species wise distribution of the Palmyra palm throughout the world:

Borassus aethiopum- Tropical Africa and Madagascar

Borassus akeassii-West and Central Africa

Borassus flabellifer- Southern Asia from India to Indonesia

Borassus heineanus- New Guinea

Borassus madagascariensis- Madagascar

Cultural symbolism

The Toddy Palm tree (another name of the tree) is the official tree of Tamil Nadu and is very revered in Tamil culture. All the parts of this mighty tree have a definite use and so it is also called "karpaha Veruksham" ("celestial tree"). The Asian Palmyra palm tree is also a symbol of Cambodia where it is a very common palm, found everywhere in the country. It can be seen growing around the famous Angkor Wat temple. In Indonesia, the Toddy Palm is revered as the symbol of South Sulawesi province. The plant didn't fail even in capturing the imagination of Bengalis, particularly in the words of Rabindranath Tagore whose nursery rhyme 'Taal Gaach Ek Paye daariye' (Tall tree standing on a single leg....) is taught in most schools in West Bengal and Bangladesh.

Rituals and cultures associated with the tree

According to Sangam Tamil literature, the Palmyra tree used to be worshipped by the residents of the Neithal landscape (the seaside and its environs). According to Alamperi Sathanar of Natrinai verse 303, a Palmyra tree was the village's gathering place, and the tree had a big trunk where God resided. The Palmyra tree can be seen in different Indian temple sculptures from the second century BCE. There is a very beautiful sculpture at the Amriteshwara temple in Amritapura, Karnataka, showcasing the seven Palmyra trees. Markings have been carved on trees to show that an arrow has penetrated the trees, and Sri Ramachandra stands holding his bow on the left. A downward moving line across all the seven trees denotes the piercing done by the single arrow.

Legends, myths, and stories related to the tree

Palmyra Tree Miracle- Once the renowned Saivite saint Sambandhar visited Tiruvothur he saw a devotee crying. The devotee grew some Palmyra Palm trees in a hope that he would use the income earned from the trees in his community service within the Shiva temple. But all the trees were male trees that could yield no fruits. People were mocking him and teased him asking when his god would yield his fruits. When Sambandhar enquired as to why he was so depressed, he told him the whole story of his 'all-male Palmyra trees'. After this, Sambandhar visited the Shiva temple and sang ten verses in praise of the Lord, and then looking at the trees he said, the male trees will yield (Kurumpai Aan Panai Eenum in Tamil). Next minute all the trees blossomed and overflowed with Palmyra fruits! Dr. R Nagasamy, a prominent historian and archaeologist, has mentioned the Sanskrit lines from the Upamanyu Bhakta Vilasam referring to the same meaning.

Tamil Youths and the toy Palmyra horses

In ancient Tamil Nadu, young Tamil boys who fell for the love of girls in their villages would use the leaves of Palmyra palm to make toy horses and ride on them on the streets to publicize their love for the girl. As a result, the parents of the girls were forced to get their daughter married to them.

Economical and medicinal uses of the tree

Economically Palmyra palm is very useful. Every part of it serves a purpose in some way. Its leaves can be used for making hats, baskets, mats, and also as writing material. Because of its extreme hardness and strength, the trunk of this tree is used for constructing bridges and buildings. The sap extracted by cutting the tree's flowers can be consumed. It can also be processed into sugar. The sap from this tree is fermented to prepare the famous Toddy drink. Odiyal, a hard chewable snack is made from the dried roots of the tree.

Muffins are made from the Palmyra sprout flour that is obtained by drying and grinding the young Palmyra shoots.

Almost all the parts of the Palmyra palm bear medicinal characteristics. The sprouts of Palmyra are boiled or roasted and consumed. These are rich in fibers. Researchers have proven that the roots, bark, and leaves of the Palmyra palm contain various vitamins, minerals, proteins, and polyphenols, hence are beneficial for consumption. Face packs made from the fruit of sugar palm (another name of the Palmyra) are very useful for treating skin inflammations like boils, prickly heat, and redness of the face. It is beneficial even for sensitive skins. A mouthwash is made from a decoction of the bark combined with salt. Also, the charcoal made from the bark can be used as dentifrice (cleaning the teeth). The root decoction is used against respiratory ailments. Young roots are anthelmintic (destroying the parasitic worms of the intestine) and diuretic. The plant possesses broad-spectrum antioxidant and antimicrobial activities and hence can treat various infectious diseases. Scientific research works suggest that the strong antioxidant properties of methanol extract of this plant might be employed in developing natural antioxidants for the pharmaceutical and agro-food industries.

Ecological aspects of the Palmyra Palm

The unique features of the roots, stem, and canopy aid in their survival during strong winds and cyclones. M. Narasimhan, former chairman of the Madras Christian College Botany department, outlined the three characteristics that help these trees survive. The tree possesses a fibrous root system but has a strong grasping capacity as these roots can penetrate 5-10 ft deep in the ground and therefore not easily uprooted. The vasculature of the stem makes the tree highly flexible. Lastly, the crown of the tree, the folded leaves and structure of the tree help it withstand strong winds. Palmyra trees help replenish the ground water and minimize soil erosion. Palmyra palm's roots go vertically into the ground and bring the bottom water to numerous levels along the path. It is considered to irrigate the soil as well as play a key role in water circulation in aquifers and rivers. However, the tree is being extensively used for construction activities. Brick kilns have also exploited it as firewood. Adding to these factors, the nonavailability of manpower to harvest its fruits has led the tree to face extinction.

The authorities of the Agriculture department across Tamil Nadu are launching massive drives to increase the Palmyra tree cover by supplying as well as planting the Palmyra nuts across the state. Other than this, different agencies at grassroots levels of the society must accelerate their extension programs in bringing awareness on Palmyra palm tree cultivation and hence its preservation.

Cultivation strategies of Palmyra tree

SVPR-1 is an improved variety of Palmyra Palm has commonly grown by farmers. The tree grows best in arid soils, deep sandy, and loamy soils. Dry areas having very little rainfall are also suitable for growth. On average, 63.25% of the total seeds germinate within six weeks of sowing. The seed selection is very important for a good yield. Sunken, bored, and weightless seeds should be rejected. Seeds may be sown directly in situ or may be raised to saplings in nurseries. In the direct sowing procedure, pits of the size 20 cm^3 are dug. Sand and soil mixtures are filled in the pits to half of their capacity, followed by covering it with dry leaves. Sowing should be done in the rainy months. Germination occurs within 3 weeks of sowing. In nursery transplanting, either a mound is formed by preparing a sand bed

1m wide and 60 cm in height or a nursery bed 2m in width and 60 cm in height is built using bricks, and seeds are sown in it with 10 cm spacing, then are covered with sand. Polythene bags are used to containerize one-year-old seedlings that are picked up from the nursery. These seedlings are finally transplanted to the main field after they attain rooting, with a spacing of 3m x 3m (1110 palms/ha). For manuring the palms, farmers use sheep penning. Before planting, each pit is filled with 10 kg FYM and this dosage is increased twice every year till it reaches up to 60 kg FYM/tree/year.

Work is not over even after cultivation. Some gaps are created in the fields which are filled up by using containerized seedlings from nurseries. Inter plowing is also done between the plants. For the collection and storage of rainwater, basin rectification is also done before the occurrence of rains. Pruning of the leaves is done in a phased manner. Palmyra also favors intercropping; can be grown together with green gram, cowpea, Bengal gram, amla, pomegranate, moringa, ber, guava, and West Indian cherry.

Palmyra palm grows very slowly. The first frond in the plant appears after five months of germination and the first fan-shaped mature leaves appear in the second year. It flowers at the age of 13-15 years when it reaches a height of 12-18m. At this stage, the padaneer (sweet sap) is extracted from the inflorescence during the 4 months from February to May. The average production of padaneer is 100-200 liters; varies in individual palms. Padaneer is extracted from inflorescence by a process called tapping. Different types of tappings are done keeping in reference, the age of the inflorescence and sex of the palm. On average 150 liters of padaneer is yielded by each tree per year, 24 kg jaggery is produced per tree per year, and from each liter of padaneer, 180-250g of jaggery is recovered.

References:

Aman, Ankita & Rajan, Rajni & Sinha, Suparna. (2018). The Palmyrah Palm (Borassus flabellifer L.): Overview of Biology, Uses, and Cultivation. *Biomolecular Reports.*

Balapure, K. M., Maheshwari, J. K., & Tandon, R. K. (1987). Plants of Ramayana. *The ancient science of life*, 7(2), 76–84.

Jana, H., & Jana, S. (2017). Palmyra Palm: Importance in Indian Agriculture. *Rashtriya Krishi (English), 12*(2), 35-40. Retrieved from http://52.172.152.24/index.php/Rk/article/view/167988

Swaminathan L. (2014). Seven trees and Rama. *Tamil and Vedas.* Retrieved April 18, 2020. From https://tamilandvedas.com/tag/seven-trees-and-rama/

Kolappan B. (2018). Standing still: how Palmyra trees withstood the force of a cyclone.

The Hindu. Retrieved April 18, 2020. From https://www.thehindu.com/news/national/tamil-nadu/still-standing-how-palmyra-trees-withstood-the-force-of-the-cyclone/article25588754.ece

Kress W. J. (2017). Arecales. *Encyclopedia Britannica.* Retrieved April 19, 2020. From https://www.britannica.com/plant/Arecales

Carr G. (n.d). Arecaceae(Palmae)- Flowering Plants Families, UH botany. *University of Hawaii Botany Department.* Retrieved April 19, 2020. From http://www.botany.hawaii.edu/faculty/carr/pfamilies.htm

Prasad G. Jamkhande, Vikas A. Suryawanshi, Tukaram M. Kaylankar, Shailesh L. Patwekar. (2016). Biological activities of leaves of the ethnomedicinal plant, Borassus flabellifer Linn. (Palmyra palm): An antibacterial, antifungal, and antioxidant evaluation. *Bulletin of Faculty of Pharmacy, Cairo University.*

Ramcharitmanas. (n.d). Kishkindha kaanda. *Ramcharitmanas.* Retrieved April 19, 2020. From https://www.ramcharitmanas.iitk.ac.in/ramcharitmanas?tid=4&tid_1=11&tid_2=8

Khatri RM, Siddiqui S, Nagamaniammai G, Athmaselvi K. Development of Muffin Using Palmyra (Borassus flabellifer) Sprout Flour. *Int J Nutr Pharmacol Neurol Dis* 2020;10:14-2

Jerry, A. 2018. A Comprehensive Review on the Medicinal Properties of Borassus flabellifer. *J. Acad. Indus. Res.* 7(7): 93-97.

Saikat, Basu & R, Sengupta & Zandi, Peiman. (2014). Arecaceae: The Majestic Family of Palms. *Encyclopedia of Earth.*

Trees of Ramayana (2022): 153-162
Editor: Felix Bast
Today & Tomorrow's Printers and Publishers (India)

Chapter-14

Indian Gooseberry Tree (*Phyllanthus emblica*)

Preeti Yadav

शिंशपा आमलकी जम्बूर् याः च अन्याः कानने लताः |

मालती मल्लिका जातिर्याश्चान्याः कानने लताः || २-९१-५१

प्रमदा विग्रहम् कृत्वा भरद्वाज आश्रमे अवसन् |

The above shloka from the Ayodhya Kanda, Chapter 91 Sarga, Verse 51, in Valmiki's Ramayana published by Gita Press which means Shimshapas (Ashoka trees), Amalakis (Amla Tree), Jambus (rose-apple trees), Malati, Mallika Jati and other creepers in the forest had been changed into dancing girls in the hermitage of Bharadwaja and they spoke as follows.

This scene is described so beautifully as it is described as all the trees are dancing like beautiful girls, here Personification Figures of speech is used very well which makes it a very beautiful scene. All the trees have their specific characters. Amla is famous for its sourness and medicinal importance, amla has one of the six tastes and it gives special property which helps to treat many diseases. Some of these trees are also described in Sundar Kanda, in the Ashoka Vatika where Sita Mata was caged by Ravana in Lanka.

Figure: The original Picture of Amla Tree. © Preeti Yadav

Introduction

Phyllanthus emblica Linn or *Emblica officinalis* is commonly known as Indian gooseberry or Amla. Phyllanthus is one of the largest Genuses in the flowering plant family *Phyllanthaceae*. The genus, Phyllanthus includes from 750 to 1200 numbers of species. Phyllanthus genus is famous for its diversity of different growth forms which includes annual and perennial herbs, shrubs, climbers, floating aquatics, and pachycaulous succulents. Cladodes are also present in some of the species of Phyllanthus. Morphology of floral structure and the number of Chromosomes have a wide range and the types of pollen of the Phyllanthus have one of the broadest varieties of any seed plant genus. One specific type of growth which is common in all the species of Phyllanthus is known as "phyllanthoid branching", which means the vertical stems bear deciduous, floriferous, and plagiotropic stems. Carl Linnaeus was the first person who described Phyllanthus in 1753, but the type was not designated.

In India, there are mainly three varieties or subspecies of the Indian Amla, all of them have their advantages and disadvantages. The three subspecies are the Banarasi amla, the Chakaiya amla, and the Francis amla. Among all three, the Banarasi amla matures before the other varieties, which means Banarasi Amla blossoms and fruits will show up faster in the landscape. In Indian Tradition systems of medicine (Ayurveda, Unani, and Siddha), Amla is considered as one of the most important medicinal trees. A specialty of the Amla Tree is that all the parts are used for the treatment of different diseases. Among all parts, the most useful and important part which is used to treat different diseases is “Fruit”.

Common Name

Amla, Indian gooseberry • Hindi: Aonla • Manipuri. Heikru • Marathi: Amla • Tamil: Nelli • Malayalam: Nelli, Nellikka • Telugu: Usiri, Usirikaya • Kannada: Betta nelli, Amalaka • Oriya: Aonla • Gujarati: આમળાં ambala • Sanskrit: Dhatri, amalaka • Mizo: Sunhlu

Taxonomic Classification

Kingdom: Plantae

Clade: Tracheophytes

Clade: Angiosperms

Clade: Eudicots

Clade: Rosids

Order: Malpighiales

Family: *Phyllanthaceae*

Genus: *Phyllanthus*

Species: *P. emblica*

Botanical name: *Phyllanthus emblica L.*

Family: *Phyllanthaceae* (Amla family)

Synonyms: *Emblica officinalis*

Chromosome number: 2n = 22 chromosomes

Trade name: Amla, Amla without seeds, *Emblica officinalis*, Nelli chettu, Nellikai.

Phyllanthaceae is a family of flowering plants in the order of Malpighiales. Picrodendraceae is the most closely related to the family *Phyllanthaceae*. The members of this family are most abundant in the tropics, with many in the South Temperate Zone.

Morphological Characteristics

The tree is small to medium in size, reaching 1–8 m (3 ft 3 in–26 ft 3 in) in height with a greenish-grey bark. The branchlets are not glabrous or finely pubescent, 10–20 cm (3.9–7.9 in) long. The Leaves are usually deciduous; the leaves are the simple, obtuse, and acute apex, subsessile, with a rounded base and closely set along branchlets, light green, resembling pinnate leaves. The flowers are greenish-yellow, borne in axillary fascicles, have six segments, but no real petals. Male and female flowers are carried separately on the same branch. The fruit is nearly spherical, light greenish-yellow, quite smooth, and hard on appearance, with six vertical stripes or furrows. The size of fruits is about 1.5-2.5cm in diameter. The fruits are juicy and fleshy. The average weight of one fruit is about 5 to 6g and 4 to 5ml in volume. The fruits are extremely acidic in nature and sour in taste. The type of fruit is capsular (drupaceous) berries with a fleshy exocarp. Mesocarp is the edible part of the fruit and the seeds are engaged by the hard stone-like part of the fruit which is the endocarp. Ripening in autumn, the berries are harvested by hand after climbing to upper branches bearing the fruits. The taste of Indian emblic is sour, bitter, and astringent, and it is quite fibrous.

Habitat

Amla is a very common plant in India. It can be easily found growing in semi-arid regions and plains of northern India. Amla can be found in both lights as well as heavy soils. It is found mostly in Northern and South Western India. Uttar Pradesh, Tamil Nadu, Rajasthan, and Madhya Pradesh are preferable subtropical areas. The fruits are available from October till May.

Geographic Distribution

Amla is a small to medium-sized tree, found in abundance in the sub-tropical mountainous regions of Southeast Asia, which includes India, Thailand, Indonesia, China. Amla is found throughout India, Pakistan, Uzbekistan, Sri Lanka, South East Asia, and Malaysia. In India, it is found mostly in Northern and South Western India. Uttar Pradesh, Tamil Nadu, Rajasthan, and Madhya Pradesh are preferable subtropical areas for amla. The geological origin of amla is India.

Evolution

Indian gooseberry or Amla is harvested from two species of *Phyllanthus*, namely *Phyllanthus emblica* and *Phyllanthus indofischeri.* Two special characters are considered for the identification of these two species are vegetative and reproductive features but molecular approaches are also important and necessary for the well precise identification which are reliable for further studies.

The fossils of *Phyllanthus* are recorded from different places. From the samples of the borehole of the deposits of freshwater of the middle Miocene in the Norway Sacz Basin, West Carpathians, Poland, extracted two fossil seeds of a *Phyllanthus*. The seeds which are extracted are similar to seeds of the fossil species *Phyllanthus triquetra* and *Phyllanthus compassica* from the Oligocene and Miocene of West Siberia. There are various sites in Poland from where *Phyllanthus* fossils arc known and record from several Miocene and Pliocene.

Genetic Diversity

Amla, the Indian gooseberry has nutraceutical properties and because of these properties, Indian gooseberry is widely grown in India. Amla is grown in both plains and sub-mountain tracts from 200 to 3000m altitudes (Pathak, 2003) all over India. Amla's processed products are very popular as it is used to make Chawanprash, ayurvedic medicines, cosmetic products, preserved juice, ready to serve the drink, sherbet, jam, fruit bar, dehydrated amla whole or powder, etc are widely marketed in India under various trade names. Identification of different varieties or genotypes of amla is very important so that customers get the best-processed products of amla. According to Pathak (2003), the best method which is used to identify different varieties is the study of leafy or fruit morphology, fruit color, etc. But these are the physical characteristics that can be affected or changed by the environmental conditions of the tree and soil type or nature in which the tree is grown. The best method to identify the varieties should not be affected or changed by the environmental conditions; therefore, molecular techniques are the most reliable method to identify the varieties of amla trees. Genetic polymorphisms unsurprisingly conquering in plants has been studied widely and is used to differentiate varieties that differ even marginally from each other. Polymerase Chain Reaction (PCR) based methods such as Random Amplified Polymorphic DNA (RAPD) (Bradeen and Havey, 1995; Sambrook and Russell, 2001) can be a powerful tool for the confirmation of plant materials under study (Warude et al., 2006).

Ecology

The two important species of amla *Phyllanthus emblica* and *P. indofischeri* from which fruits are collected are an important non-timber forest product for the indigenous Soliga community in the Biligiri Rangaswamy Temple Wildlife Sanctuary, India. Seedlings, saplings, and trees of these two congeners were monitored over three years in ten 0.1 ha plots each to assess and compare their regeneration status. The densities of seedlings and adult trees of both species were similar, but the density of saplings of P. emblica was lower than that of P. indofischeri. The size class distribution of P. indofischeri, but not of P. emblica, followed the inverse J-shaped curve typically associated with regenerating populations, suggesting higher mortality of seedlings and saplings of P. emblica than of P. indofischeri. Furthermore, re-sprouting individuals-presumably a response to damage by fire or grazing-constituted a larger proportion of the population in the case of P. emblica and may constitute a future population bottleneck. We suggest that anthropogenic pressures other than harvest could be responsible for differences in population structure between these two species, which are managed under similar harvest intensities and subject to similar disturbance regimes.

Ecological Services

Phyllanthus provides numerous services to the environment as well as to the agroforestry, from providing windbreak to shelterbelt and being as a natural shade tree in intercropping of many trees. Amla provides shelter to many insects, birds, and animals too. It supports grasses and shrubs to grow and complete their life cycle. It plays an important role in nutrient cycling, water infiltration, soil aeration, stormwater management, groundwater recharge, and it also prevents soil erosion. Its beautiful flowers attract the pollinators; it helps in the reproduction of pollinator aid flora. As its leaves filter air pollution and provide fresh air to the environment.

Economic Importance

Fruit sour and astringent, cooling, diuretic, laxative, eaten raw or cooked, also pickled, a rich source of vitamin C; containing as much vitamin C and orange juice. Seeds yield a fixed oil. Fruit, bark, and leaves are rich in tannin. Popularly used in inks, shampoos, and hair oils, the high tannin content of Indian gooseberry fruit serves as a mordant for fixing dyes in fabrics. Amla shampoos and hair oil are traditionally believed to nourish the hair and scalp and prevent premature grey hair. Wood is used for making agricultural implements, poles, and inferior quality furniture. As a Vermifuge, the Juice of the amla fruit with honey is used. The recommended dose is from 1 to 3 drachms. It is also used as an Appetizer as in the use of pickles and preserves made from the green fruits. Amla is used to treat irritability of the bladder, in retention of urine, to the forehead in cephalalgia, amla is used as a paste of the fruit alone or with *Nelumbium speciosum*, Saffron, and rose water. Applying it over the affected region. As a febrifuge and in diabetes, amla is used as an infusion of the seeds. For hiccup and painful respiration, use amla juice or extract of the amla fruit combined with honey and pipli. For hemorrhage, diarrhea, and dysentery, dried fruit of amla is the best medicine so far. A decoction prepared from the fruit combined with *T. chebula* and *T. belericais* useful in chronic dysentery and biliousness, in doses of 1 oz. once or twice daily. Various kinds of methods are used to treat diarrhea of children: A compound powder of the amla seed, Chitrak root, chebulic myrobalan, pipli, and palelone is given in suitable doses, according to age, in warm water twice daily, morning and at bedtime. Tender shoots given in buttermilk cure indigestion and diarrhea; green fresh leaves combined with curds have a similar effect. Leaves are used as infusions with fenugreek seeds in chronic dysentery and as a bitter tonic. Soak one tola of the seeds in a tinned vessel during the night. Grind it. Add cow's milk and use. This is a good remedy for biliousness. Amla is also used to treat various diseases such as anemia, jaundice, and dyspepsia: The use of dried fruit with iron. Fermented liquor prepared from the root is used in jaundice, dyspepsia, cough, etc. Take 20 to 40 grains of Dhatri Leha for anemia, jaundice, and dyspepsia. Dhatri Arista is used for jaundice, dyspepsia, indigestion, and cough.

It helps in regulating blood sugar. It is a very powerful anti-inflammatory herb, a wonderful antioxidant and a Natural Source of Vitamin C. Amla helps scavenge free radicals. Amla is powerful food for the brain and helps lower cholesterol. Amla also helps maintain the functioning of the liver, increases hemoglobin, red blood cell count. It is useful for Cough, Bronchitis, and Asthma. Amla cleanses the mouth, strengthens the teeth. Its decoction is used in hyperacidity and with honey as an anthelmintic. The presence of Amla results in enhanced cell survival decreased free radical production and higher antioxidant levels. There are various classic Ayurvedic preparations, such as Chyawanprash in which Amla is used as a chief ingredient. It helps improve intelligence and memory power. Triphala and Brahmarasayana are other classic medicines in which Amla has been used since time immemorial.

Chemical Composition of Amla Fruit

These fruits are reputed to contain high amounts of ascorbic acid (vitamin C) and have a bitter taste that may derive from a high density of ellagitannins, such as emblicanin A (37%), emblicanin B (33%), punigluconin (12%), and pedunculagin (14%). Amla also contains punicafolin and phyllanemblinin A, phyllanemblin other polyphenols, such as flavonoids, kaempferol, ellagic acid, and gallic acid.

Various types of chemical constituents are found in amla. Hydrolyzable Tannins are found in amla are Emblicanin A and B, Punigluconin, Pedunculagin, Chebulinic acid (Ellagitannin), Chebulagic acid

(Benzopyran tannin), Corilagin (Ellagitannin), Geraniin (Dehydroellagitannin), Ellagotannin. Many Alkaloids which are present in amla fruit are Phyllantine, Phyllembein, and Phyllantidine. Many Phenolic compounds are also present like Gallic acid, Methyl gallate, Ellagic acid, Trigallayl glucose. Various Amino acids such as Glutamic acid, Proline, Aspartic acid, Alanine, Cystine, Lysine are also present. Carbohydrates such as Pectin are present. Vitamin C that is Ascorbic acid is important because of Ascorbic acid, the nature of amla is acidic. Some Flavonoids are also found in amla fruit for example Quercetin, Kaempferol. Organic acids such as Citric acid also make the nature of amla acidic.

The Ayurvedic Description of Amla

According to the Ayurvedic classifications, amla fruit excerpt below properties: Rasa (taste): sour and astringent are the most dominant, but the fruit has five tastes, including sweet, bitter, and pungent Veerya (nature): Cooling, treatment of burning sensation in inflammation and fever which are considered to be manifestations of pitta (fire) agitation Vipaka (taste developed through digestion): Sweet Guna (qualities): Light, dry Doshas (effect on humor): Quietens all three doshas: Vata, Kapha, pitta, and is especially effective for pitta. Based on this, Amla has been considered the best of the Ayurvedic rejuvenating herbs. Inimitably, amla exerts a natural balance of tastes (sweet, sour, pungent, bitter, and astringent), that stimulates the brain to rebalance the three main components (water, fire, and air in the body) of all physiological functions.

Cultural Significance

The Amla tree is considered sacred by Hindus as God Vishnu is believed to dwell in it. The tree is worshiped in the event of Amalaki Ekadashi. Amla is said to have originated from the drops of Amrit which spilled on earth accidentally, because of the fight of Gods and Demons, after Kshirsagar Manthan. That is why it cures every disease.

In the Buddhist tradition half, an Amalaka fruit was the final gift to the Buddhist sangha by the great Indian emperor Ashoka. This is illustrated in the Ashokavadana in the following verses: "A great donor, the lord of men, the eminent Maurya Ashoka, has gone from being lord of Jambudvipa [the continent] to being lord of half a myrobalan" (Strong, 1983, p. 99). In Theravada Buddhism, this plant is said to have been used as the tree for achieving enlightenment, or Bodhi by the twenty-first Buddha named Phussa Buddha.

Medicinal Value

Amla contains a high concentration of vitamin C, well-known within the plant kingdom– twenty times that of an orange. It is useful for healthy metabolism, digestion, and elimination of acidity. Amla plays an important role to promote anti-inflammatory properties that cool, tone and nourish tissues and organs. It nourishes the heart and respiratory system. Amla assists natural internal cleansing and maintains a healthy colon. Amla is a natural antioxidant. It promotes healthy eyes, hair, nails, and skin. It helps to get rid of Agni (digestive fire). Amla helps to build Ojas to support a healthy immune response and youthfulness. Amla pacifies Vata (catabolism), pitta (metabolism), and kaph (anabolism) though it is especially beneficial in calming pitta (metabolism). It also promotes energy and healthy cholesterol levels and maintains healthy blood sugar levels.

Nutritional Value (100 G): Energy 58 Kilo Calories

a) Fiber 3.4%

b) Proteins 0.5%

c) Fat 0.1%

d) Carbohydrates 13.7 g

e) Calcium 50 %

f) Iron 1.2 mg

g) Carotene 9 microgram

h) Thiamine 0.03mg

i) Riboflavin 0.01mg

j) Nicene 0.2mg

k) Vitamin 600mg

Famous Tree

Famous amla tree in India and the story behind worship is the Vishnu temple. King Chaitraratha of Vaidisa and his subjects were blessed with riches due to the worship of Vishnu. Once, on Amalaki Ekadashi, Chaitraratha and his subjects worshiped Vishnu and the amla tree near the Vishnu temple, on a riverbank. He also worshiped Parashurama, a sage-avatar of Vishnu.

Story of Amla Tree

The following tale adequately describes the religious importance of amla – Once upon a time, a chandala went into the forest for hunting. He hunted many deer and birds. Feeling hungry, he saw an amla tree and climbed up the tree. This way he satiated his hunger by eating sweet amla fruits.

Conclusion

Research on the Indian traditional medicinal plants is in trend. Natural medicines have the least side effects and they are more effective in the long term. Amla has an important place in Ayurveda. Amla has special features such as antioxidants and it has a huge amount of vitamin C. It is used to treat various diseases, used as food, and very important biopharmaceutical industries. Many researchers discovered the various extracts of plants and they found that they are equally effective as other standard drugs.

References:

Amalaki Ekadashi: Worship Gooseberry Tree Embodying Lord Vishnu. Apr 21, 2019, 16:49 IST

Chaurasia, A. K., Subramaniam, V. R., Krishna, B., & Sane, P. V. (2009). RAPD based genetic variability among cultivated varieties of Aonla (Indian Gooseberry, Phyllanthus emblica L.). *Physiology and Molecular Biology of Plants*, *15*(2), 169-173.

Dasaroju, S., & Gottumukkala, K. M. (2014). Current trends in the research of Emblica officinalis (Amla): A pharmacological perspective. *Int J Pharm Sci Rev Res*, *24*(2), 150-59.

Namita, P., & Mukesh, R. INTERNATIONAL RESEARCH JOURNAL OF PHARMACY.

Sangeetha, N., Mercy, S., Kavitha, M., Selvaraj, D., Sathishkumar, R., & Ganesh, D. (2010). Morphological variation in the Indian gooseberries (Phyllanthus emblica and Phyllanthus indofischeri) and the chloroplast trnL (UAA) intron as a candidate gene for their identification. *Plant Genetic Resources*, *8*(3), 191.

Trees of Ramayana (2022): 163-172
Editor: Felix Bast
Today & Tomorrow's Printers and Publishers (India)

Chapter-15

Shami Tree (*Prosopis cineraria*)

Adesh Kumar

सालैस्तालैस्तमालैश्च खर्जूरपनसाम्रकैः।

नीवारैस्तिमिशैश्चैव पुन्नागैश्चोपशोभिताः।।3.15.16।।

चूतैरशोकैस्तिलकैश्चम्पकैः केतकैरपि।

पुष्पगुल्मलतोपेतैस्तैस्तैस्तरुभिरावृताः।।3.15.17।।

चन्दनैस्पन्दनैर्नीपैः पर्णासैर्लिकुचैरपि।

धवाश्वकर्णखदिरैः शमीकिंशुकपाटलैः।।3.15.18।।

In Valmiki Ramayana, Sarga 15 in Shloka 18 in the ARANYAKAND reads that when Lord Rama reached Panchvati, they found that the place is covered with sal and Palmyra trees including mango, jackfruit, dates, kadamba, punnaga, Ashoka, champaka, tilaka, ketaka, sandalwood, spandan, dhava, asvakarna parnash, khadira, **Shami**, kimsuka, and patala trees. It is full of wild paddy, flowering bushes, and creepers that run on the ground.

पर्णशालां सुविपुलां तत्र सङ्खातमृत्तिकाम्।

सुस्तम्भां मस्करैर्दीर्घैः कृतवंशां सुशोभनाम्।।3.15. 21।।

शमीशाखाभिरास्तीर्य दृढपाशावपाशिताम्।

कुशकाशशरैः पर्णैस्सुपरिच्छादितां तथा।।3.15.22।।

The above shloka was written in Aranyakanda, Sagra 15 at number 21 says that when Laxmana was making the hut for living, he used the branches of the Shami plant and tied them across with strong ropes.

Figure: A Shami tree *(Prosopis cineraria)*. Location- Sinsini (Rajasthan) © Adesh Kmar

Introduction:

Northwest Indian regions like the Great Indian Desert known as Thar are characterized as the regions of extremely arid climate having a very low and erratic rainfall pattern, high wind speeds, and dry atmosphere. In such regions, the common species of plants having multiple benefits is *Prosopis cineraria*. Because of its myriad virtues, this tree has proved to be a boon for the local people of these regions. *Prosopis cineraria*- a small to a moderate-size tree that belongs to *Leguminosae*, and subfamily *Mimosaceae*, is native to hot regions like Arabia and several parts of India. This plant has long been used for several functions like in folk medicines for different diseases and ailments. It is also called "Kalp Taru" of arid zones. Food, fodder, fuel, lumber, medicines, gums, and tannin may all be found in the tree. ***Prosopis cineraria* are also the state tree of two Indian states- Rajasthan and Telangana.** In local communities, this tree has vast mythological importance. In the Hindu religion, this tree is highly revered and worshiped, and because of such auspiciousness, this tree is also called Lakshmi, Shiva, Sita, and many more names.

Local Name- Sami Tree is a common Indian name. Known as Khejri in Rajasthan, Banni Mara in Karnataka, Jammi chettu in Telangana, English Name- Indian Mesquite, Sanskrit Name- Shami vriksha

Taxonomic Identification (Family Features)

Kingdom: Plantae- plants

Sub Kingdom: *Tracheobionta*- Vascular plants

Super Division: *Spermatophyta*- Seed plants

Division: *Magnoliophyta*- Flowering plants

Class: *Magnoliopsida*- dicotyledons

Subclass: *Rosidae*

Order: *Fabales*

Family: Fabaceae- Pea family

Genus: Prosopis L.-Mesquite

Species: *Prosopis cineraria* (L) Druce – Jand

Botanical Name- *Prosopis cineraria*

Trade Name: Shami tree

Genetic study: *Prosopis* genus compromise about 44 species of both trees and shrubs. These are Nitrogen-fixing, fast-growing, hardy, and drought tolerant. Almost all originated in America, and are distributed in a vast variety of habitats in several countries.

Number of chromosomes: 2n =28

Description of Shami tree: Morphological features

Prosopis cineraria are a small size tree whose height ranges between 3-5 m (9.8 to 16.4 feet). The length of roots grows up to 36m in alkaline soil. Leaves of the Shami plant are alternate, bipinnate having 7-14 leaflets 4-15mm long and 2-4mm broad on each pinnate. Thorns are straight with conical bases and are present on branches with internodes. It produces small flowers with a creamy yellow color. Flowering occurs in the month of March-June. Later seeds are developed in pods. It is an evergreen tree having an open crown and thick, rough grey bark having deep fissures.

Root: Taproot more than 3 m in length is found. Due to long taproots, the khejri trees are very less affected during floods. The bark of roots is used in leather tanning.

Flowers: Yellow, glabrous flowers are present having truncate calyx, 0.8-1.2 mm in length; corolla is 3.4 mm in length. Petals roll back in age.

Fruit: Slender, elongated (8-19mm), 4-7mm in diameter with thin pericarp segmented.

Seeds: Seeds are longitudinal, ovate, and distant. Length of seeds is 6 mm.

Habitat of Plant

This tree thrives in a wide range of soil types. *P. cineraria* are found in extremely arid conditions having a very low rainfall of about 15 cm (5.9 inches) per year. It best grows in sand and clay. The presence of this tree indicates the presence of a deep water table. P. cineraria have developed tolerance to harsh conditions like highly alkaline and salt conditions.

Distribution of Shami tree

This tree is widely distributed over the globe. In India, Shami is the state tree of Rajasthan and Telangana. In India, it is distributed in Telangana, Andhra Pradesh, Rajasthan, Delhi, Gujarat, Haryana, Uttar Pradesh, and Tamil Nadu. However, distribution in India is discontinuous. It is also the provincial tree of the Sindh provincial region of Pakistan. It is also present in Afghanistan, Bahrain, Iran, Saudi Arabia, UAE, and Yemen. The Shami tree is native to arid portions of Western Asia and South Asia and is also found in Thar deserts.

Economic Significance:

It is a multipurpose tree and it plays an important role in the economy of many rural areas in arid regions notably in the Arabian Gulf and Northwest arid regions of the Indian subcontinent. The raw pods are used in making curry and pickles. Cookies and other local dishes are made from the flour of mature pods. Dry pods and leaves are used as fodder for cattle and sheep. A mature Shami tree produces 2-5 kg of dry pods. Mesquite gum, a resin that occurs naturally on the tree is also occasionally eaten by many people. Shami is a leguminous tree and it improves fertility by fixing Atmospheric Nitrogen. It produces the highest amount of litterfall which builds up the organic matter in soil under its canopy, also increases the amount of soluble Calcium and Phosphorus, and decreases the pH of soil. So farmers grow these plants in their fields to increase the crop yield. Its crown is round in shape and dense. So it provides both shade and shelter for animals and birds in summers. Its deep long roots enable the plant to get more nutrients and moisture and make the plant free of any competition. Shami is a good source of high-quality wood for basic construction work and as fuel for local people.

Fuel yield:

Khejri tree gets ready to be lopped in 8 years of its growth. It is estimated that 2-3 kg of firewood gets available during the starting 8-10 years of lopping. Timber yield: A 20-30 years old tree produces about 40-70 kg of fuelwood in a falling period of 25 years with a 350-500 mm rainfall zone. *P. cineraria* are used as the major bee foraging plant in Gulf countries like Arabian countries. As it produces a large number of long flowers, it supports honey bees and good quality honey is produced.

Nutritive Value:

As many people are suffering from nutritional deficiency of proteins around the world and especially in Asia and Africa. *P. cineraria* is a good source of protein having about 16.5- 18.25% protein content. Therefore, Prosopis seeds are a good and cheap source of protein industrially in African and Indian subcontinent countries and they can be used as an alternate source of proteins for solving the problem of malnutrition. In addition to protein content, this plant contains a good amount of fibers (20.93%). The chemical composition of pods varies from plant to plant and is influenced by several environmental factors. The pods have low moisture content (8.55%) which increases the shelf life of pods, 18% proteins, 1.89% oil, 5.34% ash, and 20.93% fiber. The seeds contain about 10.6% oils of which 28.6% are saturated fatty esters, 68.3% are unsaturated fatty esters and 3.1% are methyl hydroxy fatty esters. The seed oil is rich in Linoleic acid (32.1%) and Oleic acid (31.3%). There are no kero, cyclopropenoid, and epoxy fatty acids or any trans-unsaturation or conjugation in oils or seeds. Moreover, the leaves are rich in macro minerals such as calcium (2.43%), phosphorus (0.16%), and potassium (0.41%). Hence, Shami trees can be used as a good source of nutrition in deficient periods.

Uses of Shami as Nutritional source

P. cineraria is extensively used for nutritional requirements in many areas of arid regions or semi-deserts. Different parts of the plant are used differently as food sources.

Vegetables

During famine periods in dry regions, leguminous Prosopis trees are used to prevent protein and mineral deficiency. People eat unripe green pods and sell them in markets as vegetables and ripened fruits are also eaten. Green, unripe pods are also used for making pickles and curry.

Flour:

The pods of *Prosopis* consist of 3 parts namely mesocarp (56%), grounded to produce flour, endocarp (35%) which is discarded with the seeds (9%). The flour is often used to make chapati, bread, cakes, and sweets when combined with wheat flour. Prosopis flour is rich in proteins (62%), dietary fiber, and low content of carbohydrates and fats with free polyphenols and carotenoid compounds. This flour contains no gluten and is a good source of macronutrients like magnesium, potassium, calcium, zinc, iron and it also contains amino acids like lysine. *Prosopis* flour is recommended by doctors for diabetes patients to maintain a healthy insulin system because the digestion of this flour takes 4–6 hours and also it contains fructose which is processed by the body without insulin.

Syrups and Drinks:

Many fermented and non-fermented beverages and syrups are made from *Prosopis* species. To produce nutritious syrup, pods are broken into pieces and boiled. Beans are simmered for 2 hours with the constant addition of a small amount of water to prevent burning. After this, pods are smashed to release more sweet pulp. The juice is now sieved and stored in clean containers for drinking directly. Some more sugar may be added to juice to produce the desired flavor.

Gum:

A type of amber-colored gum is also produced by the P. cineraria tree. It has properties similar to gum produced by acacia. The exudate gum is a water-soluble liquid and hardens slowly. Another type of interesting gum, galactomannan type, called the vimal gum is also produced by the P. cineraria.

Cultural Significance:

Shami tree is highly sacred in Hindus. It is worshiped as a part of the festival Dussehra on the tenth day. In Rajputs, the kings and high priests used to worship and liberate a jay thought to be the sacred bird of Lord Rama. On the other hand, in Deccan, Marathas used to shoot the Sami tree with arrows and collect the leaves in their turbans as a part of their culture. In Karnataka, the Shami tree is considered the tree where Pandavas hide their weapons while they were on a thirteen-year exile. When they came back, they worshiped and thanked the tree and took their celestial weapons back. In Jat traditions, the Khejri plants green and dried branches are brought home from farms on the day of Baan which is then worshiped by the marrying girl or boy's mother. An interesting description of the Khejri tree is found in a couplet which is spoken during the time of marriage in Rajasthan in Brahmin culture. When the groom comes on the horse for marriage, then he used to say the following couplet-

"Anti tutti Khejri, panofullan chayi

Shabash mere sasuji, they latkan beti jayee"

It describes the irregular shape of a tree with blooming flowers and leaves. The groom says thanksgiving words to his mother-in-law for giving birth to such a beautiful girl and offering him to marry her.

NOTE: A postal stamp on Khejri was issued by the Indian Postal Department in 1988.

Spiritual significance

At the festival of Diwali, Khejri leaves are soaked in water used for taking bath. This water is thought to be sin cleansing and auspicious. While taking bath a mantra is also chanted. Shami tree is also considered as the residence of the goddess, Devi. It is not recommended to make the bed from its wood as it is considered as evil resides in it. Such a bed is not suitable for sleeping. Kalidasa, Banabhatt, and Varahamihira have mentioned the Shami tree in their work. Sheppards don't cut this tree as they believe gods reside in these trees.

Medicinal significance of *P. cineraria*

Leaves: Farmers use leaves to make compost and use it as fertilizer for their crops. Leaves can also be used to control insects and fungus because they have some insecticidal and fungicidal activity. Humans use Shami leaves extracts to kill parasitic worms in the intestine. Burned leaves smoke can cure eye problems.

Bark: Dyes, tannins, and fibers can be obtained from Bark of Prosopis. Medicines prepared from its bark can be used to cure Stomach, Skin, and Eye problems, Rheumatism, Leprosy, Dysentery, Bronchitis, Asthma, Leucoderma, and Piles. Water-soluble extracts of stem bark contain Anti-inflammatory properties. Scorpion sting is also cured by the bark. Tasty and nutritive gum is produced by the plant.

Flowers: To prevent miscarriage in pregnant women, the Prosopis flower is pounded and mixed with sugar and taken by pregnant women.

Pod and Seeds: Urino-genital disease is treated with the use of Pods. Seeds have hypoglycemic activity. To stop the growth of armpit hairs permanently, a paste of Shami seeds is used. This paste stops the growth of hair follicles permanently. Pods are rich in protein and carbohydrates and they are a part of animal fodder. It is like dessert fruit and is one of the main ingredients of vegetables and pickel. *Prosopis cineraria* pods have nutritive values as Vitamin A and C, proteins, iron, and other micronutrients.

Shami is a member of the Panchabhringa group of trees which contains five trees- Devadali, Shami, Bhrunga, Nirgundi, and Sanaka. When a person gets cured of his disease, these five herbs are used for taking baths. The water is boiled with these herbs. This acts as a disinfectant and increases strength.

Pharmacology

The bark is useful for treating diabetes as it has antihyperglycemic and antioxidative potential. Leaves have hyperlipidaemic activity. So it is useful in controlling lipid levels. It decreases LDL and increases HDL. Dried pods have antibacterial activity against E.coli, Klebsiella pneumoniae, Pseudomonas aeruginosa, Salmonella typhi. In powdered form, this plant material possesses analgesic, anti-depressant, muscle relaxant andante-pyretic effect.

Folkore uses

To avoid unexpected abortion in pregnant women, Shami flowers are triturated and mixed with sugar candy, and given to the women. In central provinces, the bark is used for treating rheumatism (watt). In Bharwad and Punjab, pods are used for making vegetable curry. Shami plant bark is used for the treatment of osteoarthritis in western India.

Other medicinal uses

Shami Tree is used for treating vertigo and also as a tonic for the brain. On a scorpion sting, a paste of Shami bark is applied. To remove hairs, ash of fruit is applied locally. To prevent miscarriage, flowers are mixed with sugar and administered. Pods are thought to possess astringent, demulcent, and pectoral properties, hence are eaten green, dried, or after boiling. Pods serve as fodder for livestock. In times of scarcity, pulp, before ripened, is eaten as it is rich in the sweetish farinaceous pulp. The bark is used to make cakes after grinding in flour. Galls formed on the leaves and barks are used for tanning. Leaves are used for making green manure.

Traditional use of *Prosopis*: Shami plant has been used as a human diet in Rajasthan for a long time. The famous "Marwari Mewa" is nothing but the dry pods of Prosopis cineraria. Marwari Mewa reduces water craving in summers. When milch animals eat Prosopis cineraria, milk production increases rapidly.

Environment conservation:

Prosopis cineraria fix environmental nitrogen, improves fertility and texture of the soil. Because of its extensive tap root system, it does not compete for nutrients with other crop plants. Crops under the Shami canopy show good yields because of the increased nutrient quality of the soil. Because of the deep taproot system, it prevents the shifting of dunes. As it is the only commonly grown plant in arid regions, it is the most needed shade and shelter for farmers on fields and also for cattle during hard summers. Besides their pods are eaten by cattle and other animals in the desert, Shami is the main source of surviving food material for Blackbuck and Chinkara in western Rajasthan.

Famous stories and Mythological Beliefs about Shami tree

"On the 10th day of Bhadrapad in 1730, Maharaja Abhaysingh of Jodhpur sent men to cut Khejri tree in Khejarli village. A lot of fireworks were needed to produce lime for the new royal palace. Amrita Devi, a local Bishnoi woman sent them back in defense of Khejri trees. They retaliated with armed soldiers but Amrita Devi embraced Khejri trees and challenged the soldiers to ax her head to spare Khejri trees. The obedient soldiers not only severed Amrita Devi`s head but went on to kill 363 Bishnois who dared to follow the courageous lady. The news of Bishnois Sacrifice for Khejri trees reached the king who then apologized to Bishnois and assured protection to trees and wild animals in that region. "

Pandavas had hidden their weapons in the hollows of the Shami tree.

Shami leaves are a favorite of Lord Ganesha; so leaves are offered for Ganesh Pooja.

Oldest Shami tree- At least 100 years old, the Shami tree at Gupchup Ganesh temple in Pune is considered to be the world's oldest tree.

Conclusions

The Shami plant has immense benefits as it can grow in harsh environments, degraded soil and it also has several medicinal values. As observed from different studies, this plant has pharmaceutical and medicinal qualities and hence it's used to treat a variety of chronic illnesses. But, still, large research work is required. It is used as a remedy for many ailments and disorders in Ayurveda. All of its parts like leaves, bark, flowers, and fruits are used as medicines for several diseases. The Shami plant is planted to bring back the vegetation in arid regions as it promotes the growth of other plants. According to Vastu Shastra, This plant is considered to be lucky. The Indian government needs to take few steps to take proper care of this tree in deserts to control pests and insects. The number of Khejri trees has declined in the Thar Desert also in recent years. It is mainly due to lowering water levels and increased pests and insects. It is a cheaper and easily available medicinal and food source for local people in arid regions.

References

Khatri, A., Rathore, A., & Patil, U. K. (2010). Prosopis cineraria (L.) Druce: a boon plant of desert—an overview. *International Journal of Biomedical and Advance Research*, *1*(5), 141-149.Religious tradition of conservation associated with greater abundance of a keystone tree species in rural Western Rajasthan, India by Jonathan C. Hall, Ian M. Hamilton

Khatri, A., Rathore, A., & Patil, U. K. (2010). Prosopis cineraria (L.) druce: a boon plant of desert—an overview. *International Journal of Biomedical and Advance Research*, *1*(5), 141-149.

Gorain, M., Charan, S. K., & Ahmed, S. I. (2012). Role of insect bees in the pollination of Prosopis cineraria (L.) Druce (Leguminosae, Subfamily Mimosoideae) in Rajasthan. *Advances in Applied Science Research*, *3*(6), p3448-3451.

Sandison, M. S., & Harris, P. J. C. (1991). Prosopis cineraria: a multipurpose tree for arid areas. *Prosopis cineraria: a multipurpose tree for arid areas.*, (91-04).

Islam, M. W., Hassan, N. A., Bloukh, S. H., Shahwan, M., & Bhandare, R. R. (2019). Exploring the literature on Prosopis cineraria Linn. for its therapeutic potential and safety: A review. *Int. Res. J. Pharm*, *10*(7), 1-8.

Trees of Ramayana (2022): 173-181
Editor: Felix Bast
Today & Tomorrow's Printers and Publishers (India)

Chapter-16

Sandalwood Tree (*Santalum album*)

Himanshu Harsh

श्रोत्रं श्रुतेनेव न तु कुंडलेन दानेन पाणिर्न तु कंकणेन ।

विभाति कायः करुणापराणाम परोपकारेर्न तु चन्दनेन। । 27

Sandalwood is described in the sloka of volume 6, chapter 109, and sloka number 27 of Valmiki's Ramayana. The sloka is that the person's ear seems to improve by hearing knowledgeable things, not by earrings, donating something more suited to hand than it is suited by bangles. In the same way, the person's body seems to be more beautiful by helping others rather than applying sandalwood's cream on it.

Figure:- Sandalwood tree. (Photo captured in Botanical garden of Regional Institute of Education, Bhubaneswar, Odisha.) © Himanshu Harsh

Indian sandalwood is the common name for *Santalum album.* It is a religious tree with is widely used in pharmaceuticals and domestic as well as on festival occasions. In Sanskrit, Sandalwood is said as "chandanam ",

"Chandan" in Hindi and "Boga Chandan" in Assam, "suket" in Gujarat, "Gondassaro" in Odisha.

Taxonomic Position:

Kingdom: Plantae

Division: Angiosperm

Class: Eudicots

Order: Santales

Family: Santalaceae

Genus: *Santalum*

Species: *album*

Morphological Characteristics

Size: 12 to 15 meters long, and 1 to 2.5 meters girth.

Habit: the plant is mostly upright with spiraling, and can be intertwined around other plants.

Tree life: they can live approximately 100 years.

Root: they have mostly tap root, which is highly developed because of the semi-parasitic nature of plants and they take part in root grafting with the host plant which results in an exchange of nutrients from the host plant to this through root attached connection.

Stem: bark is reddish or dark brown and the inner side of it is Red. When the plant is in its early stages of development, it is smooth, but after aging, it becomes hard.

Leaves: it is opposite, sometimes alternate, sometimes ovate or ovate-lanceolate, they have 1.5 to 3-inch long leaf size, protected by a powdery bloom in the lower side of the leaf, waxy layer makes it shiny, and not any hair. Young leaves are pinkish green in color but after maturity, it becomes greenish-yellow in color

Flower: straw- yellow colored flower, but after maturity it turns to deep purplish brown, mostly axillary or terminal in position and floral organs are developed in an acropetal manner. It takes 30 to 35 days to reach the bud stage from its initial stage and 85 to 95 days from the initial stage to ripening of fruit. Its breeding system is facultatively allogamous with the variation found between species. It cannot reproduce through apomixis or parthenocarpy.

Fruit: size is 0.3 inch to 0.5 inches in diameter, color is purplish-black at maturity, succulent drupes, having single seed with brown endocarp, are fit to eat i.e., edible, shape varies from ovate to elongate, initially they are greenish but after maturity, it turns to purplish-black. Direct drying of the seeds affects their viability by reducing them. It follows the epigeal form of germination.

Habitat: there are almost 19 species of the Santalum genus, and it is widely distributed all over India. Indian Sandalwood is generally distributed from Indonesia in the east to Juan Fernandez Islands (Chile) in the west and from Hawaiian Archipelago in the North to New Zealand in the south. In India, Sandalwood is widely distributed all over the country with the southern part of Karnataka to the Northern part of Tamil Nadu being a Natural area. There are other states in India where this tree is found are: Kerala, Andhra Pradesh, and the isolated populations are found in Bihar, Gujarat, Haryana, Maharashtra, Madhya Pradesh, Odisha, Punjab, Rajasthan, Tamil Nadu, Uttar Pradesh, West Bengal, Himachal Pradesh, and Assam. Because of its fragrant, medicinal, and cultural value, it is highly useful for us and that's why most people planted it in their field also.

Origin of Sandalwood:

The sandalwood tree is native to India, Australia, Hawaii, New Caledonia, Vanuatu, Indonesia, and other Pacific Islands. But some research shows that the sandalwood tree originated in Australia. The dispersal of sandalwood seed takes place millions of years ago across different continents and islands. According to American Journal, it is because of ocean currents which help in the dispersal of seed and some migratory birds also played important role in transporting this accidentally because of its red, purple, blackish fruits, and because of the fragrance of wood and the sandalwood fruits have a thick and hard layer in the exterior which may not allow destroying the seed, consequently transferring of the seed in long distances. The world's oldest fossil of trees was found in Cairo, New York which was 386 million years old, and this is older than the forest fossils that were found at Giloba, in New York State.

Economic values: In all over the world Sandalwood is known for its heartwood and its very costly oil. Its oil can be used as antiseptic and astringent; it is useful in the treatment of headaches, stomachaches, and urinary and genital disorders.

Cultural Significance:

India is a culturally rich country, and for more than 5000 years, it practices sandalwood oil production for perfumery and medicinal purposes. The aroma of the oil is used by many religions of the world i.e., Hinduism, Buddhism, and Islam. In Vamana Purana, the wood of sandalwood should be used for worshipping Lord Shiva. According to Vaivarta Purana, Goddess Lakshmi lives in the Sandalwood tree. It is also a tradition of Hindu communities to put the sandalwood in the funeral fire to let their soul in peace which also has many scientific values. Sandalwood is also used in another way in Hindu culture by applying a paste of the wood on the face and the body on God's body for ritual bathing purposes and to make them clean and sacred. In Egypt, the wood of this tree is used for medicinal purposes, in ritual burning to respect the traditions and the Gods.

The global economy of the tree:

Sandalwood produces one the best timber and fuel in terms of quality and because of this, it is extremely important to the country's economy. In India, the sandalwood is largely produced in the south part of the country in the Deccan region. From the time of the Tipu sultan to the current time, 90% of natural sandalwood production takes place in the southern and northern parts of Karnataka and Tamil Nadu respectively. But it decreased over 70 years ago because of heavy utilization and deforestation and few plantations of this tree. This causes a global shortage of this tree and the price of its timber hike. According to IUCN, the sandalwood tree comes under the vulnerable category because of the heavy utilization of the tree. Other reports also suggest that because of smuggling, the spoiling of this tree takes place. A huge amount of sandalwood losses takes place when the spike disease attacks on the trees, it led to huge economic loss almost 700,000 sandalwood tree in Mysore and 350,000 sandalwood tree in erstwhile Coorg state suffered from Spike disease, during 1903-1916, this was later cured by arsenical solution. And now, Kerala also produces large amounts of sandalwood timbers. In a report of 2011-2012, this state produced almost 45.15 tonnes of sandalwood whereas, in that time, Karnataka produced only 3.52 tonnes of sandalwood. Because of this several traditional artisans of Karnataka got affected.

After that government of Karnataka decided for sorting of sandalwood takes place in different classification i.e., Vilayat Budh (this is a sound billet which weigh 9kg and needs 112 pieces per tonnes of sandalwood), China Budh (this is inferior billet weigh 4.5kg and supplied 224 pieces per tonnes of sandalwood), Panjam (this is billet having small size knots and hollow weigh 2.2kg and supplied 448 pieces per tonnes of sandalwood), Ghotla (the billet are small in size having sound pieces. This has no weigh limit), Ghatbadla(the billets having cracks, tiny hollows and have knotsweigh 4.5kg and supplied 250 pieces per tonnes of sandalwood), Bagadad(it is a solid piece which don't need any fixed dimension or numbers), RootsI (this is a piece weigh 6.75kg and its limit is 150 pieces per tonnes of sandalwood), RootII (it is a piece weigh 2.25 kg and its limit is 448pieces per tonnes of sandalwood), RootIII (it is small or tiny root weighless than 2.25kg), Jajpokal I(it is a hollow piece weigh 3.1kg and its limit is 320 pieces per tonnes of sandalwood), Japokal II (it is a hollow piece weigh 1.3kg per tonnes of sandalwood), Ainbagar(it is a solid , hollow, ,cracked pieces weigh 450g), China Sali(It is like a chip of heartwood of sandalwood weigh 2.25g), Ain Chilta(It is a tiny piece of heartwood), Hatri Chilta(it contains heartwood and chips can be extracted by plaining billets), Milva Chilta(it is the small piece of equal proportions of sapwood and heartwood of sandalwood), Basola Bukni(it contains tiny heartwood and sapwood pieces), Saw dust(it is a sawn powder can be extracted by sawing of the sandalwood).

Medicinal and Food value:

Sandalwood is one of the traditional medicines which holds much more importance in our day-to-day life. Sandalwood oil was used to treat skin diseases, gonorrhea, dysentery, acne, face Wash, e.t.c. It is also considered a very good sedating agent. There is the presence of certain chemicals that causes a strong odor and pleasant smell and they are alpha-Santalol and Beta-Santalols. The alpha-Santalol contains anti-bacterial properties and the Beta-Santalol contains sedative properties. Indian sandalwood contains the highest amount of alpha-Santalol and Beta-Santalol in the world.

Because of the presence of the following chemicals, sandalwood helps treat skin-related diseases such as dry skin, itchy skin, and acne. Besides this, it is also effective in treating bronchitis, laryngitis, dry cough, sore throats. It is also helpful in diarrhea, nausea, insomnia, cystic fever, hyperacidity, stress, vex, mood enhancer, dermatitis, arthritis, etc. In medicine as well as the food industry, it can be used as an antidepressant, provide relief in stressful conditions, used as a tonic to make the mind hyperactive, disinfectant genitourinary tract, stringent as well as sedative. In chewing materials like scented tobacco, zarda, gutkha, pan masala, and others, the sandalwood smell with rose smell or jasmine plays a vital role in producing fragrance in it.

Research on sandalwood:

Researchers' study shows that there is a large amount of diversity within the sandalwood species by using isozyme, RAPD, and RFLP, as in Karnataka, which shows a high amount of diversity within the population. The research was conducted in 1980 which shows that the variations are present in the color of heartwood as well as the presence of oil content in it. Another research also shows that there is variation in the presence of heartwood with the same thickness of trees in the same population and it was also found that there is also the absence of heartwood in almost 13% of the population. A study performed in the aged clonal germplasm of sandalwood shows that there is a presence of variation in oil content and the heartwood diameter. In Australia, a study conducted on 14 years old trees shows that there is no production of heartwood in 20% of the tree. There is research conducted on sandalwood tree by using Agrobacterium tumefaciens (for transforming suitable genes) and in vitro somatic embryo method to produce transgenic sandalwood which has a resistance to spike disease, and to produce more oil content and more heartwood content but the other researcher (Jones and Plummer) stated that the transgenic sandalwood cannot compete with natural sandalwood as it will quickly lose the attention of people., therefore the traditional breeding method is the best one to grow the tree.

Cultivation:

Sandalwood has succulent drupe fruit, but the fruit is easily attacked by a fungal infection that' why for processing of seed, fruit is rubbed on a rough surface and the seed is put out from there. But these seeds are hydrated, that's why drying is performed under shady areas under the direct sun's heat condition to protect seed from going to permanent dormancy stage. The diameter of the seed is 0.5-1cm and the weight is 0.1g to 0.2g. There is a fact that less the weight of seed more is the rate of germination and more is a vigorous seed.

Before sowing, the seed is put under gibberellic acid solution (500ppm w/v) for almost one day i.e., 24 hours for the proper growth of the plant. In case of choosing a medium for growth of seed, sand is the best medium and November and December is the best season for sowing of these seeds so that it can be available at the time of monsoon season (June- July). Srinivasan et al. (1992) suggested that there should be the use of sand and soil mixture in ratio 1:3, and 500g of seed /sq.m. is performed for proper germination of seed.

Sandalwood shows the epigeal form of germination, where radicals come out first from seed, then hypocotyls come out on the ground, which is swollen and fleshy. The germination of the seed begins on the 20th day and continues for up to 45 days. After reaching 3-4 leaf stages, the plantlets were transferred to the polybag for easy transportation to the market. Annapurna et al.(2004-2005) suggested getting the plantation seedling in six months, on the need to put the plantlet in 270cc container and provide the nutrient-rich compost, sand, soil, rice husks, cocopeat, and charcoal in ratio 50:25:15:5:5 with 6x6 holes/sq. inch. One can provide a suitable host for it for proper growth and continuous supply of nutrients because of its partial parasitic nature.

Ecological importance:

Sandalwood is one the crucial tree which is of intermediate size. It grows a good amount in its initial stages of life in shady areas, but the demand for light increases with its continuous growth and it becomes higher when it is at the late stages of life. It can grow 1800metres above the sea level or in rainfall between 600 to 1600mm, or cold climates also. It can grow in soils like sand, clay, red soils, laterite soils, e.t.c. but it shows good growth in red ferruginous loam. But it cannot grow in cold areas or water-logged areas. It shows self-incompatibility and the pollination takes place through cross-pollination by insects like bees, wasps, e.t.c. Birds eat pulp only and leave the remains of fruit.

The quality of heartwood oil varies highly from species to species and because of geographical regions also. Among all sandalwood species, the *Santalum album* is the best which produces good quality fragrance, aroma, timber, and oil also and it is very much demanded by the perfume industry. Genetic divert of the tree in Karnataka is more than in any other state in India. The largest plantation of *Santalum album* in the world was set up in Kimberley, Western Australia.

There are also various pests and diseases studied by various Indian researchers in *S.album*, Sundaraj (2012) found that there are 92 sap-suckers, 60 defoliators, some stem borers, 5 barks, and deadwood feeders, 3 are seed feeders, 3 dry wood feeders, and one flower feeders. But these pests are not much harmful to the sandalwood. Remadevi (2012) also performed an observational experiment on the sandalwood affected by termites, and she found that the termite causes' biodeterioration and this causes degrading the quality of wood or log, and later on she found that light causes decreasing the activity of these termites.

Tourism place:

Marayoor is one of those beautiful places where the largest amount of sandalwood is produced naturally. It is almost near the border of Tamil Nadu and Kerala. There is very pleasant weather and the average temperature in summer is up to 30 degrees Celsius and in winter it is 8 degrees Celsius. In the way of sandalwood forest, there are other cultivating areas also like tea fields and there is also a beautiful scenery of waterfalls. There is also a cave where many paintings are made and this shows that this cave was visited by "Lord Rama and Sita". There is "Rajiv Gandhi National Park" which is also a good place for tourists to spend time with friends or family. There is a waterfall named "Thoovanam Waterfalls" where people /tourists can see the beautiful scenery of nature.

Conservation:

In the present situation, IUCN (International Union for Conservation of Nature and Natural Resources) put sandalwood among the "vulnerable" species category because of heavy exploitation of these trees. Over the past few decades, it declines rapidly. In India, production of sandalwood goes down from 4000 MT to 500MT and this data is from 1950 to 2007, respectively. According to Harbaugh, species like *S. haleakele* was extensively exploited by humans which is why this species comes under the threatened species category. To stop these things, there are many organizations established like the International Sandalwood Foundation from the United States, Iliahi Foundation Of sandalwood in Hawaii. Besides this, many governments of different countries like India, Sri Lanka, Australia, Hawaii, and New Caledonia also took major steps towards the conservation of sandalwood forests.

In India, the Karnataka and Tamil Nadu government took major steps towards the conservation of sandalwood trees. They improved the existing policies to enhance the number of trees in the state. They allowed the private residents to grow the sandalwood in their lands. The Government of Karnataka also amended the act i.e., Karnataka Forest Act (2001) to allow the people to grow sandalwood as a way to save them (Dhanya et al, 2010). This act will provide the legal right of the citizen to grow the sandalwood in their garden or backyard. Following Karnataka, in 2002 Tamil Nadu also amended their Forest act of 1998, and legalized the plantation of sandalwood in private land (Dhanya et al, 2010).

Future aspects of Sandalwood:

In Australia, the production of Indian sandalwood increased rapidly with the help of a scientific method of plantation of 5000 hectares of sandalwood in 2011. They also intend to boost the sandalwood production by planting sandalwood in 2000 hectares of Western Australia.

In India, there are some organizations such as the National Medicinal Plant Board and National Horticulture Mission that are helping the government to the plantation of sandalwood with other important medicinal plants. After the success of the Karnataka government, the farmers of states like Gujarat, Andhra Pradesh, Madhya Pradesh, Maharashtra, Rajasthan, and Assam also use their land for the production of sandalwood which is about 5000 hectares.

References:

Kumar, A. A., Joshi, G., & Ram, H. M. (2012). Sandalwood: history, uses, present status, and the future. *Current Science*, 1408-1416.

Annapurna, D., Rathore, T. S., & Joshi, G. (2004). Effect of container type and size on the growth and quality of seedlings of Indian sandalwood (Santalum album L.). Australian forestry, 67(2), 82-87.

Subasinghe, S. M. C. U. P. (2013). Sandalwood research: a global perspective. *Journal of Tropical Forestry and Environment*, *3*(1), 1-8.

Venkatesha Gowda, V. S. (2011, October). Global emerging trends on the sustainable production of natural sandalwood. In Proceedings of the Art and Joy of Wood Conference, Bangalore, India (pp. 19-22).

H S Ananthapadmanabha and V S Venketeswara Gowda. 2011. Sustainable Supply of Global Sandalwood for Industry. *Proceedings of art and joy of wood conference.*

Ramesh Chandra Mishra .2011. Sandalwood: The Saviour of Ecological Balance Wealth Creator. *Proceedings of art and joy of wood conference.*

Ralph.T.H.Griffith.1873. Ramayana of Valmiki. Vol.6, Chapter 109.

Trees of Ramayana (2022): 183-192
Editor: Felix Bast
Today & Tomorrow's Printers and Publishers (India)

Chapter-17

Ashoka Tree *(Saraca asoca)*

Pratikshya Priyadarshini

वादित्ररवसङ्घुष्टं कुब्जा वामनिकायुतम्।

लतागृहैश्चित्रगृहैश्चम्पकाशोकशोभितैः।।2.10.13।।

The above shloka from the Ayodhya Kand, Sarg 10 and shloka 13 states that "The maharaja entered the inner apartment of Kaikeyi's prosperous abode filled with parrots and peacocks, reverberating with cries of kraunchas and swans and sounds of musical instruments attended with hunchbacks and dwarfs decorated with champak and Ashoka trees, bowers surrounded with creepers, picture galleries, altars and sofas embellished with ivory, gold, and silver."

अशोक शोकापनुद शोकोपहतचेतसम्।

त्वन्नामानं कुरु क्षिप्रं प्रियासन्दर्शनेन माम्।।3.60.17।।

In this shloka from the Aranyakanda, Sarga 60 and shloka 17, Lord Rama says to the Ashoka tree "O Ashoka tree, dispeller of sorrow, by quickly showing me my darling make me Ashoka (free from sorrow) as I am grief-stricken at heart."

Figure: Image of Ashoka Tree (*Saraca asoca*) © Pratikshya Priyadarshini

Scientific classification:

Kingdom: Plantae

Clade: Tracheophytes

Clade: Angiosperms

Clade: Eudicots

Clade: Rosids

Order: Fabales

Family: Fabaceae

Subfamily: Detarioideae

Genus: *Saraca*

Species: *asoca*

Common names:

Assamese: Ahok, Ashok-goch, Ashok, English: Ashokam, Ashok tree, Gujarati: Ashopalava, Hindi: Sita Ashok, Ashok, Kannada: Achenge, Karbi: Mir krem, Malayalam: Ashokam, Hema Pushpam, Marathi: Jasundi, Others: Sorrowless Tree, Sita Ashok, Tamil: Ashoka Tree, Asogam, Telugu: Asokamu

Distribution of the tree:

Asoka has its distribution throughout India, but naturally and frequently found in South India, Sri Lanka, Odisha, and Assam. The plant may also be found in the central and eastern Himalayas at elevations of up to 750 meters. Asoka tree was originated or first grown in the central areas of the Deccan plateau and also some regions of Western Ghats. It is widely cultivated in the foothills of the Himalayas, northern plains, Bengal, and the Deccan plateau in the South (Bhalerao et al.,). Their growth is ideally suited to tropical and subtropical climates. It grows well in slightly acidic and neutral soil.

Morphological Characteristics

In India, the Asoka tree has cultural and religious significance. Its name originated from the Sanskrit word, which means "without sorrow" or "gives no grief". This tree is also known as the Sita tree and tree of love. The other names of the tree are: Anganapriya, Ashopalava, Asupala, Apashaka, Hemapushpa, Kankeli, Madhupushpa, Pindapushpa, Pindipushpa, Vanjula, Vishoka and Achenge.

It is a slow-growing, small, erect, evergreen tree and its height is up to 6-9 meters. The color of its leaves is copper brown generally, but the growing leaves turned into a light green color gradually and finally turned into deep green color. The length of the leaves is around 15- 25 cms. The shape of the leaves is lance-like and becomes wavy at the edges. These leaves are mainly used for the decoration of the entrance of temples.

Asoka flowers are small and are found in clusters. They generally bloom from Feb to May months. The flowers have four oval lobes, which resemble the petals of the flowers. Along with its beauty, it produces a sweet fragrance. The color of the flower changes with the period. In the 1st stage, flowers are yellow, and then it becomes crimson red. In spring, the tree is full of green flowers, which also matches the color of the leaves. The fruits are like broad beans, which contain 6-8 grey color seeds. May and June are good months for growing Asoka trees, which are propagated via stem cutting. When we cultivate the Asoka tree on a large scale, it is difficult to propagate through seeds. Moreover, this species is now going to be extinct day by day. So, proper care should be taken to protect this tree, which has not only cultural importance but also medicinal importance.

In the Asoka tree, the flowering process takes place in the early growth phase and produces profuse flowers in clusters at the age of 6-9 years. It produces fruits from July to October months. The Ashoka tree survives for about 50 years. At the age of 20 years, it can bark. The bark is collected without cutting down the tree and with a pattern of vertical stripes. The peeled-off areas of the tree are renewed by fresh bark within one to two years. Tannins (0.57 % -7.85 %), ash (2.43 % -6.69 %), and other extracts are all found in Asoka bark (5.74 % -14.07 %). A total of one tonne of dry bark is collected per hectare from a sole crop.

Varieties of Ashoka tree:

Asoka or Sarcosa:

It is used in Ayurvedic precautions. It is grown bushy, large, and with thick bark. Its fruit looks like broad beans containing 6-8 grey color seeds. In India, these trees are going to be distinct day by day. These are mostly found in royal palaces and temples.

False Asoka:

These trees have high resemblances with the Asoka tree but it is different by its compound leaves, flowers, etc. Its scientific name is *Polyalithia longifolia*. It is commonly known as the Buddha tree, also the Indian Fir tree. Its height is up to 30 meters. It grows without branches. It has flowers of apple green color and a single fruit. This tree is effective in combating noise pollution. It is also known as the Indian Mast tree as its bark is used to make a mast for the ships.

Mythology & traditions:

The Asoka tree is considered a sacred tree by the whole people throughout the Indian subcontinents, especially in India, Nepal, and Sri Lanka. This tree has many folks, religious and literary associations in the region. This tree is highly valued for its handsome appearance, its color, and abundance of clusters of flowers.

It is mostly found in the royal palaces, gardens, and temples also throughout India. It is used in Ayurvedic precautions. It is grown bushy, large, and with thick bark. Its fruit looks like broad beans containing 6-8 grey color seeds (Borokar et al.,). In India, these trees are going to be distinct day by day.

According to Indian mythology, in the Lumbini garden, there was an Asoka tree, under which Shakyamuni Buddha was born. So, this tree is closely connected with the Yakshi mythological beings. The sculpture of Yakshini is an Indian art that is often found at the gates of Buddhist and

Hindu temples. In this sculpture, Yakshini put her foot on the trunk and put her hands around the branch of the Asoka tree. This is an artistic element of our Indian art and is used for heavy stylization. Some authors also reported that the young holding the Asoka tree might have some connection with fertility. In Buddhist monuments, it is often utilized as a decorative element, which is often found in ancient Buddhist archaeological sites. With the coming centuries, Yakshi under the Asoka tree has become a standard decorative element of Hindu culture and Buddhist monuments. This standard decorative element of Yakshini and the Asoka tree is also integrated into the architecture of Indian temples, which is named Salabhanjika. This name was given because, at that time, there was always confusion between the Asoka tree and the Sal tree (*Shorea robusta*) in ancient Indian literature.

In Hindu culture, the Asoka tree is considered a sacred tree. There are a lot of local traditions connected to it. According to various traditions and mythology, it is known that the Asoka tree is worshipped in Chaitra, which is a month of the Hindu calendar. The Asoka tree is also connected with Kamadeva, who is the Hindu god of love. He introduced the blossom of the Asoka tree among the five flowers in his quiver. From those five flowers, Asoka represents hypnotic seduction. Moreover, the Asoka tree is often described in various poetries as it has at least 16 different Sanskrit names.

In Mahakavya or various Indian poetries, the Ashoka tree is described, mainly in Ramayana because Hanuman 1st meets Sita at the Ashoka Vatika. In Vishnu Purana, the Asoka tree is described as Sita Mata was kept in the garden of Ravana's palace, which is known as Asoka Vatika or Asoka Vana. In Asoka Vatika, Mandodari, the queen of Ravana came to meet Sita Mata. At that place also, Hanuman 1st came to meet Mata Sita. In Asoka Vatika, wife of Lord Rama, Sita Devi was kept in Lanka in the captivity of Ravana. It was said before that the Asoka tree was slightly bent. It is not to provide shelter but to show respect for Sita Devi in Asoka Vatika in Ravana's palace. It is also stated that in Vaishali, Lord Mahavira claimed this world by sitting under this Asoka tree. Also, Lord Buddha was born under the Asoka tree in the Lumbini garden. This tree is also considered as a symbol of love by the God of Love, Kamadeva as He used this flower for seductive hypnosis. This tree is also connected to Yakshi, a young girl, who was standing under the Asoka tree putting her feet on the trunk and was holding the branches of the Asoka tree.

The Asoka tree is considered a sacred tree in India, Nepal, and Sri Lanka. According to Indian tradition, women pray to the tree on the 1 day of Chaitra Shukla Padyami, which is the first day of the New Year of the Hindu Calendar from March through April. Asoka Shashthi is celebrated in Bengal regions whose main reason is to protect their children from sorrow, grief, and pain. They also consume the flower washing water to calm their mind, which ultimately brings joy, and prevents grief and sorrow.

Asoka is the State tree in Uttar Pradesh. In Orissa, the Asoka flower is the state flower. In Chhattisgarh, women boil the bark in cow's milk, add sugar and consume it once a day for three days and repeat it after three months to prevent gynecological problems. The Asoka tree or Asoka Vatika where Sita Mata took shelter is now located in Hakgala Botanical garden. This place is also named Seetha Eliya, which is situated close to the city of Nuwara Eliya in Lanka.

Usages of different parts of the tree:

Asoka is an astringent and analgesic agent. It is used for medical purposes. Astringent property is used as a treatment for womb problems along with other medicine. It is highly effective in case of gynecological problems, stimulating the uterus, the endometrial, and the ovarian tissues. It is also an effective treatment for uterine bleeding and other menstrual disturbances. It has also a great effect on the circulatory system that is used for the treatment of irregular breathing of the heart, which is otherwise called arrhythmia. As a blood purifier, it helps in the prevention of different kinds of skin allergies. It is also used to prevent painful urination. It is also a natural diuretic.

Bark:

The bark of the Asoka tree is brown. The bark has also huge importance in various sectors. The dried bark contains tannins, sterols, catechol, and different kinds of organic compounds along with some calcium compounds. The powdered form of bark contains different types of elements like Aluminium, strontium, calcium, iron, magnesium, phosphate, potassium, sodium, silica, etc. Bark has also much medicinal importance. It is used in the treatment of uterine disorders, menstrual cycle, and menorrhagia (Begum et al.). The powder form of the bark can be stored in airtight containers, which should be away from both light and moisture. To prevent scorpion stings, the bark of this tree is used generally. Women use this powder by mixing it with honey to avoid any kind of women-related problems. It is useful for the treatment of the piles by boiling 90 grams of bark with 360 ml of milk, which should be consumed twice or thrice a day.

Leaves:

Leaves of the Asoka tree are also useful for human health. Leaves have antibacterial properties for which it is used as a treatment for the bacterial infection and various skin diseases in humans.

Flowers:

Flowers also have antibacterial properties which are used for the treatment of bacterial infections. The flowers of this tree contain linoleic, Oleic, palmitic and stearic acids, P-sitosterol, quercetin, apigenin- 7-0-p-D-glucoside, kaempferol- 3-0-P-D- glucoside, quercetin- 3-0-P-D-glucoside, cyanidin-3, 5-diglucoside, pelargonidin- 3, 5-diglucoside, linolenic, p and y sitosterol, leucocyanidin and gallic acid. Leaves and flowers are used by crushing them for the treatment of various skin diseases and allergies (Sadhu et al.,). It is also applicable for the treatment of inflammations, dysentery, hyperdipsia, scabies in children, and burning sensation. Due to the anticancer properties, it is also useful in cancer treatment. The powder form of flowers is also used for medicinal purposes. The powder is very useful against diabetes.

Roots:

Along with leaves, flowers, and bark, roots are also used for several medical purposes. It is used as a paste form against external inflammation and other skin diseases. It also has a useful effect against skin diseases like Eczema, Psoriasis, Dermatitis, Hyper kushta/visarpa, etc. Apart from these skin diseases, the paste is also useful for the treatment of paralysis, hemiplegic and visceral numbness. It is also used as cosmetic products like creams and face wash. It is useful in rejuvenating the skin tone and improving the complexionIt's also used to treat rickets and other rickets-related conditions, delayed bone consolidation, and calcium deficiency.

Seeds:

Seeds of the Asoka tree contain oleic, linoleic, palmitic, and stearic acids, catechol, etc. It is used as an external application for rheumathritis along with its ash.

Ayurvedic Uses:

In Ayurveda, the uses of the Ashoka tree are as follows:

Vedana sthapana (Treatment of all painful conditions)

Varnya (Improvement of skin tone)

Grahi (Improvement in digestion and assimilation system)

Daha shamanam (Treatment of excessive thirst)

Trishanashnam (Treatment of burning sensation in the body)

Krimighna (Against all infectious agents)

Shothajit (Treatment of all oedematous conditions)

Vish asrajit (Blood purifier)

Apachijit (Treatment against inflammation of lymph nodes)

Asrigdara nashanam (Excessive bleeding during menstruation)

Health benefits of Ashoka tree:

The ethanolic and water extraction of various parts of the Asoka tree is very important in the field of research also. This extraction of the bark of the tree is effective against various microbes such as *Staphylococcus aureus*, *Pseudomonas aeruginosa*, *Proteus vulgaris,* and *Klebsiella pneumoniae.* Along with this advantage, the extraction of leaves shows antibacterial activity against *E. coli.* Apart from this, it is also effective against *Bacillus subtilis*, *Pseudomonas aeruginosa*, and *Salmonella typhimurium* (P. Pradhan et al.,). It is also used against different kinds of health issues like menorrhagia, astringent, Diabetes, biliousness, dyspepsia, ulcers, uterine bleeding etc. They have different properties like a uterine stimulant, antiulcer, antidepressant, antibacterial, antioxidant, etc. It has been found that the bark contains many essential minerals such as potassium, magnesium, calcium, iron, tannin silica, and also many trace minerals. The leaf, bark, and flowers of the Asoka tree contain antibacterial and antifungal properties. The Asoka flowers are red and orange with a sweet fragrance

Arthritis: Paste is made up of the bark of the tree by soaking it with water and applied to that particular painful part by warming it slightly. Its repeated use will reduce the pain of arthritis.

Inflammation: It is also useful in case of inflammation. First of all, the bark of the tree is boiled with water, and then it is cooled down for consumption. Its consumption gives relief from burning sensations and inflammations.

Excessive bleeding: This tree has a huge benefit for the diseases which are related to women such as uterine problems, heavy bleeding, pain, reduction in fertility, etc. For the treatment of these diseases, boiled water or milk along with the bark is consumed by the women. The consumption of this liquid should be in small quantities thrice a day. During this treatment process, the usage of spices in regular food must be avoided for the betterment. This treatment is very beneficial in stopping excessive bleeding and cleanses the uterus.

Infections: The bark of the Asoka trees has both anti-bacterial & anti-fungal properties, for which it is utilized for the treatment against different kinds of allergies and various skin diseases effectively.

Tuberculosis: This disease is very painful for the patients as it gives severe pain to that diseased person. In this case, the powder form of the bark, blended with the goat milk is consumed by the patients. This gives a lot of relief to the patient.

Diabetes: In this case, to control the blood sugar level, the powder form of the Asoka flower is used vastly.

Pregnancy: In this situation, the powder of the bark of the tree is used for the protection of the unborn baby. Aside from that, it aids in the improvement of women's fertility and overall health. Using this powder, several ayurvedic medicines are also produced. However, you should only take these medications under the observation of your doctor.

Diarrhea: The powder of the bark, leaves, and flowers is very effective when taken with water during diarrhea with blood.

Insect bite: The bark is also beneficial in the case of treating the insect bite.

Other uses: The bark of the Ashoka tree is used in the preparation of tonic for purification of blood, a cosmetic for enhancement of complexion, for deworming, good medicine for curing internal piles, to get relief from headache and for various other ailments of women.

Respiratory problems: A half spoon of Asoka seeds powder is taken in a betel leaf and should be chewed twice a day. This will provide relief from respiratory problems.

Side-effects & allergies of Asoka tree:

Although there are a lot of health benefits of the Asoka trees, sometimes it causes complications for pregnant women due to the consumption of various products of this tree. So, the people who are sensitive to this type of product should use this product as per the advice of their doctors. Its overuse can also result in allergic reactions to the users.

Conservation of Asoka tree:

Asoka tree is one of the most admired and respected trees in India. It is probably due to its mythological connections. Apart from these, this tree is mainly popular due to its immense health benefits. The Asoka tree is considered a boon for women due to its medicinal values in women-related problems.

When we cultivate the Asoka tree on a large scale, it is difficult to propagate through seeds. Moreover, this species is now going to be extinct day by day. So, proper care should be taken to protect this tree, which has not only cultural importance but also medicinal importance.

Reference:

Begum, S. N., Ravikumar, K., & Ved, D. K. (2014). 'Asoka'–an important medicinal plant, it's a market scenario and conservation measures in India. *Current Science*, *107*(1), 26-28.

Bhalerao, S. A., Verma, D. R., Didwana, V. S., & Teli, N. C. (2014). Saraca asoca (Roxb.), de. Wild: an overview. *Annals of plant sciences*, *3*(7), 770-775.

Borokar, A. A., & Pansare, T. A. (2017). Plant profile, phytochemistry and pharmacology of Ashoka (Saraca asoca (Roxb.) D. Wild)-A comprehensive Review. *International Journal of Ayurvedic and Herbal Medicine*, 7(2), 2524-2541.

Pradhan, P., Joseph, L., Gupta, V., Chulet, R., Arya, H., Verma, R., & Bajpai, A. (2009). Saraca asoca (Ashoka): a review. *Journal of chemical and pharmaceutical research*, *1*(1), 62-71.

Sadhu, S. K., Khatun, A., Phattanawasin, P., Ohtsuki, T., & Ishibashi, M. (2007). Lignan glycosides and flavonoids from Saraca asoca with antioxidant activity. *Journal of Natural Medicines*, *61*(4), 480-482.

Chapter-18

Sal Tree (*Shorea robusta*)

Deepmala Mardi

1. सा निकृत्तेव सालस्य यष्टिः परशुना वने।

पपात सहसा देवी देवतेव दिवश्च्युता।।2.20.32।।

All of a sudden Kausalya fell on the ground like the branch of a Sal tree in the forest severed by an ax, like a goddess dropped from heaven.

2. स लक्ष्मण स्सन्त्वरित स्सालमारुह्य पुष्पितम्।

प्रेक्षमाणो दिश स्सर्वाः पूर्वां दिशमुदैक्षत।।2.96.11।।

Lakshmana hurriedly climbed a flowering sala tree, surveyed in all directions, and fixed his gaze on the east.

Figure: *Shorea robusta*. Date of capture- 21/04/20, GPS coordinate-22.64821 N and 86.35377¯ E, Locality- Jaduguda, Dist: East Singhbhum, Jharkhand, India). © Deepmala Mardi

Introduction

Sal tree *(Shorea robusta*) is the second most important timber after teak. Chhattisgarh and Jharkhand each have it as their state tree. It is dominant in Indian deciduous forests. The Indian Subcontinent is home to this tree. Sal trees are economically, ecologically, and culturally very important. It has been mentioned several times in Ramayana.

Botanical name: *Shorea robusta*

Common name: Sal, Sala, or Shal

Sanskrit: Ashvakarna, Chiraparna, Agnivallabha, Ashvakarna, Ashvakarnika, Chiraparna, Dhanya, Dirghaparna, Dirghashaka, Divyasara, Jaladashara, Jaranadruma, Kaushikahva, Kushika, Lalana, Latashankha, Latataru, Rala, Ralakarya, Sala, Salaniryas, Salaveshta, Sarja, Sarjakarya, Sarjarasa, Sarjjaka, Sasyasambara, Sasyasamvera, Shankataru, Shankurriksha, Shasyasambara, Shura. Sidhaka, Sureshtaka, Tarkshyapravasa, Vallivriksha, Vansha, Vastakarna, Yakshadhupa

Local name: Sal, Salwa, Sakhu, Sakher(Hindi), sal, guggillu, rala, sajara (Marathi), attam, venkungiliyam, kungiliyam (Tamil), karimaruthu, kungiliyam, maramaram (Malayalam), ashvakarna, asina, asu, bile-bhogimara (Kannada), Sal (Bengali), Sargi gatcho (Oriya), Ral, Safed dammar (Urdu), Sal, Hal (Assamese), Dieng blei (Khasi)

Taxonomic position

Class: Magnoliopsida

Order: Malvales

Family: Dipterocarpaceae

Genus: *Shorea*

Species: *S. robusta*

Features

Sal is a sub-deciduous tree that can reach up to the height of 30-35 m and a diameter of 200 cm. The younger tree has an elongated crown but as they grow it becomes more round. It has a lifespan of over 150 years. It is a slow-growing tree that is evergreen in wetter areas but in drier areas, it seasonally sheds leaves. It mainly sheds leaves between February and April month but leaves grow again between April and May month. It is one of the toughest timber available today. Sal wood has hard and coarse grains with light-colored wood but constant exposure to light can turn darker in color. The bark surface is rough and is reddish-brown. The sapwood is whitish, thick, and less durable. The heartwood becomes dark brown to black on sun exposure. The wood pores are filled with resin.

The leaves of the Sal tree are thin and light green when young but turn dark green or reddish, shiny, and leathery when matures. They are large, 10-30 cm long, and 5-18 cm broad having 1-2 cm long petiole. They are oval with a taper to the tip and rounded or heart-shaped at the base.

Flowers are small, regular, bisexual, yellowish to white in large terminal or axillary racemose panicles. Petals are 5, narrow-oblong or lanceolate, and silky outside. The stamen are numerous and shorter than petals. The ovary is superior having 3 locations each having 2 ovules.

Fruits of the Sal tree are ovoid, 1.3 to 1.5 cm long and 1 cm in diameter, pale yellowish or green in color, and is surrounded by segments of calyx which are enlarged by five unequal wings about 5 to 7.5 cm. Seeds are brown having calyx and wings.

Habitat

The Indian Subcontinent is home to the Sal tree. It is a dominant tree species in the deciduous forest which lies between 20-32¯ N latitude and 75-95¯ E longitude. It ranges from the south of the Himalayas, from Myanmar in the east to Nepal, India, and Bangladesh. In India, it ranges from Assam, Bengal, Odisha, and Jharkhand west to the Shivalik Hills in Haryana and east of Yamuna. In Nepal, it is found in the Terai region. Many protected areas are having dense forests and huge sal trees, such as Chitwan National Park, Bardia National Park, and Shukla Phatan Wildlife Reserve.

The global economy of tree

One of the most valuable timbers is sal. This tropical hardwood is strong, durable, and is resistant to fire. It is resistant to rotting, pest infestation, and the impacts of wind, water, and snow owing to its high oil content. It is widely used for construction work and railway sleepers. It is also used to make poles for electric and telephone lines, furniture, boats, agricultural implements, tool handles, liquid storage vats, etc.

Sal trees yield an oleoresin called Sal Dammar or Bengal Dammar which is obtained by tapping its trunk. It's utilized in the production of paints and varnishes. Sal dammar is also used for making shoe polishes, typewriter ribbons, carbon papers, and as cementing material for plywood and asbestos sheets. It is also used for sealing the joints or seams in boats.

Medicinal value

Shorea robusta has its use in Ayurveda, Unani and tribal medicine systems. The bark and leaves of Sal tree are helpful for ulcers, wounds, cough, gonorrhea, and leprosy. The bark powder is used in dysentery, diarrhoea, and vaginal discharge. Bark decoction is used for ear problems. Leaf juice is used for treating dysentery. To reduce pain, leaves are applied as a poultice to swollen regions of the body. Gum resins are applied on skin eruptions, infected wounds, and ulcers. Seed oil is used for treating skin problems. Fruit is used in the treatment of epilepsy, excessive salvation, and chlorosis. Fruits are used for seminal weakness, tubercular ulcers, and burning sensation. Seed powder for dental problems.

Other uses

The seed of the Sal tree is edible. It can be either roasted or boiled into porridge. It can be grounded into coarse flour to make bread. It is used as a famine food. The seeds also yield oil called Sal butter which is used in cooking and lighting. Sal butter is also used as an adulterant of ghee and is a suitable substitute for cocoa butter in the manufacture of chocolate.

The Sal tree's leaves are used to produce plates, cups, and wrapping materials. The leaves are also used to make Bidies, it is a local cigarette smoked by Adivasis. The leaves are also used as wedding invitations by keeping turmeric and rice between leaves by tribal people. The tribal people use the leaves in cooking rice cakes and meat. Branches of Sal tree are used as datun for brushing teeth.

Cultural importance

The Sal tree is considered to favor Lord Vishnu in Hindu religion. Buddha is said to have been born and died underneath the Sal tree in Buddhist tradition. It is said that a branch of the tree bent to support Queen Maya of Sakya and as soon as she touched the branch, the baby appeared. In Buddhism, the flowering of the sal tree is believed as a symbol of impermanence and the rapid passing of glory. The first line of the tale of the Heike, a story about the rise and fall of a once-powerful dynasty in Japanese Buddhism, whose second part reads "the beauty of the sala flowers shows the fact that even privileged people must collapse."

Sal tree has special importance in the festivals and marriages in the Adivasis. Sal tree is worshiped in the tribes of Jharkhand, Odisha, and West Bengal, especially in Munda, Santhal, Ho, and Oraon who follow Sarnaism, the indigenous religion of tribes. During marriages, unless the bride and groom sit under the altar made of Sal tree, the marriage is considered meaningless. Sal tree has an important role in Sarhul festival (word Sarhul means worship of Sal tree). It is also known as Baha Parb or festival of flowers which is performed under a Sal tree in a sacred grove known as Sarna Sthal or Jaher. This festival is dedicated to Mother Nature and is celebrated during the spring season in March-April when the Sal flower blossoms. The Adivasis pay their obeisance to the tree for providing food, shelter, shade, livelihood, and also protection from evil eyes all round year. The priest sprays holy water at the ending of the rites and gives sacred flowers to the villagers blessing them with health and prosperity.

Ecological importance

Sal forest covers about 11 million hectares in India, Nepal, and Bangladesh. Sal trees are major trees found in deciduous forests. It is ecologically very important. Sal trees absorb carbon dioxide and provide oxygen to the environment. They improve the air quality. They control the climate by moderating the effect of sun, wind, and water. They lower the air temperature and reduce the heat intensity in summer. They have large roots which hold the soil tightly which prevents soil erosion. The water absorption capacity of the Sal tree is high. This helps to prevent the area from the risk of flooding in extreme weather or rainfall. They have a major effect on hydrological cycles. Sal tree sheds leave yearly, these fallen leaves on the forest floor decompose and release nutrients in the soil. This helps in nutrient and mineral recycling. They act as water filters, collecting and storing water and recharging underground. The Sal forest ecosystem supports a rich and diverse variety of flora and fauna. Sal trees have been found to have an association with about five hundred undergrowth species. A special microclimate is provided by Sal forest which helps in association with undergrowth diversity. They provide habitat to a large no. of animals. Sal trees are large which provide a home to birds and monkeys. Sal forest is well known to provide shelter to peacock, tiger, leopard, elephants, and Sambar deers which are disappearing due to its habitat loss.

Conservation

Most of the species of *Shorea* are currently listed on IUCN Red List with most being critically endangered. Sal is a very important timber, due to its high demand there is the illegal cutting of forest. The rapid expansion of agriculture in forest land is also a threat to these trees. Over-exploitation, illegal cutting, encroachment, rapidly expanding agriculture, poaching, industrial development, urbanization, plantations (with invasive species), grazing, pollution, management failure, disease, and climate change has led to the loss of biodiversity of Sal forest.

These trees must be protected because they sustain a lot of biodiversity. In-situ conservation is done in the natural habitat. The areas are demarcated under rules as natural parks, sanctuaries, preservation plots, etc. Many protected areas are having dense forests and huge Sal trees, such as Chitwan National Park, Bardia National Park, and Shukla Plant Wildlife Reserve. Sustainable Forest Management (SFM) is also helpful in the conservation of these forests. The government has taken some initiatives to protect these important. The Sal forests are brought under community reserves where local people are made partners in conservation and management processes.

Conclusion

Sal trees are mostly known for their economic importance as timber. But it also has great cultural value. Sal tree is worshiped by many tribes of Chota Nagpur Plateau. The origin of indigenous tribal religion, the Sarna religion, is also related to this tree. It is an integral part of tribal culture. It provides alternate livelihood to many people living around the Sal forest, like the tribal women who go to the forest to collect the leaves and seed of the Sal tree and sell it. These tree parts have been used for curing many diseases since ancient times and are a part of Ayurveda, Unani and Tribal medicine systems. It is ecologically very important. Tropical deciduous forest contributes the most forest land in India and Sal trees are one of the most dominant species in this forest. It supports vast biodiversity. We need to protect and conserve this forest.

Reference

Choudhury, S. (2013). An Empirical Study on the Relationship Between Nature Worship and the Preservation of Environment in Some Parts of West Bengal in India. *International Journal of Social Sciences*, *2*(2), 79. https://doi.org/10.5958/j.2321-5771.2.2.002

Sarkar, A., & Dasgupta, S. (2009). Aspects of Tribal Culture in the Forest Environment of Bastar. *Studies of Tribes and Tribals*, *7*(2), 81–89. https://doi.org/10.1080/0972639x.2009.11886597

Singh, M., Sonkusale, S., Niratker, C., & Shukla, P. (2014). Micropropagation of Shorea robusta: an economically important woody plant. *Journal of Forest Science*, *60*(No. 2), 70–74. https://doi.org/10.17221/80/2013-jfs

Surabhi, G. K., Mohanty, S., Meher, R. K., Mukherjee, A. K., & Vemireddy, L. N. R. (2017). Assessment of genetic diversity in Shorea robusta: an economically important tropical tree species. *Journal of Applied Biology & Biotechnology*, 110–117. https://doi.org/10.7324/jabb.2017.50218

Trees of Ramayana (2022): 199-207
Editor: Felix Bast
Today & Tomorrow's Printers and Publishers (India)

Chapter-19

Jamun Tree (*Syzygium cumini*)

Rajalaxmi Sahoo

रसाकुलं षट्पदसन्निकाशं प्रभुज्यते जम्बुफलं प्रकामम्।

अनेकवर्णं पवनावधूत भूमौ पतत्याम्रफलं विपक्कम् 4. 28. 19।।

The above shloka from the Kishkindha Kanda, Sarga 28, shloka number 19 in Valmiki's Ramayana published by Gita Press captures a still where Rama describes the beauty of the rainy season to Lakshmana after killing Bali and declaring Sugriva as the king. Rama arrived at the mountain of Malyavan to reside.

He said to Lakshmana: 'Now that the rainy season has started, see the sky covered with mountain-like (huge) clouds. The sky has absorbed the ocean water through the Sun rays and carried it in its womb for nine months (from Kartika to Asarha). It transports water, which would be the foundation of all juices. The sky with its gentle winds sighs; its ash-colored clouds painted with red sandal paste in the form of the glow of twilight appear like a passionate lover. This earth scorched by the heat and then flooded with fresh rainwater, radiating heat, appears like my Sita shedding tears burning with grief. The mountain streams of rainwater carry freshwater swiftly to the ocean along with the deposits of red mineral rocks of the mountain. The black bees like Jambu fruits full of sweet juice. People share them to their heart's content, while the Mango fruits take multiple colors on getting the ripened drop on the ground shaken by the wind. " After hearing this, Lakshmana again expressed his opinion with due respect to handsome Rama that grief can weaken our efforts, which then becomes our enemy. In moments of grief and difficulty, we need to hold on and reinforce our minds so that we may survive, like a drowning man that grabs on a tiny straw in hope of not drowning. And in this way, Lakshmana advised Brother Shri Rama to keep patience and hope for the best.

Figure: Picture of Jamun tree taken in Nayagarh district, Orissa. © Rajalaxmi Sahoo

Jamun tree is widely grown in large parts of India from Indo-Gangetic plains in the north to Tamil Nadu in the south, also found in Sri-lanka.

Introduction

The tree, scientifically called *Syzygium cumini*, Jambu Phalinda in Sanskrit, Jambu in Hindi, or the Indian Blackberry in English, is among India's few native trees, although it may also be seen in Bangladesh, Nepal, and Pakistan. However, this is the only fruit that is completely associated with India. The genus *Syzygium* is a flowering plant belonging to the *Myrtaceae* family, comprising about 1200-1800 species. This tree's natural range is rather large from Africa and Madagascar through southern Asia east through the Pacific. This tree has the highest level of diversity found from Malaysia to north-eastern Australia, where many species are very poorly known and taxonomically not clearly described. It includes many species mostly from evergreen trees and shrubs. Many species are grown as ornamental plants for their attractive glossy foliage and also for their edible fruits that can be eaten fresh or used in jams and jellies. Some plants are used as economically most important species e, g. clove *Syzygium aromaticum* of which we only use the unopened flower buds as an important spice. These spices are planted worldwide throughout the tropics which has become several invasive species in some island ecosystems. Many several species of this plant bear edible fruits for humans, animals, and birds some of which are named "rose apple". Around 52 species are found in Australia and are generally known as Lilly pillies, brush cherries, or satinash. At times *Syzygium* was confused with the genus Eugenia (ca 1000 species), but later due to higher diversity in neotropics, many species that were formerly classified as Eugenia are included in the genus *Syzygium*. Now the international group of researchers, formed in April 2016 working on Syzygium to produce a monograph of *Syzygium*.

Syzygium cumini, often known as Malabar plum or black plum, is an evergreen tropical tree that is sometimes confused with blackberries, a fruit of a different order. This plant has been spread overseas from India to other tropical former British colonies.

In Florida, this tree was introduced in 1911 by USDA which is still grown in Suriname, Guyana, and Trinidad and Tobago. In Brazil, it was introduced by Portuguese colonized and dispersed spontaneously in some places by various native birds such as thrushes, tanagers, and great kiskadee. This is considered an invasive species.

Different Names

Botanical name: Syzygium cumini, English name: Black plum, Java plum, Malabar plum, Hindi name: Jambol, Jambul, Jamun, Sanskrit name: Jambu, Local name: Jamukoli, Jambas, Jambolan, Rajaman, Trade name: Kala jamun, Neredu, Naval, Jamali, Other names: Jamblang, Jambolan, Duhat, Plum, Kavika, Jamelonguier, Punjabi names: Jamalu, Telugu name: Saval naval, Malayalam name: Naval, Bengali name: Kala jam, Kannada name: Nerale

Taxonomic position:

Kingdom: *Plantae*

Division: *Magnoliophyta*

Class: *Magnoliopsida*

Order: *Myrtales*

Family: *Myrtaceae*

Genus: *Syzygium*

Species: *S. cumini*

Binomial Name -*Syzygium cumini*

Morphological Characteristics

Jamun: The humble fruit with a unique position in Hindu tradition and culture.

Jamun is a slow-growing tree, medium to large size up to a height of 30 m and girth is 3. 6mt and can live up to 100 years and more. The tree's upper bark is light greyish and smooth. And at the base of the tree bark becomes rough dark grey. The wood of this plant shows water resistance. The leaves have a soothing aroma and are like turpentine. At the young stage leaves are pinkish and slowly change into a leathery, glossy, and dark green with yellow-colored midrib. These features of leaves allow it to offer dense shade and contain rich nutrient value and are also used as foliage for animals. Its dense foliage provides shade and ornamental value with its water-resistance wood that can be also used put motors in boreholes and railway sleepers.

Flowers of these trees start within the season from March to April and are very tiny white-colored giving aromatic fragrance and around 5mm in diameter.

The *S. cumini* grows in subtropical and tropical parts of India and is found in many Indian subcontinents and widely distributed forest trees found in Sri Lanka, Malaysia, Bangladesh, and Australia. Jamun is dark purple. Its shape is oval. Fruit is generally fleshy and has a seed inside. The tree only bears fruit once a year and the fruits have a sweetish sour flavor.

When this fruit ripens its color slowly changes from pink to shining crimson red and finally to black color. Another variant of this tree produces white color fruit. This fruit has a strong astringent flavor that tends to color the tongue purple. The extract of fruit seed is used in alternating healing systems like Ayurveda, Unani and Chinese medicine. It is effective against hyperglycemia in diabetic rats; Wine and vinegar made from this fruit offer a huge source of vitamin A and vitamin C. This fruit has also found a place in a book in 1889 'the useful native plants of Australia' records that this plant was referred to as durobbi by Indigenous Australians.

Fruit Information:

Jamun is a leathery fruit and delicious plum that is rich in iron, vitamin A and vitamin C. This seasonal fruit is very nutritious with its unique shape and color available in Asia.

Jamun is also called "Fruit of God", and has a vast significant place in Hindu religion and mythology. When contrasted to other seasonal fruits papaya, guava, banana, and orange, it has high antioxidant content like.

Jamun is low in calories and can be preferred as a healthy snack. It promotes natural bowel movement and helps in improving digestion. Jamun juice contains high bioactive phytochemicals that lower the risk of liver disease and cancer and hence proving very effective in the potential treatment of Diabetes. Other various names of this fruit are Indian blueberry, Jaman, jambol, doowet, jambolan, faux, pistachier, *Eugenia cumini*. This fruit holds an important place in summer fruits that has many health and medicinal benefits. This high fiber content of Jamun will keep you satisfied and make you feel full for a longer time which will help an individual to lose weight first. This is why many nutritionists advise including this fiber-rich food in the diet for healthy weight loss. We can also use the seeds of this fruit by making it dry and powder it to consume regularly before meals to fight diabetes very effectively. Besides the seeds, we can also use leaf, bark, and fruit to make medicines and most commonly used in folk medicine for diabetes. It also gives relief from swelling and inflammation of the stomach, gastritis, constipation, diarrhea, and flatulence and proving extremely beneficial for curing digestive disorders, especially from indigestion and acidity issues.

Habitat:

Syzygium cumini are mainly found native to the Indian subcontinent and adjoining part of south-east Asia. This species is widely distributed all over Bangladesh, Pakistan, Nepal, Sri Lanka, Malaysia, the Philippines, and Indonesia.

Evolutionary history of Plant:-

It is believed that this fruit has originated in Neolithic times when man consumed wild berries, wild plums, and nuts as a staple food.

In India, Jamun is referred to as " Fruit of God " because during Lord Rama's 14 years of exile from Ayodhya he ate several berries and plums including Jamun those days.

The oldest Jamun tree is located near Kodaikanal lake garden in shola road which is of around 500 years old and has become the main region of tourist destination in the past few decades.

Usage in medicinal and food value:-

S. cumini fruit is a miraculous fruit that works great in diabetes and very effective in diabetic people. It is wonderful medicine for people who suffer from hyperglycemia. Because of its low hyperglycemia index, it maintains proper sugar levels in the human body. As this fruit is rich in iron it acts as a natural blood purifier and it ensures proper blood supply of oxygen blood throughout the body.

The astringent property of this fruit makes skin healthy glowing and free from acne and pimples. This fruit is rich in various chemicals and contains many compounds like gallic acid, oxalic acid, etc. that help us to fight many diseases against malaria, microbial and bacterial infection. It is used in lung-related treatments and can cure problems like cough, asthma, and bronchitis. It also reduces abdominal pain, dysentery, etc. It has the potential to protect the body from free radicals that cause mainly cardiovascular diseases and are good for overall body health. This plant is used to treat a variety of ailments like generalized weakness, treating anemia, and improving sexual weakness because of its aphrodisiac nature. The bark of this plant is beneficial for the effective treatment of females suffering from leucorrhoea, depression, exhaustion, and nervous related disorders. This is also effective in the treatment of mouth ulcers, sore throat, and pancreas-related ailments. It reduces Kapha and pitta dosha but aggravates Vata dosha.

PARTS USED:

- Seeds
- Leaf
- Bark
- Fruit

Economic importance of *Syzygium cumini*:

Syzygium cumini is cultivated all across India because of its numerous health benefits. It is known to be an indigenous and one of the important minor commercial crops to India. It is a very tall evergreen plant and is usually grown as a wind breaker or shade.

As this fruit is very good for diabetic patients, it gets sold at a higher price in the market compared to other fruits. This is a seasonal fruit and hence its cultivation is favored at a certain particular season of the year i.e. from March to April month of summers only. This is also called Ram Jamun in some parts of India, cultivated in both tropical and subtropical areas by the small farmers and gets a good amount of profit.

Major Jamun producing states:-

India ranks 2nd position in Jamun production in the world. In India, Maharashtra is a major Jamun producer followed by Uttar Pradesh, Tamil Nadu, Gujarat, Assam, and others. Although no commercial improved varieties developed in *S. cumini* production the Ram Jamun is the most cultivated one because it has small seeds with a good amount of pulp and big size with sweet and juicy. There is another variety in UP, Varanasi which is found to have no seeds. Fruits with little bigger seed and small size mature lately.

Cultural and Mythological Significance

Syzygium cumini is one of those trees that is held in veneration not only in Ramayana but also by Buddhists and is often planted near Hindu temples because it is regarded as sacred to Lord Krishna and Lord Ganesha.

In the **Srimad Bhagavad Gita** commentary verse (10.30.25) it was mentioned that in the right foot of Krishna the four symbols of jambu are found as mentioned by Sri Rupa Chintamani by Srila Visvanatha Chakravarti Thakura. It is often compared with Lord Krishna and Lord Ram's skin color is the color of Jamun.

In the story of the great epic Mahabharatha, it is also mentioned the name of Jambhul Akhyan, which is related to this fruit. In Maharashtra, the leaves of Jamun are used as marriage pandals for decorations. A song from the film 'Jait re Jait' mentioned this fruit`s name as' Jambhul Pikalya Zadakhali. '

The Puranas divides the cosmos into seven continents, but the central position was occupied and called Jambudvipa, the island of jambu or Jamun. This shows the importance of this tree due to which the Hindus and Buddhist cosmologies put a giant Jamun tree in the middle of the world. In Southern parts of India, in Telugu culture, the eyes of beautiful girls are compared to this fruit. This tree gives life to many animals and birds like fruit bats, jackals by providing fruits as an important part of their diet, and its tiny white flower is used abundantly by honey bees. This plant holds a special place in Ramayana because of its sacred qualities and medicinal value. Lord Megha, the "god of clouds," is supposed to have descended upon the world in the guise of a Jamun, which explains why the fruit is as black and stormy as the violent monsoon clouds. These are big beautiful trees that could easily survive summer and remain leafy and provide shade to people this is why Britisher chose it to plant for the avenues of New Delhi when they were building a new capital.

In ancient Sanskrit texts, this was mentioned that a wine called jambu asava was made from this ripened fruit. In the state of Andhra Pradesh, both fruits, as well as wood from this plant, are used widely in all auspicious work starting from marriage to agriculture. Wood is used to make bullock cartwheels and other agricultural equipment and the timber of this plant is used to make doors and windows. Hindus use a branch of this tree to inaugurate the marriage preparation before beginning and plant it near the pandal of marriage to avoid any evil eye on this work.

Injuries, Pest and Diseases

Dialeurodes eugenia commonly known as whitefly damages the tree in all parts and is found in all parts of India. The fruit affected by this fly appears wormy on the surface. However, there are a variety of methods for controlling this fly like maintaining the sanitary condition around the *S.cumini* tree. Pluck and remove all the affected parts from the tree so that it would not damage the nearest part. The soil around the tree trunk should be dug up so that the maggots in the affected tree hibernating in the soil would get destroyed. The leaf-eating caterpillar would destroy the tree and would be only controlled by spraying Roger 30. Other pests rather than this insect harm the Jamun tree seriously and damage the leaf, branch, and tree-like monkeys, squirrels, parrots, and crows. Diseases like Anthracnose, a fungal disease, affect the plant and make leaf spots and fruit rot. These affected parts show symptoms of small scattered spots, light brown or reddish-brown color spots, and ultimately rot the fruits and shrivel.

Stories and Myths related to Jamun

Panchatantra Story: The monkey and the crocodile

Once upon a time, there was a monkey that lived on the banks of a river in a Jamun tree. The Jamun tree produced fruit throughout the year and the monkey spent his days happily eating the fruit playing on the tree. A crocodile emerged from the river one day to relax under the shade of a Jamun tree. "Oh crocodile," the monkey exclaimed when he spotted the crocodile. Welcome! You are welcome to stay with me. Please accept my humble meal of Jamun fruits from my tree." The Jamun fruits were quite good to the crocodile, so he ate them. "Oh monkey, the Jamun fruits on your tree are really wonderful," he replied. Is it possible for me to come back tomorrow for a little more? "You are my friend as from today. You are welcome to eat here at any time ", the monkey responded. The crocodile came to see the monkey all the next day. The two buddies would spend the day conversing and munching Jamun fruits, which were juicy and delicious.

One day the crocodile took some Jamun fruits home for his wife so that she could also taste the Jamun and told her about his new friend who lived on that Jamun tree. Crocodile's wife was overjoyed eating this fruit and she was very cunning and thought to herself, "These fruits are so sweet than the monkey who is eating these fruits every day I'm confident his meat would have been much more delicious.". So she thought to herself how she could eat the monkey and planned to act sad and depressed. When her husband asked about the reason for depression she trickly lied that the doctor had advised her to eat a monkey's heart to recover her health as she has become very weak or else she would die soon. She requested her husband to bring that monkey to her or else there is no hope. The crocodile was aghast and agony filled his heart. He never wanted to betray his friend. The crocodile tried to reason her but she argued and never listened, instead stopped eating. The crocodile had to fulfill her wish. Then he went to his friend and said that his wife loved the fruit he had given and invited him for the dinner tonight. Hearing this monkey was delighted and happily agreed to come but the only problem was that he can't swim, then how he will cross the river and go. The crocodile said to come and sit on his back and go. The monkey accepted at once and set off. As they approached the center of the river, the crocodile started going deeper into the river. Monkey started doubting and asked about the matter. Then the crocodile replied sadly and told everything that how they were going to kill him.

The monkey paused for a moment before saying, "oh dear friend! Why didn't you say that earlier? I would have happily given my heart to you to carry that to your wife. But now I kept my heart on top of that tree only and requested him to go back and get his heart. The stupid crocodile trusted him and turned around. They were on their way to the riverside. As soon as they arrived, the monkey leaped off and climbed the tree, laughing at the crocodile. He told him to go back to her and tell her that her husband is not only foolish but also deceitful.

References

Singh, K. (2011). *The Sunset Club*. Penguin Books India.

Singh, J. (2016). Jamun (Java plum): Syzygium cumini. *Ayur Times*, 1.

Chagas, V. T., França, L. M., Malik, S., & Paes, A. M. D. A. (2015). Syzygium cumini (L.) Skeels: a prominent source of bioactive molecules against cardiometabolic diseases. *Frontiers in pharmacology*, *6*, 259.

Bijauliya, R. K., Alok, S., Sabharwal, M., & Chanchal, D. K. (2018). Syzygium cumini (linn.)-an overview on morphology, cultivation, traditional uses, and pharmacology. *international journal of pharmaceutical sciences and research*, *9*(9), 3608-3620.

Ayyanar, M., & Subash-Babu, P. (2012). Syzygium cumini (L.) Skeels: A review of its phytochemical constituents and traditional uses. *Asian Pacific journal of tropical biomedicine*, *2*(3), 240-246.

REGE, S. (2003). Crocodile and the Monkey. *The Practice of Sociology*, 286.

Trees of Ramayana (2022): 209-218
Editor: Felix Bast
Today & Tomorrow's Printers and Publishers (India)

Chapter-20

Arjuna Tree *(Terminalia arjuna)*

Hiramoni Ojah

अथवाऽर्जुन शंस त्वं प्रियां तामर्जुनप्रियाम्।

जनकस्य सुता भीरुर्यदि जीवति वा न वा।।3.60.14।।

ककुभः ककुभोरूं तां व्यक्तं जानाति मैथिलीम्।

यथा पल्लवपुष्पाढ्यो भाति ह्येष वनस्पतिः।।3.60.15।।

The above Shloka mentioned in Aranya Kanda - The Forest Trek, Chapter [Sarga] 60 reads that when Rama expressed sorrow for Sita's separation, he starts searching for her in the forest and goes on asking every single plant, tree, and animal, in a kind of emotion. Rama says "Oh, Arjuna tree if you know my lady love who loves or fond of your beautiful Arjuna flowers, who has a slender waist and is the daughter of Janaka, is whether living or not?".

How the Kakubha tree (Sanskrit name of Arjuna tree) shines or laden with creeping plants, tender leaves, and flowers which is well known by Maithili (another name of Sita) and whose thigh is compared with the trunk of the Kakubha tree.

एष फुल्लार्जुनश्शैलः केतकैरधिवासितः।

सुग्रीव इव शान्तारिर्धाराभिरभिषिच्यते 4.28.9।।

The above Shloka mentioned in the Kishkindha Kanda Chapter [Sarga] 28- states how Rama praises the rainy season for a heavenly elixir is showered for all the living beings. The Shloka means- "This Mountain is fully bloomed with Arjuna flowers which are like the garlands on the chest of Sugreeva. It also smells with Ketaka trees' flowers like those of the fragment items which are brought for Sugreeva's anointment. Pouring all kinds of water by Sugreeva after the death of his enemy Vali, this mountain is also being anointed by heavy rain".

Figure: Arjuna tree (*Terminalia arjuna*) (Date: 18/04/2020). © Hiramoni Ojah

Introduction-

The genus '*Terminalia*' includes nearly 250 species that are distributed in tropical regions. And in India 24 species of Terminalia have been reported (M. K. Singh et al., 2013). Out of these 250 species, 4 species are found in Andaman and Nicobar islands. Almost 6 species are reported which are used in Indian Medicine. The generic name 'Terminalia' was named from the Latin word Terminus, which means the leaves grow the branch or shoot terminal and it intermixes with the flowers. *T. arjuna* is native to the Indian subcontinent. The trees under this genus contain many secondary metabolites that are rich in flavonoids, tannins, etc, and also contain natural deposition of calcium oxalate. Traditionally, people use its bark for curing many diseases such as diabetes, diarrhea, heart diseases, cough, tumor, asthma, etc. Arjuna tree is important for the rearing of Tasar silkworm. The *Terminalia* is abundant in Africa and Asia, especially in India, Sri Lanka, Cambodia, Burma, and Vietnam, extending into New Guinea, Malaysia, and up to Polynesia, northern Australia, and tropical America. Approximately 24 species of Terminalia have been reported in 2003 from different states, adding two new species.

Scientific name- *Terminalia arjuna*

Sanskrit name- Kakubha

Trade name: Arjun chhal

Common (Indian) names- White Marudah, white murdh (English name), Arjun, Arjuna(Hindi), Sadada(Gujrati), Sadura(Marathi), Sahajo (Odia), Vellamatta (Tamil), Yerra maddi (Telugu), Orjun (Assamese), Arjhan(Bengali), Arjuna(Punjabi), Neer maruthu (Malayalam).

Taxonomic position-

Kingdom: Plantae

Subkingdom: Tracheobionta

Division: Magnoliophyta

Class: Magnoliopsida

Subclass: Rosidae

Order: Myrtales

Family: Combretaceae

Genus: Terminalia

Species: Arjuna

Morphological Characteristics

The *T. arjuna* is a large deciduous, evergreen tree. It may grow to a height of 60 to 85 feet, that is, almost 20 – 25 meters. *T. arjuna* usually has a buttressed trunk and has a wide canopy at the crown and drooping branches. The lifespan of an Arjuna tree is almost 50 years and above. The bark is often grey in color and smooth in nature. In mature trees, the bark peels off in thin layers or small patches which are often darker in color (B. Boyogueno and A. D, 2010). The color of sapwood is reddish-white and the heartwood is dark brown (M. K. Singh et al., 2013). The wood is generally hard, heavy, and strong (Hossain et al.). The flowers are sessile and are grouped in axillary spikes. The panicle is up to 9 – 13 cm long with 2.5 – 6 cm long branches. The rachis is short, hairy, and white. The calyx is cream in color and glabrous. It is densely covered with small short hairs inside. It has five short triangular lobes. The *Terminalia arjuna* tree is bisexual or hermaphroditic with male and female flowers borne on the same plants. The flowering season starts in April and continues up to June or August.

The fruit of Arjuna is a fibrous woody drupe. It is about 2.5 - 5 cm in size. The drupe is greenish yellow when young and it becomes dark brown when mature. It has five wings that are projecting out, veined, and are hard. The fruiting season starts from July to February. Leaves are alternate to opposite, oblong-lanceolate, thick coriaceous. Leaves are up to 8 cm long and are serrulate. Leaves are simple. The above portion of a leaf is light green in color and pale green below. Venation is reticulated with a prominent midrib. The root system of *Terminalia arjuna* is having a short distance from top to bottom. As the tree grows, the taproot starts to disappear.

The Combretaceae family consists of about 600 species, out of which 20 species belong to shrubs, lianas, and trees which are distributed in tropical and subtropical regions. The subfamily contains 19 genera which include Combretum and Terminalia. Genus Terminalia belongs to the family Combretaceae which includes 250 species distributed throughout humid, tropical, and subtropical regions around the world.

Terminalia genus generally consists of hard large wooded trees. In India, the other related species to *T. arjuna* are *T. chebula, T. bellrica,* and *T. ciliata.* All these trees have a common family, the Combretaceae family. *T. tomentosa* is known as Indian laurel. It is a large deciduous tree. It may grow up to 30 meters tall. This tree is also known as the Crocodile Bark tree due to its bark pattern. *T. chebula* is known as Black myrobalan. This tree is native to Southwest China and south Asia that is India and Nepal. It has many medicinal and economical values. The fruits are used to dye cloth and in tanning leather. In Ayurveda, it is the main ingredient of *Triphala*, which is used in curing liver dysfunction. *T bellirica* is another large deciduous tree of the genus *Terminalia*. It can reach a height of 50 m and a width of 20 m, and it has no branches. The color of the bark is ashy grey or bluish. The fruit extracts have germicidal and antibacterial activity. *T. catappa* which is known as tropical almond is a large tree distributed throughout Tropical Asia and the Indian Ocean. The bark and leaf parts are used as medicine for anti dysentery and anti digestion. *Terminalia myriocarpa* is known as East Indian almond. It has many economical uses such as dye or tanning, agroforestry, charcoal, etc. *Terminalia elliptica* grows up to a height of 30m. The wood is used for furniture, boat-building, and musical instruments. The stem is used to store water. The bark is used in curing diarrhea.

Phytochemistry

Comprehensive chemical analysis on different parts of *T. arjuna* was performed using standard processes such as UPLC, HPLC, and LC-

ESI-MS/MS. The bark extract of *T. arjuna* revealed the presence of biochemical compounds which are important in medicinal as well as physiological activities. The different chemical constituents found in the bark and stem are - tannins, phenolics, triterpenoids acid, flavonoids, phytosterol. The important constituents of bark are terminoic acid, arjunolic acid, and Arjun glucoside 1, 3 (Soni et al., 2019).

Habitat

Arjuna is a large deciduous tree. In India, it is found in Bihar, the Northeast region, Uttar Pradesh, Delhi, Madhya Pradesh, and the Deccan region near rivers, ponds, and banks of streams. It grows well along a bank of streams, rivers, and on fertile alluvial loam and wet, marshy areas. In a small village named Manipur of Jammu and Kashmir two trees each of 26 feet and 32 feet in girth which is 5 feet from the ground have been reported (Paarakh and P. M, 2010; Gupta et al, 2018). As all trees required a suitable environment to grow well, this tree also required a suitable environment such as soil and climatic conditions. Arjuna trees can be generally grown in all types of soil. But it mostly prefers humid, red lateritic, and fertile soil to grow well. This tree can also grow well in drought conditions and also frost resistant. The maximum temperature required for growing is from 26p C to 35p C and the minimum temperature is from 17p C to 25p C. The soil should have the capacity for good drainage. It requires a variety of soil types to grow well. It requires a pH of 5.5 to 7.0 and performs well on slow-draining clay and loam soils. They can tolerate soil salinity, wet soil condition, and seasonal flooding.

Geographical distribution

In India, it is common in almost all parts. It reaches the northward under the Himalayan tract. It is found in Sri Lanka, Burma, and Bangladesh, and peninsular India. About 54 species of *Terminalia* are distributed naturally throughout eastern, southern, and western Africa. The *Terminalia ivorensis* and *T. superba* are the two most important species found in Central and West Africa. Some of the species of the genus Terminalia can grow at high altitudes also. But most of the species grow well at an altitude which is less than 2000 meters above sea level. The climatic conditions in which the Terminalia trees grow vary from place to place with the average rainfall. The species occurring in the forest area requires >2000 mm per annum rainfall seasonal rainfall and the species occurring in Savannah zones require moderate rainfall around < 1200 mm per annum.

Cultivation of *Terminalia arjuna*

T. arjuna is easy to cultivate in all types of soil. They can be grown manually through air layering, root suckers, ripe seeds, coppicing, etc. At the initial stage after cultivation, it starts to grow slowly and later on starts to grow faster. It attains a height of approx. 2 to 3 meters in almost 3 years after cultivation (Gupta et al., 2018). Because both male and female flowers grow on the same plant, self-pollination is not possible. So, the pollens are pollinated by wind or with the help of several insects. For seed propagation, the newly fallen seeds should be collected as the seeds present in the tree may not be mature fully. And some of the fallen seeds are paralyzed by some insects, which lead to low viability. To avoid this problem, sometimes seeds are collected by cutting off the branches from the tree. The seeds are taken out of the fruit by placing them in a heap, sprinkling them with water, and covering them with leaves or grass. After a few days, the seeds can be extracted manually when the fruit wing is stripped off. Before sowing in beds, the seeds are soaked in water for 48 hours. The plant should be planted early in the rainy season.

Evolution

One of the phylogenetic studies over the biogeographical history of the Combretaceae family suggested that Combretaceae was diversified at 110 mya. The study of the family Combretaceae was done by using the DNA sequences. This family was further divided into sub-tribes. Terminaliinae is one of the subtribes which arises at 46.4mya. In this subtribe, *Terminalia* is the largest genus which comprises two clades – clade I and clade II. Clade I diverged earlier around 39mya and consisted of New World species. Clade II diverged later on after clade I around 17mya. Clade II comprises Old World species. *Terminalia* is known as the Crown age of New World which age is estimated at around 39mya. From this study, it was also suggested that *Terminalia* is a paraphyletic clade (Gere et al, 2012 March).

Pest and diseases

Few studies on pests and diseases affecting *Terminalia* spp. are done. There are many insect species associated with *Terminalia* spp. but, at present, no widespread complications have arisen. However, some common species in the area are very dangerous, affecting the early stages of trees.

Medicinal uses

The therapeutic qualities of the tree may be found in every part of it. This herb is used in Ayurvedic and Unani medicine systems. According to Ayurveda, it helps in ulcers, heart disease, rupture, urinary incontinence, pain, and asthma. According to Yunani's system of medicine is used internally and externally for urine discharge. It has also been used as a cardiotonic in heart failure, ischemic, cardiomyopathy, myocardium necrosis and has been used to treat a variety of human illnesses, including blood problems, anemia, arthritis, and viral sickness, as well as to maintain overall health. It is also useful in hypocholesterolemic, antibacterial, antimicrobial, and antioxidant, antiallergic, antifertility, and anti-HIV activities. Parts used in the treatment are leaves, bark, fruit, and flower. The taste of the bark part is bitter. Arjuna bark powder and its liquid extract are very safe for ulcer and their protection action is compared with ranitidine. It increases the heart's ability to pump blood by strengthening the cardiac muscles. It has cardioprotective activities, which help maintain good cardiovascular functions and speed up the recovery process of cardiac damage. Numerous clinical and therapeutic studies have shown that Arjun bark has a potent antioxidant.

Economic importance

Arjuna trees have much economical importance. They are used as timber, fuel, and tannin, pharmaceutical, and animal fodder. The timber is mainly used for making carts, agricultural tools, tool handles, and water troughs, boat building, mine props, etc. It is also used for structural purposes such as oars, house buildings, masts, water traps, and transmission poles. It is also suitable for making tea chests and plywood in the second grade. They are also used as a fuel resource. Wood is used to make excellent firewood and charcoal with high calorific value. The fallen leaves are used as manure by the local people and the fruit is used as fuel (Pandey, A. K et al, 2009). One of the studies revealed that the concentration of tannin in different parts such as leaves, barks, roots, and fruits are present in different amounts (Wadhai et al, 2019). The fruits and barks are used as a source of dyeing material and tanning. One study suggested that the leaves contain 7.73 ± 0.29 % of total phenol and 6.58 ± 0.23 % of total tannins and the bark contain 12.23 ± 0.33 % of total phenol and 11.90 ± 0.37 % of total tannins (Deshmukh et al., 2019). Arjuna leaves are used to feed the tropical Tasar silkworm that is *A. mylitta D.* It is considered the backbone of the Tasar silk industry. The leaves of Arjuna trees are also used as fodder for animals such as goats, cows, etc. The bark is used in pharmaceutical industries to cure fever, fracture, ulcers, and dysentery.

Ecological importance

Due to the huge canopy offered by *T. arjuna,* during the germination stage of riparian tree species, it provides adequate shade and retains soil moisture.It also acts as keystone species. Due to its inflorescence, *T. arjuna* is used in parks or gardens for attraction. They are also planted as ornamental trees and for shade in parks and avenues.

Cultural Importance

Arjuna is one of the sacred shrines of India. It has acquired social and religious holiness over time. Lord Vishnu and Lord Ganpati donate the leaves and flowers of this tree on various holy festivals. It has been used in Ayurvedic formations from ancient times.

Stories related to *T. arjuna*

Lord Krishna and the Arjuna Trees: The story from the Bhagavatam- The following story represents how Lord Krishna delivered two Gods from a curse through which they had been born as Arjuna trees on earth. When mother Yashoda tied infant Krishna with a rope to a larger wooden mortar because of his naughtiness. As an infant, Krishna could not sit quietly in one place so he jerked at the rope and started to crawl. On seeing two Arjuna trees standing next to each other, he decided to pass through them with the mortar. After this, the mortar gets stuck in between the trees. When little Krishna pulls the rope which is tied with the mortar, the two trees get uprooted. And from this, two people fell at Krishna's feet bowing and offering prayers. They were Manigriva and Nalakuvara, the sons of Kubera. They were rich and meaningful as they were, prone to wine and women. Once, when they were so busy, the great Sage Narada passed away. Having consumed much alcohol, and associated with beautiful women, they failed to show proper respect and acceptance in the sage. Enraged and shocked at this unpopular behavior, Sage Narada was shocked that they would live forever like the two Arjuna trees in Gokul. Hearing this, the women of Nalakuvara and Manigriva rushed to apologize for the behavior of their husbands, urging Sege to return the curse. Finally, Sage Narada repented and said "The curse once given cannot be reversed. It can only be changed or its effect reduced. Now, that prophecy was fulfilled. Released from their curse, Nalakuvara and Manigriva thanked Lord Krishna.

Conservation

The *Terminalia arjuna* has not been evaluated by the IUCN Red List as their population is abundant in nature. The rearing of Tasar silkworm will get reduced if proper maintenance of *Terminalia* species is not undertaken. Due to overexploitation of timber, leather, and in the pharmaceutical industry population of some of these species are highly threatened. Hence, conservation of the existing genus *Terminalia* is urgently needed. The genetic diversity can be conserved by in situ and ex-situ approaches. By preserving the seeds or pollen, it can be conserved. In India, they are rapidly depleting due to deforestation. So, we have to preserve it for the future.

Conclusion

Terminalia arjuna is one of the widely used trees from the ancient period because of its medicinal property. It is one of the most economically valuable trees as it provides innumerable goods and services to humans. *Terminalia arjuna* is one of the keystone species as its removal from an ecosystem can damage overall diversity. Due to its various uses, we may lose it in the future. So, we must preserve this valuable tree for the future.

References

AG Deshmukh, AR Pawar, Varsha Tapre, and SD Deshmukh (2019). Comparative Evaluation of quality parameters in leaves, fruits, and bark of *Terminalia* sp. International Journal of Chemical Studies; 7(2): 64-69

Amalraj, A., & Gopi, S. (2017). Medicinal properties of Terminalia arjuna (Roxb.) Wight & Arn.: a review. *Journal of traditional and complementary medicine*, *7*(1), 65-78.

Begoude Boyogueno, A. D. (2010). *Characterization of Botryosphaeriaceae and Cryphonectriaceae associated with Terminalia SPP. in Africa* (Doctoral dissertation, University of Pretoria).

Gere, J., Maurin, O., & Van der Bank, M. (2012, March). Phylogenetic relationships within sub-tribe Terminaliinae (Combretaceae). In *SOUTH AFRICAN JOURNAL OF BOTANY* (Vol. 79, pp. 187-187). PO BOX 211, 1000 AE AMSTERDAM, NETHERLANDS: ELSEVIER SCIENCE BV.

Gupta, S., Bishnoi, J. P., Kumar, N., Kumar, H., & Nidheesh, T. (2018). *Terminalia arjuna* (Roxb.) Wight & Arn.: Competent source of bioactive components in functional food and drugs. *J Pharm Innov*, *7*(3), 223-231.

Hossain, M. A., Rokeya, U. K., & Biswas, D. Physical and Mechanical Properties of Arjun (*Terminalia arjuna*) Grown in Bangladesh.

P.K. Srivastav, Priya Ranjan, and S.S. Sinha; conservation of *Terminalia* genetic resources: the principal source of non-wood forest products in India

Paarakh, P. M. (2010). *Terminalia arjuna* (Roxb.) Wt. and Arn: a review. *Int J Pharmacol*, *6*(5), 515-534.

Pandey, A. K., & Kori, D. C. (2009). Variations in tannin and oxalic acid content in *Terminalia arjuna* (Arjuna) Bark. *Pharmacognosy Magazine*, *5*(18), 159.

Singh, M. K., Sharma, M., & Sharma, C. L. (2013). Wood anatomical variations in some *Terminalia* species of Assam. *Int J Bot Res*, *3*(2), 13-18.

Soni, N., & Singh, V. K. (2019). Efficacy and Advancement of *Terminalia arjuna* in Indian Herbal Drug Research: A Review. *Trends in Applied Sciences Research*, *14*, 233-242.

Vijayasankar, R., & Khan, I. A. (2011). Identification of *Terminalia* Species from India using Macro-morphological Features. *Planta Medica*, *77*(05), P_1.

Wadhai, M., Ayate, D., & Ujjainkar, V. V. (2019). Estimation of tannin content in leaves, bark, and fruits of *Terminalia arjuna* Roxb. *International Journal of Farm Sciences*, *9*(1), 61-63.

Index